Copenhagen Chic

Urban Chic

Series Editor: Susan Ingram, York University, Toronto, Canada

The Urban Chic series is premised on the fact that a new wave of urban change is afoot. It is a series of 'locational histories of cities' fashion' that use unique spaces of specific cities to show the interplay between fashion in its art historical understanding as clothing or dress, on one hand, and fashion more broadly conceived as social change, on the other. Each volume seeks to establish how a city's urban imaginary has evolved in dialogue with the fashion system, and how cultural institutions involving dress, design, and particular looks and styles have informed those imaginaries.

Published previously:

Berliner Chic: A Locational History of Berlin Fashion, by Susan ingram and Katrina Sark (2011)

Wiener Chic: A Locational History of Vienna Fashion, by Susan Ingram (2014)

Montréal Chic: A Locational History of Montréal Fashion, by Katrina Sark and Sara Danièle Bélanger-Michaud (2016)

L.A. Chic: A Locational History of Los Angeles Fashion, by Susan Ingram and Markus Reisenleiterner (2018)

Copenhagen Chic

A Locational History of Copenhagen Fashion

Edited by
Katrina Sark

Bristol, UK / Chicago, USA

First published in the UK in 2023 by
Intellect, The Mill, Parnall Road, Fishponds, Bristol, BS16 3JG, UK

First published in the USA in 2023 by
Intellect, The University of Chicago Press, 1427 E. 60th Street,
Chicago, IL 60637, USA

Copyright © 2023 Intellect Ltd

All rights reserved. No part of this publication may be reproduced, stored in a retrieval system, or transmitted, in any form or by any means, electronic, mechanical, photocopying, recording, or otherwise, without written permission.

A catalogue record for this book is available from the British Library.

Copy editor: MPS Limited
Cover designer: Tanya Montefusco
Cover image: Copenhagen 2022, photo by K. Sark.
Production manager: Laura Christopher
Typesetter: MPS Limited

Print (hbk) ISBN 978-1-78938-866-4
Print (pbk) ISBN 978-1-78938-783-4
ePDF ISBN 978-1-78938-784-1
ePUB ISBN 978-1-78938-785-8

Urban Chic
ISSN 2053-7077 | Online ISSN 2053-7085

To find out about all our publications, please visit our website. There you can subscribe to our e-newsletter, browse or download our current catalogue and buy any titles that are in print.

www.intellectbooks.com

This is a peer-reviewed publication.

Contents

List of Illustrations	vii
Acknowledgements	xiii
Introduction: Fashion Culture	1
Katrina Sark	
1. Scandinavian Chic	20
Katrina Sark	
2. Copenhagen Fashion History	56
Marie Riegels Melchior	
3. Fashioning Sustainability	77
Else Skjold and Frederik Larsen	
4. Fashioning Functionality	94
Trine Brun Petersen and Maria Mackinney-Valentin	
5. The Bearded Queens of Copenhagen	112
Anders Larsen and Maria Mackinney-Valentin	
6. Fashion in Film	131
Katrina Sark, with research contributions by Bjørn Utoft Sørensen, Emilie Thomsen and Izabella Andersen	
7. Fashion in TV Shows	166
Katrina Sark and Izabella Andersen	
8. Innovation and Technology	181
Katrina Sark, Bjørn Utoft Sørensen and Emilie Thomsen	
Conclusion	197
Katrina Sark	
Notes on Contributors	199

Illustrations

We would like to acknowledge the generosity of the copyright holders of the images in this book. If any have not been properly credited, please contact the publishers, who will be happy to rectify future editions.

I.1	The Emperor's New Clothes statue in Odense, 2020, photo by K. Sark.	2
I.2	Hans Christian Andersen (HCA) statue in Odense, 2020, photo by K. Sark.	2
I.3	HCA museum plaque, 2020, photo by K. Sark.	2
I.4	HCA museum, Odense, 2021, photo by K. Sark.	4
I.5	HCA Childhood Home, Odense, 2021, photo Sebastian Stolz, with permission.	4
I.6	HCA Childhood Home, Odense, 2021, photo by Sebastian Stolz, with permission.	5
I.7	HCA Childhood Home, Odense, 2021, photo by Sebastian Stolz, with permission.	5
I.8	HCA Childhood Home, Odense, 2021, photo by Sebastian Stolz, with permission.	6
I.9	HCA Childhood Home, Odense, 2021, photo by K. Sark.	6
I.10	HCA statue at Tivoli amusement park in Copenhagen, 2019, photo by K. Sark.	9
I.11	Copenhagen's biking culture, 2020, photo by K. Sark.	12
I.12	Copenhagen Fashion Week 2020, photo by K. Sark.	12
I.13	Table: Fashion cities in the Urban Chic book series, developed by K. Sark.	14

1.1	Arne Jacobsen display of chairs at the Design Museum in Copenhagen, 2019, photo by K. Sark.	25
1.2	Kolding Design School 2021, photo by K. Sark.	26
1.3	SDU campus in Kolding, photo by K. Sark.	27
1.4	Textile weaving looms at the Royal Academy in Copenhagen, 2019, photo by K. Sark.	29
1.5	VIA University College in Herning, 2020, photo by K. Sark.	29
1.6	Design Museum in Copenhagen, 2019, photo by K. Sark.	32
1.7	Handbags embroidered by Queen Margrethe II of Denmark, exhibited at Koldinghus, 2021, photo by K. Sark.	33
1.8	Founders of MANND and Else Skjold at the Geological Museum in Copenhagen, 2019, photo by K. Sark.	34
1.9	Geological Museum in Copenhagen, 2019, photo by K. Sark.	34
1.10	Kate Fletcher at the Geological Museum in Copenhagen, 2019, photo by K. Sark.	34
1.11	Fashion collection of the Design Museum in Copenhagen, 2019, photo by K. Sark.	35
1.12	Fashion collection of the Design Museum in Copenhagen, 2019, photo by K. Sark.	35
1.13	Danish design label inside a garment at the Horsens Industry Museum, 2020, photo K. Sark.	39
1.14	Herning Textile Museum 2020, photo by K. Sark.	39
1.15	Herning Textile Museum 2020, photo by K. Sark.	40
1.16	Arne Jacobsen suite 606 at the Radisson Royal Copenhagen Hotel, 2021, photo by K. Sark.	41
1.17	Arne Jacobsen's lobby and winding staircase at the Radisson Royal Copenhagen Hotel, 2021, photo by K. Sark.	42

ILLUSTRATIONS

1.18	Arne Jacobsen's Royal Copenhagen Hotel during World Pride 2021, photo by K. Sark.	43
2.1	Thorvaldsen's Museum facing Vindebrogade, June 2021, photo by Marie Riegels Melchior.	57
2.2	Close-up of the painted motifs on the walls of Thorvaldsen's Museum, photo by Marie Riegels Melchior.	58
2.3	The department store Magasin du Nord, 1918. Photo by unknown photographer, Magasin du Nord Museum, with permission.	59
2.4	Wonderful Copenhagen poster, 1959, by Viggo Vagnby, with permission.	63
2.5	Strøget, the main high street of Copenhagen, 1963, photo by Aage Sørensen/Ritzau Scanpix, with permission.	66
2.6	Nørgaard på Strøget, 1978, photo by Susanne Mertz/BAM/Ritzau Scanpix, with permission.	67
2.7	Live transmission from Copenhagen Fashion Week in February 2007, photo by Marie Riegels Melchior.	73
3.1	CEO Cecilie Thorsmark presenting the Copenhagen Fashion Week "Sustainability Action Plan" in January 2020, photo by Frederik Valdemar Kjeldgaard, with permission.	87
3.2	Circular Fashion Days exhibition organized by the Lifestyle & Design Cluster at CIFF during Copenhagen Fashion Week 2021, photo by K. Sark.	89
3.3	Circular Fashion Days exhibition organized by the Lifestyle & Design Cluster at CIFF during Copenhagen Fashion Week 2021, photo by K. Sark.	89
3.4	MANIFESTO: student exhibition at the program New Landscapes for Change, Fashion, Clothing & Textiles, displayed at the 70% less CO_2 exhibition at the Royal Danish Academy, from 7 October 2021 to 14 January 2022. Photo by the Royal Danish Academy, with permission.	90
4.1	Nørgaard paa Strøget store front in Copenhagen 2022, photo by Trine Brun Petersen.	100

4.2	"Ganni Girls" in frilly dresses and practical footwear. Collection "GANNI × Selfridges: Let's Go Outside," photo by Clare Shilland, with permission by Ganni.	101
4.3	Knit-designer Lærke Bagger's knitted dress 2021, on display at the Design Museum in Copenhagen in 2022, photo by K. Sark.	105
4.4	Henrik Vibskov store in Copenhagen, 2022, photo by Trine Brun Petersen.	107
4.5	Henrik Vibskov store front in Copenhagen, 2022, photo by Trine Brun Petersen.	107
5.1	Jaxie, Copenhagen, 2018, photo by Jack Ashley Benn, with permission.	113
5.2	Fru Bryn, Copenhagen, 2021, photo by Anders Larsen.	119
5.3	Maj, Copenhagen, 2021, photo by Noah Kaber, with permission.	121
5.4	Brynhildr, Copenhagen, 2021, photo by Anders Larsen.	125
5.5	Brynhildr, Copenhagen, 2021, photo by Fru Bryn, with permission.	126
5.6	Jack, Copenhagen, 2021, photo by Anders Larsen.	127
5.7	Noah, Copenhagen, 2021, photo by Anders Larsen.	128
6.1	Asta Nielsen exhibition at the Brandts Museum, Odense, 2020, photo by K. Sark.	134
6.2	Costume workshop at Koldinghus 2020, photo by K. Sark.	140
6.3	Copies of the original costumes from *A Royal Affair* (2012) on display at Koldinghus, 2020, photo by K. Sark.	140
6.4	Koldinghus Castle, 2019, photo by K. Sark.	141
6.5	Dolls at HCA Childhood Home in Odense, 2021, photo by K. Sark.	142
6.6	Helsingør castle, north of Copenhagen, 2019, photo by K. Sark.	143
6.7	Danish graduation hat, photo by Izabella Andersen.	147
6.8	Old sewing machine, Tidens Samling Museum, Odense, 2020, photo by K. Sark.	149
6.9	HCA Boulevard, Copenhagen, 2010, photo by K. Sark.	149
6.10	Magasin du Nord in Copenhagen, 2010, photo by K. Sark.	152

ILLUSTRATIONS

6.11	Danish graduation hat, photo by Mia Petersen, with permission.	160
6.12	Danish graduation hat, photo by Mia Petersen, with permission.	160
7.1	Old television sets, on display at the Horsens Industry Museum, 2020, photo by K. Sark.	171
7.2	Øresund tunnel-bridge that connects Denmark and Sweden, 2019, photo by K. Sark.	173
7.3	Christiansborg, Danish Parliament, 2010, photo by K. Sark.	175
8.1	Kerne Milk storefront in Nørrebro, Copenhagen, 2022, photo by K. Sark.	182
8.2	Artikel København store in Copenhagen, 2021, photo by K. Sark.	185
8.3	Artikel København, 2021, photo by K. Sark.	185
8.4	Artikel København, 2021, photo by K. Sark.	185
8.5	Kvadrat fabrics at Illum Bollinghus in Copenhagen, 2022, photo by K. Sark.	186
8.6	Kvadrat logo on a bag at Res Res conscious fashion store in Copenhagen, 2022, photo K. Sark.	186
8.7	*X-Ray Fashion* installation, 2018, photo by MANND, with permission.	187
8.8	*X-Ray Fashion* installation, 2018, photo by MANND, with permission.	187
8.9	*X-Ray Fashion* installation, 2018, photo by MANND, with permission.	187
8.10	*X-Ray Fashion* poster, photo by MANND, with permission.	188
8.11	*X-Ray Fashion*, photo by MANND, with permission.	189
8.12	The making of *X-Ray Fashion*, photo by MANND, with permission.	189
8.13	Career Day at the Aarhus City Hall (designed by Arne Jacobsen) organized by the Lifestyle & Design Cluster in collaboration with Danish design schools and universities, 2019, photo by K. Sark.	190
8.14	"Fashion Tech & Fashion's Sustainable Growth Layer" exhibition in Copenhagen, August 2019, photo by K. Sark.	192

8.15	"Circular Fashion Days" exhibition and panel discussion on regenerative practices organized by Johanne Stenstrup at CIFF during Copenhagen Fashion Week in August 2021, photo by K. Sark.	193
8.16	"Circular Fashion Days" exhibition and panel discussion on regenerative practices organized by Johanne Stenstrup at CIFF during Copenhagen Fashion Week in August 2021, photo by K. Sark.	194
C.1	HCA statue with kids, Copenhagen, 2010, photo by K. Sark.	198

Acknowledgements

We would like to express our deepest gratitude to DIS Copenhagen and SDU Kolding for their generous support of the publication of this book.

Introduction: Fashion Culture

Katrina Sark

The iconic Danish fairy tale author Hans Christian Andersen (1805–75) has several stories that pertain to fashion, including "The Galoshes of Fortune" (1838), "The Red Shoes" (1845) and "The Shirt Collar" (1848), but none so persistently quoted and relevant as "The Emperor's New Clothes" (1837), in which an emperor and his courtiers are too afraid of losing prestige and power to admit that the two textile weavers and dressmakers they invited to make fashionable new designs for the Emperor are gaslighting everyone by pretending to make clothes, which are in fact invisible. Because the power elites have been told that only those well suited for their privileged positions will be able to see these invisible clothes, they try to save face by lying, pretending that the invisible fabrics and designs are exquisite and continuing to reward the weavers with more silk and gold. Only a child from the village is innocent and honest enough to ask why the Emperor is naked, while all the courtiers continue pretending that nothing is wrong for fear of losing power. This parable is well suited as a metaphor for the contemporary unethical fashion industry and was recently applied to the current climate crisis in Malena Ernman's *Our House Is on Fire: Scenes of a Family and a Planet in Crisis* (2018), where she referred to her daughter Greta Thunberg's climate activism as follows:

> She saw what the rest of us did not want to see. [...] She saw the invisible, colourless, scentless, soundless abyss that our generation has chosen to ignore; the greenhouse gasses streaming out of our chimneys, hovering upwards with the winds, and transforming the atmosphere into a gigantic, invisible garbage dump. She was the child, and we were the emperor. And we were all naked.
> (Ernman 2018: 37–38)

The fairy tale lesson can also stand as an effective metaphor for the greenwashing too prevalent in the global fashion industry, as many brands, companies,

CEOs and CSR managers continue to gaslight consumers with the pretence of transparency despite the urgent need for environmental and social change (Figures I.1–I.3).

FIGURE I.1: The Emperor's New Clothes statue in Odense, 2020, photo by K. Sark.

FIGURE I.2: Hans Christian Andersen (HCA) statue in Odense, 2020, photo by K. Sark.

FIGURE I.3: HCA House museum plaque, 2020, photo by K. Sark.

INTRODUCTION

Hans Christian Andersen (HCA) has shaped not only Danish culture and other literary cultures around the world but he also has a direct link to fashion culture and fashion history. Despite a difficult childhood due to poverty in Odense, on the island of Fyn in the middle of Denmark, Andersen's imagination and creativity were nurtured and cultivated by his father, a local shoemaker, and his mother, who washed clothes for a living. Despite their poverty, Andersen's parents encouraged their son's love of literature and theatre. As Tansy Hoskins explained in *Foot Work* (2020), for centuries shoemakers were important members of their local communities because they provided a vital service,

> working out of small home workshops where they were aided by their wives, children, and apprentices. [...] Shoemakers also had high levels of literacy and enjoyed an unusual degree of autonomy because they could set their own hours and pace of work.
>
> (Hoskins 2020: 51)

Moreover, while fashion production remained localized and community-based, it permeated all other cultural fields and remained interconnected with the cultural fabric of cities and communities, as people valued what they wore, took better care of their clothes and knew who made them. "On Sundays, [my father] made me panoramas, theatres, and transformation pictures, and he would read me pieces out of Holberg's plays and stories from the *Thousand and One Nights*," Andersen recalled in his autobiography, translated as *The Fairy Tale of My Life* (1847), "and those were the only moments in which I remember him as really cheerful, for in his position as an artisan he did not feel happy" (quoted in Slotnik 2016).

There are several buildings in Odense that HCA lived in before moving to Copenhagen as a teenager. His yellow birth house is now incorporated into the new HCA Museum that pays homage to his fairy tales (Figures I.4 and I.5). Andersen's humble childhood home, where he lived from the age of two (1807) until fourteen (the longest stretch of time he lived in one place), was comprised of just one room, much of which was taken up by the shoemaker's workbench, a bed, and the turn-up bench on which young Andersen slept, "but the walls were covered with pictures, on the chest of drawers there stood beautiful cups, glasses, and knickknacks, and above the workbench, by the window, there was a shelf with books and songs" (Slotnik 2016). Andersen grew up making costumes for puppets and enacting plays on the model stage his father had built for him, before heading to Copenhagen, where he perfected his gift for "spinning magic from the mundane" (Slotnik 2016), where his first play, *Love on St. Nicholas Church Tower*, was produced at a local theatre, and where his stories were published and reached beyond the literary and cultural scenes of Copenhagen (Figures I.6–I.9).

FIGURE I.4: HCA museum, Odense, 2021, photo by K. Sark.

FIGURE I.5: HCA Childhood Home, Odense 2021, photo by Sebastian Stolz, with permission.

FIGURE I.6: HCA Childhood Home, Odense, 2021, photo by Sebastian Stolz, with permission.

FIGURE I.7: HCA Childhood Home, Odense, 2021, photo by Sebastian Stolz, with permission.

FIGURE I.8: HCA Childhood Home, Odense, 2021, photo by Sebastian Stolz, with permission.

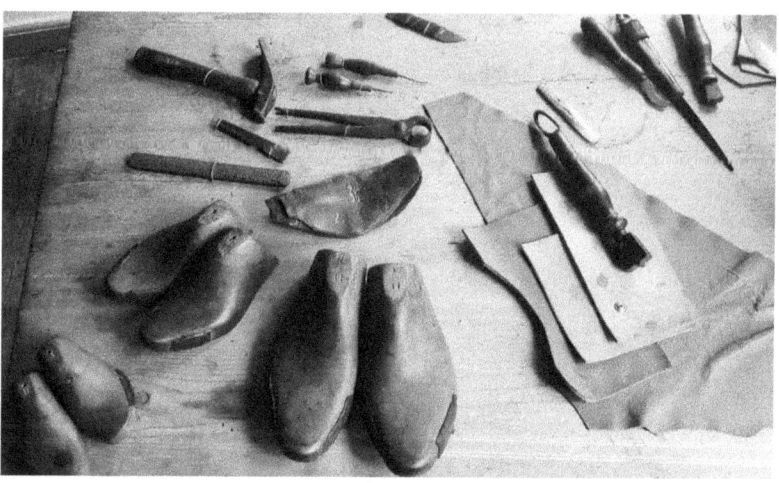

FIGURE I.9: HCA Childhood Home, Odense, 2021, photo by K. Sark.

According to historian Anders Larsen, a contributor to this book, in Andersen's later years, after he had achieved fame and recognition through his fairy tales and joined the upper echelons of the Copenhagen high society that spent large portions of their disposable incomes on fashion, Andersen became quite the fashion victim, spending hours getting dressed and having his hair curled. At times, he was even ridiculed for his appearance.

Andersen has become a major part of Danish cultural export and the cultural branding of Denmark. So, to understand the fashion culture of Copenhagen today, we need to look far beyond its fashion systems of production, consumption and economic value to also engage with cultural meaning, narrative and mediated imaginaries and the locational significance of cultural practices and expressions. I argue that it is precisely in the locational intersections between fashion, art, craft, creativity and visual and narrative storytelling, as well as local histories, that fashion culture can be researched and analyzed to reveal many significant interconnections and new perspectives on the ways in which locational fashion cultures are shaped, cultivated and preserved.

Henrik Spandet-Møller, a Danish fashion industry expert, used Andersen's metaphor from "The Emperor's New Clothes" to argue that Denmark does not have a "fashion culture" (i.e. industry) the way France, Italy and Japan do; rather, it "only has a trading culture" (Spandet-Møller 2011: 36). This view was based on a narrow economic interpretation of fashion cultures (more precisely, fashion systems), one that is supported by academic and non-academic literature on fashion capitals and fashion cities that measures the economic value of fashion production and consumption as it accumulates capital and centres around traditional fashion capital cities, such as London, Paris, Milan, New York and Tokyo. Denmark is indeed different from France, Italy and Japan in how its fashion system operates, but as this book demonstrates, it is not for the lack of a fashion culture. As Kate Fletcher reminded us, "in the collective cultural consciousness, fashion *is* consumption, materialism, commercialization and marketing," and sadly that is also the "view of fashion from many within the sustainability lobby, where there persists a reluctance to imagine fashion outside a commercial context that trades on novelty and status anxiety for economic return" (Fletcher 2015: 18). That is why a "consumer society fails to value activities that cannot be marketed," since in a consumer society "ideas about fashion are organized around commerce and consumerism," as well as economic growth, scalability and status symbols (Fletcher 2015: 18). Breaking away from this limited view of fashion culture is one of the main goals of this book.

Copenhagen Chic is a critical inquiry into the Copenhagen fashion culture, and by extension also the Danish fashion industry and fashion system, through a contemporary and historical analysis of fashion, media and cultural landscapes to expand our understanding of fashion and of culture. It looks at Copenhagen's relationship with fashion through history, contemporary practices and trends, queer identities, performativity and artistic, literary, filmic and television narratives and representations, as well as attempts to innovate industry practices through new technologies. It also challenges perceptions of Copenhagen fashion as inherently sustainable by pointing to the hypocrisy of conventional, unsustainable paradigms and business practices that unethical marketing promises greenwash; yet it also showcases the idealism, engagement, and grit of leading and upcoming Danish innovators – all the while situating these developments in their local, national and global contexts. This book also highlights how the fashion industry remains under-researched due to its situation in the experience rather than the knowledge economy.

The Urban Chic book series was created exactly in opposition to the narrow view of what fashion and fashion culture can be. In many contexts of our daily life, fashion is reduced to a consumer commodity – a fast and mass-produced traded article of textile waste made obsolete within an unjust and unsustainable economic fashion system. But fashion is so much more than its market value – it is also a culture in its own right, and this book, along with the other books in the Urban Chic book series, demonstrates that by shifting the focus towards the cultural analysis of fashion and, as has also been done with literature, art, film, media, architecture, design, branding and other cultural fields, deconstructing its many layers of meaning. It is in the interpretive work of cultural analysis that fashion culture becomes a field of study and a methodology. Since the publication of the first volume in this series, *Berliner Chic: A Locational History of Berlin Fashion* (2011), which I co-authored with Susan Ingram, the Urban Chic books have been a collaborative effort to re-define fashion as urban culture, to map out the cultural significance of fashion in cities with rich fashion histories and contemporary fashion scenes, and to investigate the many intersections between fashion and other cultural fields, in order to widen our understanding of fashion and culture. As in the other books in the series, this volume maps out the ways in which fashion culture intersects and interconnects with other cultural fields amalgamated in a city and incorporates both historical and contemporary fashion landscapes (Figure I.10).

This book investigates Copenhagen culture through the lens of fashion. To understand Copenhagen fashion culture – or what we call Copenhagen Chic – it is important to first distinguish between "Copenhagen," "Danish," "Scandi or Scandinavian," and "Nordic" design and fashion, and how these descriptions have been used in different contexts for different audiences today, which is the subject of the first chapter. This clarification of geographical designations also helps to situate and contextualize Copenhagen among the other fashion cities in the series to map out and analyze the various elements that constitute a fashion city with a fashion culture and explain why Copenhagen is certainly one as well, which I do later in this introduction. But first, I will define how I use fashion culture as a methodology and a research field.

INTRODUCTION

FIGURE I.10: HCA statue at Tivoli amusement park in Copenhagen, 2019, photo by K. Sark.

Fashion culture as a methodology

Over the past fifteen years, my work has advanced an interdisciplinary methodology that analyzes the fashion culture of cities as a research field inspired by cultural analysis. Berlin, Vienna, Montréal and Los Angeles are all cities that are not traditionally considered global fashion capitals but nonetheless have vibrant fashion cultures, scenes, histories, industries, media and technological innovations. This methodological approach always begins with literature reviews (in this case what has been published about Copenhagen and Danish fashion in English and Danish). Interviews with fashion professionals in the local fashion industry, fashion education and other cultural fields combined with an analysis of literature, films, television shows and other media in which the city and its fashion play a key role. Finally, the key components and organizations of the local fashion industry and fashion scene are mapped out. By looking at the intersections of place and history, culture and economies, multimedia, innovation and technology, I argued (in *Montréal Chic* in 2016) that it is precisely the preservation and cultivation of a local fashion culture as a cultural heritage that allows cities to sustain healthy fashion economies, industries, scenes and networks. Through this interdisciplinary work, I understand fashion culture as the amalgamation of a city's fashion identity based on the interconnected web of histories, branding, industries, labour conditions, gender, race, class politics, identity negotiations, cultural scenes, topographical transformations, gentrification, social and political change and economic development, as well as visual, narrative and social media representations. Fashion culture is highly multidisciplinary and cannot be narrowly defined in economic or social terms, or in terms of developments, trends or fluctuations. While it is connected to fashion systems, fashion culture is more than the economic and social systems that surround various fashion industries. Fashion culture exists beyond economic instabilities, even though it can be impacted by economic and political decisions, such as government subsidies, cuts or policies applied to the fashion sector. More importantly, fashion culture is more than just the post-Second World War organization of industrial labour around production centres and the production output of a city's traditional industries. Fashion culture is always in flux and evolving, but it does not start or end depending on its market value; in fact, it exists and evolves beyond market values; otherwise, it would not stand the test of time or continue to evolve.

I locate the methodology of fashion culture at the multidisciplinary intersections of cultural analysis, cultural history and the analysis of media representations of fashion in urban contexts. I investigate the ways in which fashion can be re-inscribed with cultural values independent from its material or trend-driven value or obsolescence. By examining existing and available primary and secondary sources, consulting both historical and contemporary data and conducting interviews with specialists, experts, archivists, designers and other professionals, I map out, compare and analyze the research that emerges from the intersections of fashion and other cultural areas, including film, television, social media, art, museum collections and exhibitions, technology, industry practices and misdemeanours, as well as networks of key players and influences in local fashion scenes and industries. This mapping of intersecting and interdisciplinary research data allows for certain patterns to become visible and prominent in their respective locational contexts that would otherwise not be apparent without a wide interdisciplinary lens. It is both the breadth of the research and the detailed interconnections between the various case studies that yield a more nuanced understanding of fashion cultures than their economic capacities.

After mapping out the local fashion culture of a city, we can then compare them to other cities and their fashion cultures, to see larger national, transnational and global patterns and influences that can transform the ways in which we assign meaning and value to fashion and to culture. Fashion culture may be distinct from fashion industries, economies and systems but, like them, it can also be analyzed and interpreted as a cultural field. Its intersections with other cultural products and scenes reveal distinct characteristics of the respective cities and their relationship to fashion. These characteristics allow us to distinguish how fashion cultures are formed, maintained and re-negotiated. Approaching fashion culture as a field of study goes beyond its economic value as a system of production, consumption or circulation and towards an amalgamation of a city's cultural heritage. The interwoven relationship between fashion and culture is a key to conducting this type of analysis. As a methodological approach, fashion culture can be used as an investigative tool to map out fashion cities and their locational and cultural histories. Despite the vague and varying usage of the term fashion culture in fashion studies, it is possible to bring it down to one common denominator, namely that of the cultural analysis of fashion, in all its multidisciplinary, multimedia and multidimensional facets and folds, as it pertains to a given location. Unfolding these layers can help us understand our cultures, our cities and ourselves better.

Fashion cities with fashion culture

For this volume on Copenhagen, I teamed up with fashion scholars and industry experts to construct a portrait of Copenhagen's fashion culture from the perspectives of its history, sustainability, contemporary practices, various intersections of fashion and identities, media representations and technological innovations. This volume examines the ways in which Copenhagen inhabitants engage with fashion today – for example, the way biking to work affects sartorial practices, and comfort is valued as highly as elegance. How does Copenhagen fashion relate to branding conceptions of "Danish," "Scandinavian" or global fashion? And what is it about Copenhagen culture at large that has shaped its fashion culture in unique ways? Copenhagen has been repeatedly celebrated for its unique fashion, design, innovation and sustainability practices, yet no comprehensive study exists in English about the history of Copenhagen fashion and its current innovation and sustainability drive. Books about fashion in Denmark include Andersen (1977), Bech (1989), Cock-Clausen (1994), Jensen (2013) and Melchior (2013), but they are all in Danish and do not have a specific focus on Copenhagen. In this volume, we provide a historically grounded and research-based combination of insider expertise and an outsider comparative perspective to focus on specific case studies that reveal unique glimpses into the cultural fabric of the city and its fashion. Throughout this book, we conceptualize Copenhagen fashion culture as Copenhagen Chic, which is to say informed by, but also different from, the existing discursive and historical conceptualizations of "Danish" fashion and design, as well as "Nordic" and "Scandinavian" fashion and design. The way Copenhagen Chic is contextualized in the various discourses and histories of design and fashion in the first chapter allows us to distinguish Copenhagen fashion culture as a distinct cultural field of study (Figures I.11 and I.12).

FIGURE I.11: Copenhagen's biking culture, 2020, photo by K. Sark.

FIGURE I.12: Copenhagen Fashion Week 2020, photo by K. Sark.

It is not a coincidence that, in 2005, the Danish government was the "first among the Scandinavian countries to introduce a fashion policy" (Melchior 2011: 183). Similar initiatives took place around the same time in Montréal before the Quebec government subsidies turned from the fashion sector towards the IT sector; in Berlin, where the Berlin Senate under the leadership of Mayor Klaus Wowereit officially adopted the creative economy to help the bankrupt, still reconstructing and gentrifying city transition into a political, cultural and economic capital, and even incorporated its fashion promotion into the "Be Berlin" city branding campaigns (Sark 2023); and in Vienna, where in the contemporary municipal funding structure it has been incorporated into a massive city branding campaign in response to the turn to the creative economy. In the first decade of the new millennium, many fashion cities with a history of either textile or fashion manufacturing that were transitioning from the loss of manufacturing jobs to generate new creative economy jobs were competing with Tokyo for the glamorous title of "fifth" fashion capital, after Paris, London, New York and Milan, by boosting their fashion economies with subsidies, policies, reports, new organizations, fashion weeks and many other publicity events and branding campaigns. All of them poured government subsidies into their fashion industries and put economists and business leaders in charge, who often deprioritized academic research (especially in the areas of ethics and sustainability) in favour of profitability, export and brand globalization strategies. Essentially, none of them reached the desired economic status of "fifth" fashion capital before the government funds dried out and the governments reprioritized their investments into other sectors. None of the government funding at that time went into making the local fashion industries more sustainable. But nonetheless, all of them experienced a brief spike in their fashion systems, boosting their fashion scenes, institutions and media, generating new foundations in many fields of fashion creativity, and thus also boosting their fashion cultures.

What became apparent when analyzing the government funding strategies of the early 2000s, as I argued in *Montréal Chic* in 2016, was that it is not enough to pour money into boosting local fashion industries – once the subsidies ran dry, the networks and organizations were often dismantled without building any sustainable structures or bridges. What these investing strategies were missing was a close collaboration with sociologists, material historians, cultural analysts and other scholars, who not only understand fashion as a socio-economic system but also as a culture. As Else Skjold and Frederik Larsen put it in the third chapter of this book, the transition to a knowledge-based economy lost out to the short-term advantages of an experience-based economy. In *Montréal Chic*, I argued that focusing on the preservation and cultivation of a local fashion culture as cultural heritage (which Vienna came closest to doing because it included the fashion sector into its annual municipal cultural budget) allows cities to sustain more flexible fashion economies and fashion scenes. As design historian Anders V. Munch has pointed out, in Denmark both design and fashion have moved between the Ministry of Trade and Ministry of Culture since the 1950s, but the Ministry of Culture has a smaller budget, so investments from both sides are necessary.

In *Montréal Chic*, I outlined the most common elements that constitute a fashion city by comparing Montréal, Berlin and Vienna, their fashion cultures and fashion economies (2016: 163–64). Like these cities, Copenhagen also experienced a government-led boost in its fashion sector as part of the early 2000s transition to the creative economies, which repositioned the role of fashion not only as an economic priority but also as culturally relevant. But again, as in the other cities, merely subsidising the local fashion industry in the hopes that it will trickle down to the creative designers, researchers and young people with an innovative potential to make the industry more economically, socially and environmentally sustainable, while at the same time continuously rewarding the most competitive, hierarchical, exclusive, or unethical actors in the industry does not generate a lasting impact. Rather, cultivating a vibrant local fashion culture based on locational cultural heritage promoting the cultural value of fashion, and not merely its economic output, impacts the long-term evolution of the city and its culture. I developed the following chart to map out the key components in the fashion cities I researched for the Urban Chic book series (Table I.1).

TABLE I.1: Fashion cities in the Urban Chic book series, developed by K. Sark.

		Montréal	Berlin	Vienna	Copenhagen
1.	Local designers	✓	✓	✓	✓
2.	Suppliers and manufacturers	✓	✓	✓	✓
3.	Retailers, boutiques	✓	✓	✓	✓
4.	Fashion events and festivals	Festival Mode & Design	Mercedes-Benz Fashion Week	MQ Vienna Fashion Week	Copenhagen Fashion Week, Global Fashion Agenda
5.	Fashion in museums	✓	✓	✓	✓
6.	Special fashion organizations that promote designers and the fashion industry	CCMQ, Bureau de la Mode	Create Berlin	Departure, Unit F	Lifestyle & Design Cluster, DM&T
7.	Fashion schools	8	10	5	6
8.	Fashion magazines	*Elle Québec, Dressed to Kill, Clin d'Oeil, Lou Lou*	✓	✓	*Elle Denmark, Eurowoman, Scandinavian Vogue*
9.	Fashion professionals (photographers, models, stylists, etc.)	✓	✓	✓	✓
10.	Trade shows	No	Premium, Neonyt	Modepalast, Blickfang, Modecenter	Copenhagen International Fashion Fair (CIFF), Revolver

INTRODUCTION

These ten criteria can be found and mapped out for many different cities around the world. In the early 2000s, economists and strategists put in charge of distributing the government subsidies used similar criteria to map out and boost the respective fashion sectors of Berlin, Vienna and Montréal. But I define fashion cities as cities with a vital and evolving fashion culture capable of transcending fluctuations in global markets and government subsidies, or unpredictable economic recessions (as, for example, resulted from the COVID-19 pandemic). Fashion cities with evolved fashion cultures have robust cultural and fashion networks that are based on collaboration and mutual support, rather than on competition and hierarchies. The most successful fashion cities manage not only to transition from the loss of their manufacturing infrastructure, labour and production systems, but to reconceptualize themselves as creative platforms for research, innovation, knowledge, education, experimentation, creativity and sustainability. They build on their existing fashion histories (re-tellings of the past) and heritage (objects that have survived from the past), and they incorporate that past into their present and future, without creating fragmented or competing factions, but rather by fostering an environment of collaborative creativity and channeling it into a holistic fashion culture. Copenhagen has all the potential and the necessary components to be a fashion city with a holistic fashion culture, and in many ways, it is already ahead of many other fashion cities. But its fashion culture will always remain in the making – and the next decades, post-COVID-19, and after adopting its sustainability agenda, will demonstrate to what extent it can learn from both its own past and culture and those of other fashion cities, and move forward.

What Copenhagen has done differently from the other fashion cities I have observed over the years is to use the initial government investments in the early 2000s to boost fashion and design education and transform its trade schools into universities to prepare its graduates for the creative economies (as I discuss in more detail in Chapter 1, and as Else Skjold and Frederik Larsen outline in Chapter 3). In the early 2000s, graduate programs with research requirements were created in fashion and design schools across Denmark. The Danish Design Museum in Copenhagen invested in research and exhibitions on fashion and began acquiring its own fashion collection (even though only a small fraction of it has been on display). Yet, at the same time, most design schools also stopped teaching fashion history, leaving its graduates, and many educators, vulnerable to major cultural blind spots around cultural appropriation, cultural insensitivity, colonial practices and legacies, as well as a general lack of knowledge about equity, diversity and inclusivity (EDI), not to mention industry practice. Nonetheless, critical fashion studies with a focus not only on environmental but also on social sustainability are in development in Denmark and beyond, and the initial investment into education has produced industry leaders, educators, researchers, policy advisers and consultants (some of whom are contributors to this book), as well as designer-activists, who are now driving the sustainability agenda forward and gradually transforming the landscape of fashion. But the sustainability turn was rather an uncoordinated and unforeseen side effect of the initial fashion policy because most of the government funding still went into industry subsidies and events, and actually worked against the desired sustainability agenda by boosting fast fashion companies, corporations and traditional business practices, and making fast fashion one of Denmark's top export commodities.

As Else Skjold and Frederik Larsen argue in the third chapter, 2020 was an important turning point in many respects, including the introduction of a sustainability agenda, which was adopted by Copenhagen Fashion Week, Copenhagen International Fashion Fair (CIFF) and other progressive industry players in Denmark and beyond. After being accused of greenwashing and ethical gaslighting (Matthews 2020; Campione 2017), the Copenhagen Fashion Summit rebranded itself just before the COVID-19 lockdowns as the Global Fashion Agenda with a new CEO, but there is not yet any demonstrable change in its organizational practices. One step in the right direction at their first post-COVID event in October 2021 was inviting more diverse representatives of the fashion industry to speak at their panels and consult more with researchers. However, the theme of the event was "Prosperity vs. Growth," and despite their claim to "challenge" these concepts, their exclusionary, for-profit business model has not changed, their content remains restricted behind a paywall, and one of their main sponsors is Nike. Similarly disturbing is the choice of the "Sustainability Manager" from Bestseller, the Danish fast fashion conglomerate, as the chairperson of the task force put together by the Danish Ministry of Industry, Business and Financial Affairs to "make Danish fashion and textiles even greener" (Christiansen Weigel 2021). The paradoxes of the sustainability battles in Denmark and beyond are endless and need further investigation (Sark and Gotthardsen 2023).

But the transition is only just beginning, and the development of a more circular and ethical fashion industry is currently unfolding alongside the prospering fast fashion business practices, which are still unregulated. What we see in Copenhagen, as in Denmark as a whole, are two competing fashion industries with very different goals: a fast fashion empire led by Bestseller and other corporations that want to maximize profits at the expense of labour rights and environmental degradation in the Global South, and a slow and mindful fashion movement characterized by de-growth, made-to-order, zero waste and the circularity-focused practices of a growing sustainability industry that is trying to educate consumers to make more ethical choices. Currently, these two contradictory industries coexist, and they will continue to do so and compete for customers until the government intervenes to make it illegal to produce unethical fashion – unfortunately by which time it will most likely be too late to prevent environmental damage in light of the impending climate crisis. Both industries are currently fuelled by new generations of designers, industry professionals and creative young talents educated at Danish design schools. But as Else Skjold pointed out, many of the design students no longer want to contribute to an unsustainable fashion economy, as discussed in Chapter 1, and are increasingly seeking out more sustainable education and professionalization opportunities. Government-funded organizations such as the Lifestyle & Design Cluster are assisting in bringing research, circularity transitions and technological innovation to Danish fashion and design companies, as well as helping design and fashion graduates find their place in Danish fashion and design industries (discussed in more detail in Chapter 8). But this transition has only just begun and is unfolding very slowly considering that the deadline for the UN Sustainable Development Goals (SDGs) has been set for 2030.

Chapter overview

This volume is the first comprehensive study of Copenhagen fashion culture and aims to inspire future generations of thinkers, creators and practitioners in fashion and design fields to make their industries more ethical and just by reconceptualizing how we understand fashion and culture. Our chapters provide both a broad perspective on Copenhagen fashion and, simultaneously, also a more in-depth analysis and critique with the aim to provide insights into the historical and current transformation of Copenhagen's fashion and to expand the understanding of fashion. In the first chapter, I outline the discursive, historical, geographical, educational and museal representations of Copenhagen, Danish, Scandinavian and Nordic fashion and design practices and their histories of self-branding. In the second chapter, Marie Riegels Melchior focuses on the history of Copenhagen fashion after the Second World War. The third chapter is co-authored by Else Skjold, a sustainable fashion design educator and researcher at the Royal Academy of Copenhagen, and Frederik Larsen, a sustainability consultant and co-founder of In futurum. They examine Copenhagen's path towards "Fashioning Sustainability," including the missed opportunities and resistance that have affected its development since Denmark's transition to an experiential economy. The fourth chapter is co-authored by Trine Brun Petersen, head of research of the Royal Collection and Maria Mackinney-Valentin, an educator at the Royal Academy in Copenhagen. Their chapter, "Fashioning Functionality," looks at the contemporary fashion practices of Copenhageners through analysis of several Copenhagen-based brands. The fifth chapter examines queer fashion practices through the case studies of three bearded drag performers in Copenhagen. It includes a queer history that is closely tied with the city's fashion history and is co-authored by the Copenhagen historian and educator Anders Larsen and Maria Mackinney-Valentin. The sixth chapter engages with representations of fashion in Danish films set in Copenhagen and provides a cultural history of Danish cinema through the lens of fashion. It is co-authored by Katrina Sark with the assistance of her former students at SDU, Bjørn Utoft Sørensen, Emilie Thomsen and Izabella Andersen. The seventh chapter looks at representations of fashion in Danish television shows and is co-authored by Katrina Sark and Izabella Andersen. The eighth chapter concludes the book with a focus on innovation and technology, co-authored by Katrina Sark, Bjørn Utoft Sørensen and Emilie Thomsen. Our hope is that this book inspires readers to see fashion and culture in new ways and to expand the limits of creativity and sustainability in their own work.

REFERENCES

Andersen, Ellen. *Danske drageter. Moden i 1700-aarene*. København: Nationalmuseet og Nyt Nordisk Forlag Arnold Busck, 1977.

Andersen, Hans Christian. "The Emperor's New Clothes." *Andersen's Fairy Tales*, www.gutenberg.org/files/1597/1597-h/1597-h.htm. Accessed 13 Mar. 2023.

Bech, Viben. *Danske dragter. Moden 1840–1890*. København: Nationalmuseet og Nyt Nordisk Forlag Arnold Busck, 1989.

Campione, Chiara. "Copenhagen Fashion Summit: How NOT to Make the Fashion Industry More Sustainable." *Greenpeace*, 11 May 2017, www.greenpeace.org/international/story/7575/copenhagen-fashion-summit-how-not-to-make-the-fashion-industry-more-sustainable/. Accessed 13 Mar. 2023.

Christiansen Weigel, Camilla. "New Task Force Will Make Danish Fashion and Textiles Even Greener." *Ehrvervsministiriet*, 11 Apr. 2021, https://em.dk/nyhedsarkiv/2021/marts/ny-taskforce-skal-goere-dansk-mode-og-tekstil-endnu-groennere/?fbclid=IwAR0FVV8PN-CUWTm1f9TiJrV0UAIt2pgf1SOYytzJ0PJS7q6uudtOs7aeMcl4. Accessed 13 Mar. 2023.

Cock-Clausen, Ingeborg. *Moden i 1890–1920. Historicisme og nye tider*. København: Nyt Nordisk Forlag Arnold Busck og Nationalmuseet, 1992.

Ernman, Malena. *Our House Is on Fire: Scenes of a Family and a Planet in Crisis*. New York: Penguin, 2018.

Fletcher, Kate. "Other Fashion Systems." *Routledge Handbook of Sustainability and Fashion*, edited by Kate Fletcher and Mathilda Tham. London: Routledge, 2015, pp. 15–24.

Fletcher, Kate, and Mathilda Tham, editors. *Routledge Handbook of Sustainability and Fashion*. London: Routledge, 2015.

Hoskins, Tansy E. *Foot Work: What Your Shoes Are Doing to The World*. London: W&N, 2020.

Ingram, Susan and Katrina Sark. *Berliner Chic: A Locational History of Berlin Fashion*. Bristol: Intellect, 2011.

Jensen, Kristoffer. *Beklædningsindustriens møde med globaliseringen. Brancheorganisationer og individuelle virksomheder under press, perioden 1960–2000*, Odense: University of Southern Denmark, 2013.

Kent, Sarah. "How Copenhagen Became Fashion's Sustainability Capital." *Business of Fashion*, 28 Jan. 2020, www.businessoffashion.com/articles/sustainability/how-copenhagen-became-fashions-sustainability-capital/. Accessed 13. Mar. 2023.

Mathews, Brett. "Clean Clothes Slams Global Fashion Agenda over Summit." *Apparel Insider*, 12 Oct. 2020, www.apparelinsider.com/7707-2/. Accessed 13 Mar. 2023.

Mathews, Brett. "Greenwash Not Growth is Fashion's Problem." *Apparel Insider*, 22 Jan. 2020, www.apparelinsider.com/greenwash-not-growth-is-fashions-problem/. Accessed 13 Mar. 2023.

Mathews, Brett. "How Can We Fix a Broken Industry?" *Apparel Insider*, 8 Dec. 2020, www.apparelinsider.com/how-can-we-fix-a-broken-industry/. Accessed 13 Mar. 2023.

Melchior, Marie Riegels. "From Design Nations to Fashion Nations? Unpacking Contemporary Scandinavian Fashion Dreams." *Fashion Theory*, vol. 15, no. 2, 2011, pp. 177–200.

Sark, Katrina, and Sara Danièle Bélanger-Michaud. *Montréal Chic: A Locational History of Montréal Fashion*. Bristol: Intellect, 2016.

Sark, Katrina. *Branding Berlin: From Division to the Cultural Capital of Europe*. London: Routledge, 2023.

Sark, Katrina, and Tanja Gotthardsen. "Bæredygtighedsparadokser i modesystemer." *Grønne designkulturanalyser: Perspektiver på bæredygtighed*. Odense: SDU University Press, 2023.

Sark, Katrina, and Tanja Gotthardsen. "Digital Multilogue on Fashion Education – Workshop on Fashion Paradoxes." *Chic Podcast*, Episode 33, 26 Oct. 2021, www.anchor.fm/chic-podcast/episodes/Episode-33—Digital-Multilogue-on-Fashion-Education—Workshop-on-Fashion-Paradoxes-e19bk6d. Accessed 13 Mar. 2023.

Skjold, Else. *Fashion Research at Design Schools*. Kolding: Designskolen Kolding, 2008.

Skjold, Else. "The Fashion Industry Is So Yesterday." *Politiken*, 9 Aug. 2020, www.kglakademi.dk/sites/default/files/downloads/news/feature_politiken_9.8.2020.pdf. Accessed 13 Mar. 2023.

Slotnik, Daniel E. "Sprung from Poverty, the Tales of Hans Christian Andersen Endure." *The New York Times*, 4 Aug. 2016, www.nytimes.com/interactive/projects/cp/obituaries/archives/hans-christian-andersen. Accessed 13 Mar. 2023.

Spandet-Møller, Henrik. *Danish Fashion Going Global*. Hellerup: Henrik Spandet-Møller/HSMH Holding ApS, 2011.

Urban Chic Book Series, www.urban-chic.net/. Accessed 13 Mar. 2023.

1

Scandinavian Chic

Katrina Sark

The discursive and historical context in which Copenhagen fashion and design co-habit, along with other locational and symbolic demarcations, have been written about in academic literature as separate fields of research. This chapter bridges the discourses of design and fashion, examines the wider context, terminology and usage practices of the designations "Scandinavian" or "Scandi" and "Nordic" design and fashion, maps out design and fashion education in Copenhagen and locates Copenhagen fashion in academic and popular literature. I begin with an overview of the ways in which Danish, Scandinavian and Nordic design have gained wide international recognition since the 1950s and how these concepts and branding strategies relate to the history of Danish fashion, with a particular focus on the role of Copenhagen as a cultural centre. I investigate why the locational markers of "Danish," "Scandinavian" and "Nordic" have been used interchangeably at different times, what they evoke and how they serve as markers of self-identification, self-mythologizing and international branding.

This chapter maps the history of fashion culture in Copenhagen onto already existing cultural histories of Danish design and fashion because a comprehensive study of its fashion and its connection to design history does not yet exist. It also connects the multidisciplinary research field and methodologies of design culture, developed by my colleagues at the University of Southern Denmark (SDU) out of the fields of design history and design studies, with fashion culture to help extend the critical studies of fashion beyond economic fashion systems. Thus, by connecting Copenhagen's discursive, theoretical, practical, historical and current fashion culture to design culture in Denmark and Scandinavia, we can see the intersections of cultural practices and narratives emerge that are not usually apparent when analyzed as separate fields of research. By weaving in multidisciplinary literature reviews, cultural histories, media and branding analysis and comparing them to institutional practices various funding structures, a multidimensional perspective on fashion culture emerges that cannot be reduced to a mere economic denominator. This type of research takes time and requires a level of comfort with interpreting often conflicting and contradictory data, but it also allows for a more holistic and complex understanding of fashion and culture.

Terminology, history and geography

What is called "Scandinavian Design" – in reference to Scandinavian, Nordic, Danish and Copenhagen design, furniture, décor, fashion and style – can be traced back to international exhibitions in the 1950s, but Mirjam Gelfer-Jørgensen found two "Nordic" Exhibitions of Industry and Art in 1872 and 1888 in Copenhagen, which were followed by two collaborative exhibitions at the 1889 and the 1900 Paris World Fairs, where the Nordic countries exhibited together "in order to strengthen the sense of community" and mark the "special character of each country" (Gelfer-Jørgensen 2006: 19). The terms "Nordic" and "Scandinavian" often refer to the general geographical area of northern Europe that includes Denmark, Sweden, Norway and in some cases Finland, but in strict geographical and linguistic terms, Finland is not considered part of the Scandinavian peninsula – geographers refer to it as the Fenno-Scandinavian area. In design, however, Finland is often included under the designation of "Design in Scandinavia," while Iceland, Greenland, Åland and the Faroe Islands are considered part of the Nordic countries but not part of Scandinavia. The terms are often used interchangeably, but in practice "Nordic" is the preferred term the nations refer to themselves both in local and transnational references (both in local and transnational references like the Nordic Council, Nordic Press Association, Nordic Innovation, etc.), while "Scandinavian" is the term originally preferred by the Anglo-American media and then adopted by the Nordic countries for international (self-)branding purposes. According to Anders Larsen, historically Denmark had very close ties to the Holy Roman Empire, even though the Danish king remained independent, and much of the cultural influence came from Germany (the Danish royal families of the fifteenth to nineteenth centuries came from the House of Oldenburg and the House of Glücksburg). But following the Schleswig Wars of 1848 and 1864, and the rising anti-German sentiments (*Tyskerfejden*), which also coincided with growing Romantic narratives that glorified a common Scandinavian past (pan-Scandinavism), it could also be argued that the Danes became Scandinavian in order not to be regarded as German.

Design historian Anders V. Munch borrowed the term "self-exoticization" from fashion studies to describe how Danish design developed a strategy of self-fashioning performed according to the international, more or less flattering expectations of a preserved, cultural unity (Munch 2017: 51). The self-fashioning discourse of Danish design has been traced to as early as 1900, which demonstrates how critics and designers were central in shaping the Danish design culture later reproduced for foreign audiences by the exhibitions and books of the 1950s and 1960s (Munch 2017: 51). Munch also notes that, as we know from postcolonial research and works such as Graham Huggan's *The Post-Colonial Exotic: Marketing the Margins* (Huggan 2001: 13), "exoticism describes a particular mode of aesthetic perception – one which renders people, objects, and places strange even as it domesticates them, and which effectively manufactures otherness even as it claims to surrender to its immanent mystery" (quoted in Munch 2017: 59). Self-exoticization in post-Second World War Danish design discourse was a response to an "already formed curiosity about Denmark as an exotic exception to global developments," but one that presented

> a different kind of exoticism to orientalism or dreams of remote paradise islands because it refers to a part of the European cultural heritage, i.e. Old World exotica. But it is still a lost world, a former crafts-based society, invoked by objects and images.
> (Munch 2017: 59)

Thus, the self-branding narratives in Copenhagen's fashion and design scenes that continue to intermingle the geographical demarcations of Nordic, Scandinavian (or Scandi) and Danish design are less about locational accuracy or specificity and more about evoking well-established narratives of design cultures.

In New Nordic branding, the interplay between the well-established tradition of "Scandinavian Modern" and the trendy "New Nordic Design" has been examined by Anders V. Munch and Niels Peter Skou, who argue that the "New Nordic Design must be seen as (part of) a lifestyle trend" (Skou & Munch 2016: 2). The New Nordic branding created a "design destination" for tourists and creative professionals (Skou & Munch 2016: 3), in many ways inspired by the success of New Nordic cuisine, with the opening of the restaurant Noma in 2003 in Copenhagen and the launch of the *New Nordic Kitchen Manifesto* in 2004, and with official backing by the Danish government and the Nordic Council of Ministers in order to position "Scandinavia as a cultural region with a special potential for creativity and a heightened level of aesthetic understanding" (Skou & Munch 2016: 5–6). Again, the terms "Nordic" and "Scandinavian" were used interchangeably to signal various co-operations and regional affinities and simultaneously also construct a narrative and consolidate its reputation for quality products and experiences associated with the locational histories and cultures. Similarly, the "Meet the Nordics" fashion events curated by Kim Grenaa as part of the Copenhagen Fashion Weeks for several years leading up to 2020 showcased and marketed many Danish brands, along with a few brands from neighbouring countries. Including both slow fashion brands and fast fashion brands positioned to greenwash themselves to fit the bill highlighted the perceived sustainability that the term "Nordic" conveyed.

One of the most comprehensive investigations into the origins of "Scandinavian Design" was conducted by Widar Halén and Kerstin Wickman in their edited book, *Scandinavian Design Beyond the Myth: Fifty Years of Scandinavian Design from the Nordic Countries* (Halén & Wickman 2006). Their collection revealed the way that "Nordic solidarity," which solidified during the Second World War, then led to a number of post-war joint exhibitions, starting with the Nordic Decorative Arts Congress in Copenhagen in 1946, followed by gatherings in Oslo in 1948, Stockholm in 1950, Oslo in 1952, and concluding with a conference in Helsinki in 1954 (Halén 2006: 8). What bonded the northern European countries together in issues of design at that time was post-war reconstruction and the housing shortages (Halén 2006: 8). British design historian Kevin Davies has established that the term "Scandinavian" design was launched in England in 1951, when the Nordic countries presented a collaborative exhibition of industrially produced design and decorative arts entitled "Scandinavia at Table," organized by the British Council of Industrial Design in London, accompanied by a simultaneous commercial exhibition, "Scandinavian Design for Living," at Heal's department store (Halén 2006: 9). The "Triennale" exhibitions in Milan during the 1950s also contributed to the creation of the concept "Scandinavian Design" as the style of the modern Nordic countries (Halén 2006: 15). Thus, in the design world, "Scandinavian" design was a branding term that emerged from several international design exhibitions and consolidated after the North American success of the "Design in Scandinavia" exhibition that toured the United States and Canada between 1954 and 1957 and prompted the international press to push Danish, Swedish, Finnish and Norwegian design into the international media spotlight.

In the 1950s, when the Danish Ministry of Culture was founded, marking a centralized attempt to canonize Danish culture, and shortly after the post-war creation of the welfare state economies in Denmark, Norway and Sweden, Edgar Kaufmann Jr., curator at the Museum of Modern Art (MOMA) in New York, praised the collaboration of the Nordic countries in presenting their joint designs. Kaufmann was impressed by the smaller scale of the Danish design industry in comparison to the US manufacturing system and believed "Scandinavian Design" to be "the last refuge of a consistent set of aesthetic and cultural values" through "closer contact to users and their everyday practice," which was "being erased by mass production and commercialisation elsewhere" (Munch 2018: 48). Thus, Danish design practices were celebrated in the United States through deliberate locational marketing and branding of place – specifically under the common umbrella of "Scandinavian Design." This and similar international reviews elevated "Scandinavian Design" beyond the realm of design culture and helped construct an almost mythical legacy of connecting design practices to values associated with post-Second World War social democracy, modernity, welfare state and quality craft that to this day inform the international conceptions of life in Scandinavian countries, which may not always reflect actual day-to-day reality and struggles but nonetheless still fuel global imaginaries and are reproduced in marketing and branding strategies.

According to Jørn Guldberg, who studied the discourse of "Scandinavian Design,"

> From the mid-1950s, Scandinavian commentators, critics, historians, and others simply adopted the discourse of "Scandinavian Design" after it had been elaborated, refined, and made sophisticated abroad. Actually, two different discourses exist: a commercial one in which "Scandinavian Design" stands for a general brand, and a design cultural one referring to the elements of the continuity issue. This double discourse also invokes a conception of the post-war decades as a "Golden Age," the legacy of which is now being considered a yoke by contemporary designers and exporters.
>
> (Guldberg 2011: 58)

The tendency to group design and industrial production by nations or regions has always been part of international exhibition practices, something Stina Teilmann-Lock has traced back to the exhibition culture of the Great Exhibitions, starting with the Crystal Palace in London in 1851 (Teilmann-Lock 2016: 164). Teilmann-Lock's research shows that the American and British press coined the concept of "Swedish Modern" at the 1939 World Fair in New York, in reference to Swedish handicrafts, such as furniture, pottery and textiles, and used it interchangeably with "Scandinavian" aesthetics in design. When "Danish Modern" and "Danish Design" became more prominent labels in the 1950s (Teilmann-Lock 2016: 164), the language of "Scandinavian" and "Danish" design was also used interchangeably. Sales catalogues and promotional materials were full of references to the "Danish," or occasionally "Scandinavian," values of quality, good taste, simplicity, social harmony and so forth (Teilmann-Lock 2016: 164). Ironically, the blurring of the geographical locations and categories happened just as the national – Danish, Swedish, Norwegian and Finnish – design cultures were gaining international renown and a reputation for high quality and modern innovation and establishing themselves locally through design museums and educational institutions. Even though the term "Scandinavian Design" briefly receded in popularity with the onset of postmodernism in the 1970s and 1980s, it made a comeback in the 1990s, with a new wave of exhibitions, symposia and articles devoted to it, as well as with designers reclaiming its significance in their own output and manufacturers using it for marketing strategies (Halén 2006: 7). Thus, the legacy

FIGURE 1.1: Arne Jacobsen display of chairs at the Design Museum in Copenhagen, 2019, photo by K. Sark.

and heritage of "Scandinavian" and "Danish" design developed simultaneously but was used for different purposes to both capitalize on local cultural values and diversify them with international prestige. Adhering to both local and international symbolic and cultural design capital allowed Denmark, and its capital Copenhagen, to position themselves at the forefront of innovation and style (Figure 1.1), which Copenhagen continues to promote to this day.

Design and fashion education

In design education, the discipline of design history was developed in Denmark in the 1970s, paving the way for design studies which examine various design processes, practices, theories and histories. More recently, design culture which emerged as its own discipline around 2000, focuses on design's contemporary manifestations with an "emphasis on the deep understanding of design objects and their interrelationships with the multiple actors engaged in their shaping, functioning, and reproduction", as well as their mediation and representation in the digital world (Julier & Munch 2019: 1).

Danish design history is usually traced back to the furniture designer and educator Kaare Klint, the pioneer of Danish Modernism (also known as the "Danish Modern" movement and style) who founded the furniture department at the Royal Academy in Copenhagen in 1924. Klint and his contemporaries were "inspired by the humanist aims of the Bauhaus movement in Germany, but they felt that Bauhaus buildings and furniture designs were in practice not particularly humanistic" or affordable, and the Danish Modern movement was partly an attempt to "do what the Bauhaus hadn't" (Kingsley 2012: 57), namely, to make "good furniture that everyone could enjoy" and to "make better homes for the masses" by making them both "well-made and affordable" (Kingsley 2012: 64). Originally, "Danish Design" was a term to identify and celebrate Danish modernist furniture (Hansen 2006, quoted in Teilmann-Lock 2016: 159). Danish design is typically characterized by its "minimalist aesthetic and unity of lifestyle," including a "focus on design as culture and everyday practice," featuring "flexibility through multi-functionality" and aiming "to enhance the experience and meaning of everyday routines" (Munch 2018: 51). As "affordable luxury," it also had the often-paradoxical task of "releasing art from the golden frames and into the design of everyday objects," such as well-designed furniture, lamps, utensils and household items (Munch 2018: 51). Part of Danish design culture is the "consistent focus on aesthetic detail" as a "sign of cultural integrity when a society showed the capacity to care about the design of all the minor objects for everyday use" (Munch 2018: 51). Munch also notes that "there is a fine line between aesthetic enhancement of the ordinary object and the alienation of it as a more conceptual work of art" (Munch 2018: 52), meaning that there is a paradoxical relationship between elevating everyday objects into the realm of art or design heritage, thus making them exclusive and unaffordable, and imposing a value on, and deriving cultural capital from, things made for everyday use.

FIGURE 1.2: Kolding Design School 2021, photo by K. Sark.

FIGURE 1.3: SDU campus in Kolding, photo by K. Sark.

"Danish" design education, including fashion design, continues in Danish design schools and universities to this day, for example at the Royal Academy in Copenhagen and at the Kolding Design School, where "design is now taught as a social practice – as a way of organizing the way that we act in societies" (Kingsley 2012: 63), which today also increasingly includes considerations of sustainability. The University of Southern Denmark (SDU) in Kolding offers programmes in design culture and economics, social design and interaction, participatory design, as well as design management. Its design culture programme is grounded in design history, theory and analysis, and in 2015 a fashion studies profile was added to its design culture and economics programme. While the programme includes one course on the history of Scandinavian design (including Danish design), the general approach to design and fashion studies at SDU is very international.

As Anna Dahlgren outlined in the introduction to *Fashioned in the North: Nordic Histories, Agents, and Images of Fashion Photography* (2020), fashion education in Denmark is primarily concentrated at the design schools because

> Danish universities have no independent fashion studies programs, but fashion is taught as a component of other visual representations within art history and design studies, and as part of material culture studies within history, European ethnology, and social science programs. At the design schools, fashion design and fashion studies have more prominent status in relation to educational programs for fashion designers, where it is generally taught as a specific design practice. Among the best-known

design schools teaching fashion are the Royal Academy Designskolen Kolding and Margrethe-Skolen. Some elective courses are also offered on fashion and luxury business at the Copenhagen Business School and on fashion as a cultural and historical phenomenon at University of Copenhagen.

(Dahlgren 2020: 12)

Margrethe-Skolen was renamed the Scandinavian Academy of Fashion Design in 2017. In 2008, Else Skjold, a sustainable fashion design educator and contributor to this volume, who at the time taught sustainable fashion design at the Kolding Design School and is now heading the new MA programme in sustainable design at the Royal Academy in Copenhagen, published a report on *Fashion Research at Design Schools* (2008), explaining that the Danish Ministry of Culture formulated the goal that "by 2010 the design schools should be accredited with status as universities" in order to meet the "changes in the fashion industry that now require fashion designers to be knowledge workers rather than only hands-on clothing production experts" (Skjold 2008: 11). She argued that it was essential to "establish networks and more binding partnerships with selected educational institutions or fashion companies in Denmark and abroad, in order to be able to have co-funded research projects and to share knowledge" (Skjold 2008: 18). After fashion production was outsourced, innovation became a buzzword for politicians in their efforts to secure a future for the Danish economy, thus entrusting fashion educators with the task to "produce ideas, concepts, and design solutions that demand a high level of education, skills, and creativity" (Skjold 2008: 31). With the transition to the creative economies, profit from the creativity of individuals and their creative labour was valued "as a raw material" that could sustain "European economies in the future" (Skjold 2008: 32). According to this creative economy, innovation "happens when creativity and the organization of money, knowledge, and value flows meet," but according to Skjold this does not occur automatically by just placing different professions together (Skjold 2008: 32), and the true challenge for a functional creative economy based on innovation lies in finding the right formula for mixing business, knowledge and creativity (Skjold 2008: 33). I would add that this is, in a nutshell, a formula for a successful fashion culture, with a particular emphasis on knowledge, research and creativity.

The design education reforms that began in 2003 changed the Danish education structure to include bachelor's and master's degrees, "to enhance the level of business understanding as well as internationalization of the design education" to match some of the highest international levels (Spandet-Møller 2011: 45). Spandet-Møller recommended as part of his 2011 report that part of the internationalization of education should be in the form of exchange programs and international traineeships, as well as "better cooperation with the business world through communication and partnership" (Spandet-Møller 2011: 45), which the Lifestyle & Design Cluster has taken up as part of its mandate (discussed in Chapter 8). He also suggested interdisciplinary cooperation between universities, business schools and fashion design schools, with the possibility to attend courses across the schools (Spandet-Møller 2011: 45), which has not yet been adopted as a common practice. If there is any cooperation between schools or research projects, it happens at the individual level (Figures 1.4 and 1.5).

FIGURE 1.4: Textile weaving looms at the Royal Academy in Copenhagen, 2019, photo by K. Sark.

FIGURE 1.5: VIA University College in Herning, 2020, photo by K. Sark.

In her analysis of the ways in which creativity can be connected to national identity and branding, Lene Tanggaard, the current rector of Design School Kolding, found that in Denmark, "the concept of creativity is often linked to stories about collaboration, quick interchange of knowledge, learning across sectors and the conceptualization of new products and designs" (Tanggaard 2016: 376). In her research and analysis, creativity is understood as "the ability to think differently, innovatively, and appropriately," and the "Danish model of creativity" is grounded in "flexibility" and the "ability to adapt and work within a framework that offers freedom of movement" (Tanggaard 2016: 386). Fashion culture is the intersectional amalgamation of fashion research and development, intergenerational networks of creative talent and researchers and cultural heritage. All components have to be sustained and connected in order to build a sustainable fashion culture.

In August 2020, during the Copenhagen Fashion Week that took place during the COVID-19 pandemic, Else Skjold published an opinion piece entitled "The Fashion Industry Is So Yesterday" in one of Denmark's leading newspapers, *Politiken*, in which she announced the opening of her new MA programme at the Royal Academy of Copenhagen. The focus of the program is "inclusion, responsibility, and sustainability in response to a deeply irresponsible fashion industry" (Skjold 2020). The pandemic amplified the problem that the global fashion industry's focus on the trend-driven seasonal production and consumption of fast fashion with almost instantly diminished value of clothing is not ethical. As a fashion design educator, Skjold noted that, for many years, fashion and textile design students have expressed "a lack of motivation to work in the fashion industry, simply because they cannot see the point in helping to destroy our climate through what they do" (Skjold 2020). These talented young people, who represent the next generation of designers and industry leaders, and whose creativity fuels the current creative economies, have for a long time felt excluded, voiceless and disempowered. The educational responses not only to the crisis in the fashion industry but also to fashion education already have had an impact on the future of fashion in Denmark. Skjold's philosophy of design centres on the understanding that the usability of clothing is now more important than its novelty value. Her approach to sustainability focuses on repair, maintenance, adjustment and re-design (Skjold 2020). At the time we were writing this book, the first cohort of the new MA program at the Royal Academy was working on their third-semester projects, where they learn to collaborate with external partners such as museums, brands, municipalities and other organizations to help them pursue their artistic vision and sustainability focus. Their graduation collection produced at the end of the fourth semester in the summer of 2022 was presented to the public during Copenhagen Fashion Week (see Sark and Skjold podcast conversation on sustainable fashion education, *Chic Podcast*, 2020).

Since moving to Denmark in the summer of 2019, I have re-developed the fashion studies stream at SDU. The two most pressing issues in fashion studies that I have identified to date are sustainability and decoloniality, especially regarding the ways in which fashion studies, including fashion history and fashion theory, is taught. It quickly became apparent that without decolonizing old, exploitative, transactional and unsustainable ways that people and the planet have been and are still treated in the global fashion industry in particular, and in global market economies in general, there cannot be any sustainable fashion systems, or a new generation of ethically minded and creative researchers, experts and professionals who can address the climate crisis effectively, reform the broken systems and rebuild the industry in a more just and inclusive way. What the new generation of fashion and design students need is a holistic understanding of history, environmental and social sustainability, critical media literacy, knowledge of theoretical frameworks to make their analytical work more informed and grounded, and a global perspective and digital skills that transcend the classroom. The responsibility of educating and empowering young people so that they are able to reform the global fashion industry, empower others in the industry and produce actual social change and sustainability was a tremendous responsibility. I had to develop a methodology and a pedagogy for making fashion studies more ethical, just, intersectional and decolonial. While decoloniality is still not part of mainstream education in many European countries with colonial histories, putting decolonial education into concrete practice and bridging it with sustainability, in and beyond the classroom, will be the next big step in this paradigm shift for all of us in the years to come. Bridging decoloniality and sustainability in institutional practices, in schools, museums and industries will be an ongoing project for the foreseeable future. Educating the next generations of creative professionals to be better equipped to change the fashion industry is an ongoing goal in fashion and design education.

Fashion in museums

When it comes to fashion collections in Danish museums, Anna Dahlgren lists the following institutions in Copenhagen and across Denmark:

> The National Museum of Denmark holds the largest dress collection in the country representing what people from different social groups wore from the late seventeenth century until the present. The museum's ethnographic collection has one of the largest collections of Inuit dress in the world. The Design Museum Denmark holds the country's largest collection of Danish as well as international fashion design and textile

design. The holdings from the twentieth and twenty-first centuries have a strong focus on Danish fashion design. The museum also holds the largest collections of print, drawings and magazines representing fashion's visual culture in the country. Finally, the Textile Museum Midjylland [in Herning] holds a collection of fashionable dress from the twentieth century onwards representing the local Danish mass fashion industry, which in the latter half of the twentieth century was located in the provincial towns of Herning, Ikast and Brande. Fashion photography is collected unsystematically by the Royal Library and by art museums with a modern and contemporary focus, such as Louisiana Museum of Modern Art [north of Copenhagen], the National Gallery of Denmark, and Brandts Museum of Art and Culture [in Odense].

(Dahlgren 2020: 14)

The Design Museum in Copenhagen (Figure 1.6) closed its doors during the first COVID lockdown in March 2020 for reconstruction and reopened in the summer of 2022. Unfortunately, its fashion collection is not available in a digitized format yet, so very few people have seen its vast collection and understand its historical and cultural value and contribution to telling the story of Denmark, and perhaps also Copenhagen, as a fashion culture. Tidens Samling Museum of Everyday Life in Odense also has a large collection of fashion items. The Koldinghus hosts the annual exhibitions that the Kolding Design School undergraduate and graduate students produce for graduation, as well as other travelling fashion and textile exhibitions, including Queen Margrethe's own embroidery collection (Figure 1.7).

FIGURE 1.6: Design Museum in Copenhagen, 2019, photo by K. Sark.

FIGURE 1.7: Handbags embroidered by Queen Margrethe II of Denmark, exhibited at Koldinghus, 2021, photo by K. Sark.

In conjunction with the V&A exhibition "Fashioned from Nature," which was on display at the Geological Museum in Copenhagen from April to September 2019 and included a strong focus on sustainability in fashion, the Geological Museum was used in August 2019 for the presentation of the graduation collections of several Danish fashion design schools, whose design students were tasked with collaborating with fashion industry innovators, including the founders of MANND and many other companies (discussed more in Chapter 8), and a keynote address by sustainability educator Kate Fletcher, introduced by Else Skjold (see Sark podcast conversation with Fletcher and Skjold, *Chic Podcast*, 2019). This event took place a year before Copenhagen Fashion Week (in collaboration with In futurum consultancy) launched its sustainability agenda, and this interdisciplinary and inter-generational exchange had a lasting impact on Copenhagen fashion (Figures 1.8–1.10).

Museums play a key role in the formation and cultivation of a city's fashion culture, not only as institutions for fashion exhibitions, education, preservation, conservation, history and heritage but also as facilitators of intercultural exchange between researchers, creative professionals and industry leaders. Curatorial and collecting practices around fashion and textiles have vastly improved in Denmark in the past twenty years. According to Marie Riegels Melchior, it was considered "sacrilegious" when in the 1990s, the National Gallery in Copenhagen hosted an exhibition showcasing the works of Danish couturier Erik Mortensen. Two decades later, from October 2014 until February 2015, the National Museum

FIGURE 1.8: Founders of MANND and Else Skjold at the Geological Museum in Copenhagen, 2019, photo by K. Sark.

FIGURE 1.9: Geological Museum in Copenhagen, 2019, photo by K. Sark.

FIGURE 1.10: Kate Fletcher at the Geological Museum in Copenhagen, 2019, photo by K. Sark.

hosted a provocative exhibition entitled "Fur – An Issue of Life and Death," asking its visitors whether it is ethical to breed and hunt animals when fur clothing is no longer necessary to survive the cold in the western European context. The question was written on a wall outside the large, heavy glass door separating the special exhibition from the rest of the museal collections and inviting visitors to reflectively engage and participate in the display in what has been described as the "new museology" approach to exhibition practices (quoted in Melchior 2015: 483). The Design Museum in Copenhagen has traditionally collected dresses with a focus on "craftsmanship" rather than fashion, while the National Museum has always focused on folklore. It was only in recent years that the Design Museum established a permanent fashion collection (Figures 1.11 and 1.12).

As my research on fashion cities has revealed, establishing a museum dedicated solely to fashion history and fashion culture is a hard battle many fashion researchers, curators and scholars have lost because fashion either falls through the cracks of not being art, craft, design or industry, or is still not taken seriously by the administrators in charge of budgets and exhibition space allocation. Combined with a lack of resources and competing hierarchies with other artefacts of art, culture and design, fashion is usually deprioritized in museums that hold other collections despite the fact that fashion exhibitions have become successful blockbusters that attract new museum-goers, who would not otherwise enter a museum. But as many fashion historians and curators have proven, showing a city's history through the materiality of textiles and fabrics that have been made, worn and preserved by the people in these cities, which is to say through its fashion culture, is one of the best ways to understand history. The multiple narratives told through clothing and fashion are often comprised of complex webs of colonial legacies and contradictory relationships that get to the core of the paradoxicality of human nature and vulnerability more than other historical objects. But if it were possible for museums to assume a

FIGURE 1.11: Fashion collection of the Design Museum in Copenhagen, 2019, photo by K. Sark.

FIGURE 1.12: Fashion collection of the Design Museum in Copenhagen, 2019, photo by K. Sark.

more active role in sustaining a healthy fashion culture of a city, by digitizing their collections, making them more accessible to wider audiences and not only specialized researchers, broadening their programming to include more links to contemporary fashion scenes and generally taking on the duties of bridging fashion history, heritage, culture and innovation, it would allow them to have a much more meaningful role in the cultivation of current fashion cultures.

Danish fashion in academic research

Copenhagen, or København in Danish (*købe* means to buy or purchase, *havn* is harbour), has by definition always been a mercantile trade centre, the harbour of tradesmen or merchants and the textile trade has always been a major part of the economy, dating back to King Christian IV's (1588–1648) attempt to establish a textile industry in Denmark, which initially failed despite state subsidies due to the high price of imported silk. But with the beginning of the colonial expansion and trading with India and Sri Lanka starting in 1616, cotton textiles became one of the staples of the trading culture and economy (Krarup podcast). The Industrial Revolution played a central role in establishing Denmark, together with other European countries, as manufacturing hubs with networks of textile and clothing production that stretched across the globe long before the term globalization was invented. Denmark's colonial past also plays an important role in its self-conceptualization as a trading nation and has wide-reaching repercussions on its educational and economic hierarchies, and now also its sustainability projects. I argue that without decoloniality, there cannot be a sustainable fashion culture.

In the first half of the twentieth century, Danish fashion mirrored international fashion systems, most notably in Paris, through local fashion magazines (including the monthly journal *Modejournal Chic*), trade journals and mail-order catalogues. Starting in 1911, Daells Varehus offered access to affordable, ready-to-wear fashion and other home consumer goods, and department stores and fashion shows were introduced to the country in 1911 by the Copenhagen-based department store Fonnesbech (Melchior 2020b: 46). According to Melchior, in the early 1930s, it was reported that the first fashion show in Denmark had taken place in September 1911, with live mannequins that presented the new collection of the Fonnesbech department store to an exclusive group of invited guests. Her research also shows that

> The following year, Nimb, a restaurant and entertainment destination connected to Tivoli Gardens, became the preferred location for fashion shows, first for Fonnesbech

and beginning in 1913 for the department store Magasin du Nord. These first shows were "theatrical presentations" held just once a year, but by the end of the 1910s, they had become biannual events hosted by an increasing number of department stores and local fashion houses, held at luxurious venues such as Nimb and The Palm Garden at the exclusive Hotel D'Angleterre. Thus, the role of the fashion show in the local fashion system was less structured and ritualized in these formative years. The fashion shows were consumer-oriented, and as in Paris, were intended to stimulate customers to buy from the new season or take elements from it to update their existing wardrobe.

(Melchior 2020b: 49)

Before the youth quake of the 1960s, Copenhagen fashion followed Paris trends. Magasin du Nord had a salon dedicated entirely to couture, and local designers such as Holger Blom, Jean Voigt and Jørgen Bender found their inspiration in the French couture houses of Dior, Balenciaga and Cardin. Until the 1960s and 1970s, Danish fashion was "on the receiving end of fashion in an international fashion system context" (Melchior 2020b: 48).

The term "Scandinavian" was not used in reference to Danish fashion until 1966 when *Dansk Textil Messe* was renamed *Scandinavian Textile Fair*, and *Dansk Mode-Uge* was renamed *Scandinavian Fashion Week*, using the term "Scandinavian Look" in its marketing and branding materials (Lyngbye Pedersen 2012: 125). This changing of names was due to growing exports of Danish clothing and a more direct communication with international buyers. Melchior found that after the 1950s a discourse emerged that tried to identify and negotiate what constitutes Danish fashion, albeit without any clear conclusions, but a national self-awareness began to emerge in the Danish fashion industry (Melchior 2020: 135). Other scholarly attempts to define Danish fashion in the context of Danish design history include Stine Teilmann-Lock's examination of "Made in Denmark" labels, where she found that:

Until the 1950s Denmark was internationally respected only for its fairy tales and its bacon. But from the 1950s onwards design came to constitute another source of worldwide recognition. Today, fashion is a successful branch of Danish design: it produces the largest annual turnover and the greatest export of any of the creative industries in Denmark. And one thing that characterizes the many different styles of Danish fashion is that they all come with the labels "Danish Design" or "Designed in Denmark" sewn onto the clothes or attached to the price tag. Similar labels may be found on clothes from Sweden, Britain, France, and Italy as well as from numerous other Western countries where clothes have been designed – though not manufactured.

(Teilmann-Lock 2016: 156)

Despite the homogenizing efforts to unify design histories and practices under the umbrella of "Scandinavian Design," Teilmann-Lock argued that simultaneously, throughout the twentieth century, design became a "central element in the national identity of many European countries" with categories such as "British Design," "Italian Design" and "Danish Design" that have "acquired a certain mythic status in the rhetoric of both business and culture" (Teilmann-Lock 2016: 157). Government efforts to promote national design initiatives to either stimulate economic growth or enhance social and cultural development placed design in the global economy, while simultaneously playing a "central role in policies of nation-building" (Teilmann-Lock 2016: 158). She explained the evolution of linking design objects with their geographical origins and the development of nation states, and the change in global manufacturing practices that detached design practices from production locations:

> Traditionally, design products would be naturally linked to a geographical place, either a city or a region. It lies in the names of many fabrics: cashmere, denim (de Nîmes), damask, suede, and so forth. After the rise of the nation state the bond was adopted and sustained at the level of the nation. It would be understood on the international market that a pair of "Italian" shoes had been designed, prototyped, produced and exported from Italy according to Italian ways and standards. [...] However, today the law promotes the estimation of design according to its value as an "asset" in the national "economy of knowledge" and as a token of "cultural capital."
> (Teilmann-Lock 2016: 162)

Thus, according to Teilmann-Lock's research, "Danish Design" became "a label that celebrated the idea of design – as a material product – originating in a particular national culture, contributing to an international image of a national cultural identity," but with a changed denotation because "it is no longer an endorsement of the idea of cultural origins," but rather the designation of a "brand," as Danish design products "have lost the implicit physical attachment to the country that defines their status," and are no longer promoted as "hand-made in Danish workshops" (Teilmann-Lock 2016: 165). This development in design discourse and practices explains the reluctance of many Copenhagen-based fashion professionals to limit themselves strictly to "Danish" design, especially as most of it is no longer produced in Copenhagen or Denmark, and the continued preference to use "Danish" and "Scandinavian" labels interchangeably depending on the sphere of influence (Figure 1.13).

The first textile trade show, *Jydsk Textil Messe (Jutland Textile Fair)*, took place in August 1947 in Herning, the emerging post-war textile hub in Jutland (Figures 1.14 and 1.15), and was open to consumers as well as professional buyers (Lyngbye

FIGURE 1.13: Danish design label inside a garment at the Horsens Industry Museum, 2020, photo K. Sark.

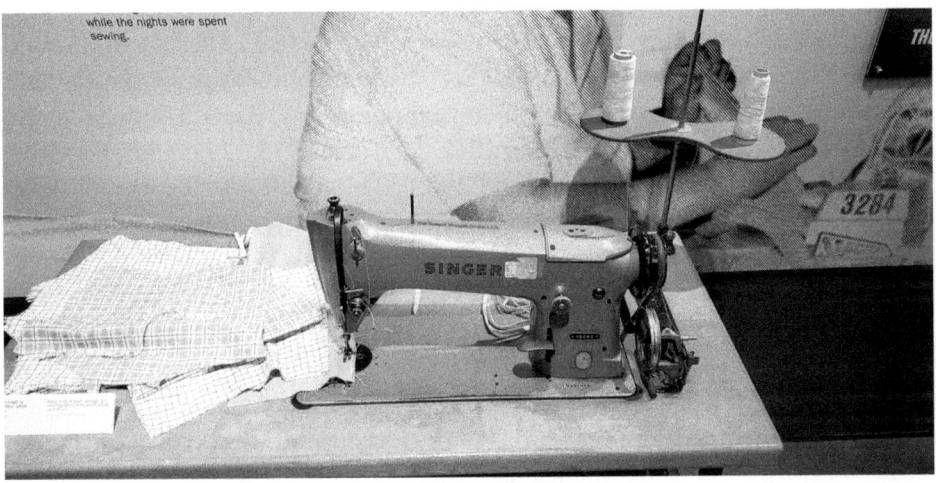

FIGURE 1.14: Herning Textile Museum 2020, photo by K. Sark.

Pedersen 2012: 116). By 1950, it was renamed *Dansk Textil Messe* (*Danish Textile Fair*) and turned into a closed trade fair for the national retail industry (Lyngbye Pedersen 2012: 121), which from 1950 onwards was capable of mass-producing clothes in standard sizes, thanks to the Marshall Plan investments in European industries (Lyngbye Pedersen 2012: 122). Birgit Lyngbye Pedersen's research also shows that the concepts of "fashion and society" were linked in the post-Second World

FIGURE 1.15: Herning Textile Museum 2020, photo by K. Sark.

War period, as the modern production industry became more attentive to consumers' needs and as "clothes became a main component of the way consumers built their social identities," as the "Danish industry developed from class fashion into consumer fashion" (Lyngbye Pedersen 2012: 123) (see also Sark podcast episode on Herning Textile Industry, *Chic Podcast*, 2020). This development was well represented in the famous Danish TV series *Matador* (1978–82), discussed in Chapter 7.

The post-war economic miracle years of the 1950s generated a textile and fashion boom across Denmark (and western Europe in general), with a textile production concentration around the cities of Herning, Ikast and Brande in central Jutland. In the 1950s, clothing imported into Denmark rose dramatically, and the Clothing Industry Association (founded in 1920 to oversee finance, operations and education) wanted to boost the local Danish clothing industry (Lyngbye Pedersen 2011: 144) by establishing the Danish Men's Fashion Council in 1958 and the Danish Women's Fashion Council in 1959 that "consisted almost exclusively of Copenhagen manufacturers, except for the president, and manufacturer, Tage Vangaard who had his dress factory in Aarhus" (Lyngbye Pedersen 2011: 152). The Council organized the first Danish Women's Fashion Week in May 1958, a year before the Council was formally established, at which 46 manufacturers showed their collections to buyers (Lyngbye Pedersen 2011: 154). The first *Dansk Mode-Uge* (*Danish Fashion Week*) presented ready-made clothes and was organized in Copenhagen in 1964 as a precursor to *Dansk Textil Messe* in Herning. Thus, as Lyngbye Pedersen pointed out, Copenhagen was the centre of fashion (and fashion weeks) and Herning that of textiles (and Danish textile fairs). Then in late 1966, the internationalization turn came, and the *Dansk Textil Messe* was renamed *Scandinavian Textile Fair*, expanding its reach beyond Danish boutiques and department stores to Scandinavian consumers.

Development strategies in the design and fashion sectors followed the dual path of simultaneously building up a national Danish industry and tradition, while also responding to the cultural exchange and internationalization that characterized western Europe in the aftermath of the Marshall Plan-induced economic miracles through capitalist expansion, modernization, innovation, mass communication, pop- and subcultures and cultural new waves – with Copenhagen catching, riding and sustaining these cultural new waves and generating what would be known as the youth quake or mod culture of the 1960s and 1970s. According to Anders Larsen, the post-war era also marked a change in cultural reference points – before the Second World War, Denmark and Copenhagen were very influenced by Paris and Berlin, and after the war by London and Hollywood. Copenhagen quickly recognized its potential in acquiring cultural and economic capital through internationalization. This transition was particularly apparent in architectural developments like Arne Jacobsen's SAS Royal Copenhagen Hotel, which opened in July 1960, and for which he designed all the interior design objects, including his famous egg chairs, lamps, textiles and all other items including the cutlery. Today, only one room, 606, has been preserved in its original state with the original Arne Jacobsen furniture and design objects (Figures 1.16 and 1.17).

FIGURE 1.16: Arne Jacobsen suite 606 at the Radisson Royal Copenhagen Hotel, 2021, photo by K. Sark.

FIGURE 1.17: Arne Jacobsen's lobby and winding staircase at the Radisson Royal Copenhagen Hotel, 2021, photo by K. Sark.

Jacobsen's SAS Royal Copenhagen Hotel is a true testament to both the "Danish" design legacy, as well as the "Scandinavian" international boom in air travel (SAS stands for Scandinavian Airlines System) and the anticipation of mass tourism for international events in Copenhagen. It was inspired by New York's Park Avenue skyscrapers and was the largest and tallest building in Denmark until 1969, and the second skyscraper in Copenhagen, after the Hotel Europa, which was built in 1955 and is now Danhostel. The SAS Royal Copenhagen Hotel was originally designed with its own bus terminal, which connected travellers with Copenhagen Airport in Kastrup, linking Copenhagen to international modernism, both through air travel and the building's design (Munch 2012: 104–05). Danish architects were often designers who created "a concentrated total design" for "ordinary use in the community" (Munch 2012: 110), which also consolidated Copenhagen as an architectural frontrunner in Europe, something it remains to this day (Figure 1.18). This transition towards internationalization is also apparent in cinematic representations of Copenhagen in the 1960s and 1970s, as the city became more and more cosmopolitan, international and modernized (discussed in Chapter 6). However, gentrification did not start until the 2000s.

As Marie Riegels Melchior's research confirms, the internationalization of the Danish clothing and textile industries can be traced back to the 1960s and 1970s, when Danish manufacturers began "integrating professionally trained fashion designers in the production of Danish ready-to-wear," and as "the clothes turned into branded goods, labeled with the name of the fashion designer in

FIGURE 1.18: Arne Jacobsen's Royal Copenhagen Hotel during World Pride 2021, photo by K. Sark.

addition to the manufacturer's company name" (Melchior 2010b: 15). Danish fashion was characterized as "functional, wearable, and fashionable," as well as "highly modern, young, and priced at a level accessible to a wider group of people compared to the clothes from international fashion houses" (Melchior 2010b: 17). The 1960s and 1970s also generated a "profound transformation of the global fashion and clothing industry," as fashion "morphed from a privileged domain of artistic creators," or *couture*, into a ready-to-wear and boutique-fashion culture, allowing new manufacturers and brands to gain market share and flooding the local markets with more imports, which "gave professionally trained fashion designers a central role during the 1960s, either as employees in the manufacturing industry or as owner-managers of their own companies" (Melchior et al. 2011c: 215). After the fall of the Berlin Wall in 1989, the Danish textile manufacturing industry could no longer compete with cheap labour in eastern Europe and Asia. By the 1990s, many Danish clothing manufacturing companies had to shut down "if they had not managed to move their production facilities abroad or convert their companies into so-called 'concept houses' (meaning becoming wholesalers of clothing focusing on design, distribution, marketing, and retail, rather than manufacturing)" (Melchior 2010b: 17). Similar dismantling of the local manufacturing industries happened in textile centers all over Europe and North America and created a vacuum or a complete recession in many economies.

In 2005, the Danish government started investing more strategically in the fashion sector in an attempt to establish Copenhagen as "the fifth global fashion cluster," with a particular focus on "business-oriented" fashion education to gain market share, and by developing and subsidizing a network of fashion organizations to "improve the cohesion of the national industry, and to coordinate and promote the brand-building of Danish fashion" (Melchior 2020: 138). At this time, many design schools in Denmark were converted to universities because the "Danish fashion industry lacked a high level of systematic and research-based knowledge in its work with innovation" (Melchior et al. 2011c: 218).

Inspired by Joseph Pine and James Gilmore's book *The Experience Economy* (1999), which links cultural and commercial sectors for future economic potential in terms of "new jobs related to creativity and design, export growth, and business development," the Danish government saw future growth not in "selling products alone, but in selling stories, experiences, and identities to consumers" and included the fashion industry among the cultural industries central to the "linkage between design and business" (Melchior et al. 2011c: 217) in response to globalization and the loss of manufacturing jobs. Once again, innovation, knowledge sharing, knowledge centres and design education became central to boosting post-industrial economic growth and the creative economy. This transition to a creative economy included the establishment of the Danish Fashion Institute (DAFI) in 2005, with joint government and industry support to coordinate and promote Copenhagen Fashion Week and later Copenhagen Fashion Summit. The latter was formed in response to media exposure of the dangerous working conditions and child labour among the suppliers of leading Danish and Swedish retailers and in preparation for the UN climate summit held in Copenhagen in 2009, as well as to "promote and strengthen the perception of a specific Danish fashion through seminars, assistance for start-ups, support for exhibitions, fashion awards, fashion design talent scouting, and so on" (Melchior 2020: 139). One of the first initiatives of DAFI was to commission a report entitled the "DNA of Danish Fashion," which found that

Danish fashion had an "identity problem, a problem of belonging, historically, and in an increasingly global world," and that "Danish fashion does not seem very distinctive" (Melchior 2011: 61). Nonetheless, a Danish "fashion design industry sector had emerged as a post-industrial success story," not merely "subject to government regulation aimed at improving industry performance or protecting labour," but also directly linked to cultural policy (Melchior et al. 2011c: 216). By 2009, the Danish fashion industry's trade association was renamed from the Federation of Danish Textile and Clothing (*Dansk Textil og Beklædning*) to Danish Fashion and Textile (*Dansk Mode og Textil*) because traditionally the industry "shied away from using the term fashion and designated itself as a clothing or apparel industry," because "fashion" was regarded as a "foreign, elite, and female phenomenon" (Melchior et al. 2011c: 214). It currently has about 350 members spread across Denmark.

In his 2011 report on the state of Danish fashion, Henrik Spandet-Møller announced that "Copenhagen is not the world's fifth most important fashion hub," and recommended that Copenhagen should focus on remaining the "fashion center of Scandinavia" instead, before losing that position to Stockholm just as, due to a "lack of cooperation and strategic alliances in Denmark to create one industrial fashion fair platform" (Spandet-Møller 2011: 39), it had lost the competitive strategy implementation to Berlin with the relaunch of the Bread & Butter fashion fair, which was replaced by NEONYT, the international sustainable fashion fair, which moved to Frankfurt in 2022. Berlin's Bread & Butter was able to take the lead by developing a "competitive strategy against its Danish competitors while the Danes were engaged with focusing on rivalry with their local competitors only" (Spandet-Møller 2011: 40). Spandet-Møller argued that "rather than investing most efforts and government funds into 'invisible emperor suits', let Denmark focus on global marketing of original design of good quality at commercial prices to most international consumers" (Spandet-Møller 2011: 39), which it has done through its fast fashion conglomerates like Bestseller. With the 2005 FORA Report, which boasted "innovative thinking for policy makers" and announced that Denmark should aim to become the fifth fashion hub with Copenhagen as a centre, Danish media and various fashion stakeholders started identifying Copenhagen as the fifth biggest fashion hub after Paris, New York, London and Milan (Spandet-Møller 2011: 39). Copenhagen City Hall used to host more than half Fashion Week shows since 2006, demonstrating just how coordinated the political investment and support of the Danish fashion industry was in the early 2000s (Spandet-Møller 2011: 38). Copenhagen Fashion Week continued to display "Nordic efforts" and position itself as "international and Scandinavian" rather than Danish, while simultaneously promoting "Danish and Scandinavian identity and heritage" as an "effective tool to distinguish brands from international mass production and to give the brands authenticity" (Spandet-Møller 2011: 39).

To this day, Copenhagen is known as a centre for fashion events, fashion media, networking and international outreach, while the fashion industry, or rather what remains of it after most of the production and manufacturing was outsourced to the Global South, is still concentrated in Jutland. This duality underpins not only the Danish fashion industry but also its fashion culture. Nonetheless, Copenhagen plays a key role in the landscape of fashion. The interplay between "Danish" and "Scandinavian" design and fashion and their cultural legacies continues to fuel the branding narratives of Denmark and Copenhagen as fashion locations, with fashion branding and city branding often used to boost their cultural significance. Even though Copenhagen did not succeed in becoming the fifth fashion hub, the government-subsidized business policy did strengthen the fast fashion industry as the country's fourth largest export industry, arguably creating a much bigger challenge of how to transition that industry towards a circular economy. The COVID-19 pandemic and ensuing multiple order cancellations by Danish and international (fast) fashion brands like Bestseller and others, which brought the supply chain and garment workers practically to the point of starvation, revealed at whose cost Danish fashion companies have remained economically afloat, with several even reporting profits during the pandemic (CGWR Report 2020). The Penn State Center for Global Workers' Rights (CGWR) set up a COVID-19 tracker to hold international brands accountable for paying for their manufacturing orders, and the list of companies that "Made No Commitment to Pay in Full for Orders Completed and in Production" included the Danish conglomerate Bestseller, which was instead forcing their suppliers to provide discounts (CGWR 2021).

Since the publication of the "DNA of Danish fashion" report in 2005, there have been many attempts to describe Danish fashion – by academics who have conducted surveys, by expats and Danish authors who have written about life in Denmark, and by social media influencers and stylists who work with both Danish and Scandinavian brands. In analyzing Danish fashion consumption patterns, Julie Sommerlund's research reveals two important findings: first, that the Danish welfare system, characterized by general equality and prosperity, high labour costs and hence fewer people able to afford domestic help, influenced people's fashion choices to be more practical and pragmatic; and second, that the more egalitarian gender relations in Denmark, where women work more and have more childcare than in other countries, also had an impact on Danish fashion consumption choices (Sommerlund 2011: 165). Again, there was a clear emphasis on multifunctionality, as clothing had to be "versatile and usable," able to be "washed at home in a machine," made of "natural fibers, without intricate buttons or delicate lace," not in need ironing, allowing unrestricted movement to be able to move on a bicycle, suited for menial tasks such as doing one's own laundry and cleaning the house and adaptable (Sommerlund 2011: 172). Thus, in a collective effort to make fashion more versatile, functional, flexible and pragmatic, and often taking inspiration from the furniture design of the Danish Modern period, Danish fashion did not separate dressing up and down (Sommerlund 2011: 176–7). Such practical demands on clothes made them distinct from other fashion cultures in that they had to be comfortable, easy to maintain and "able to move through a variety of aesthetic contexts" while remaining fashionable, "chic, elegant, minimalist" (Sommerlund 2011: 177). While her research was helpful in identifying some of the common denominators of Danish fashion, Sommerlund's analysis also raised a number of questions because it focused exclusively on cis-women and mothers and did not account for fashion worn in Denmark that is not designed in Denmark, nor for a modernist design aesthetic. The close discursive and aesthetic connection between Danish fashion and Danish (furniture) design has been fuelled by references to their "flexibility through multi-functionality," highlighting a "minimalist aesthetic and unity of lifestyle," with a "focus on design as culture and everyday practice" (Munch 2018: 50).

In 2005, DANSK magazine (2002–22) described the identity of Danish fashion as having a dual character that was both fashionable as well as practical (Melchior 2020: 139). Perhaps Danish fashion achieved that paradoxical balance between refinement and everyday accessibility and comfort that Danish design aspired to. Danish fashion or style has been described as minimalist, practical, understated but elegant and increasingly also sustainable, despite the persistence of fast fashion and thus greenwashing. The interplay between all the definitions of Danish fashion and what Copenhagen fashion represents in the Danish imaginary is a productive tension that allows Copenhagen fashion culture to constantly evolve. Since the 1970s, Copenhagen has transitioned from a clothing and fashion manufacturing centre to an experience economy hub centred around tourism, creative industries and design services. Its museum exhibitions, fashion festivals and other cultural offerings make the city a destination for fashion consumption and fashion experiential economies.

Danish fashion and design in popular culture

In an attempt to condense Danish fashion into a few highlights in his international bestseller, *The Little Book of Hygge: The Danish Way to Live Well* (2016), Meik Wiking claimed that "there is a Danish art to master being stylish and casual at the same time" (Wiking 2016: 102). He argued that Danish fashion is "sleek, minimalistic, elegant but not highly strung," and "a sweet spot between hygge and minimalistic functional design" usually consisting of scarfs for men and women, "the bigger the better," which the "Danes love so much that some Brits have been referring to the Danish TV drama *Borgen* [discussed in Chapter 7] as 'scarf watch'" (Wiking 2016: 104). He also described Danish fashion as "stylish but monochrome," and that the key to "surviving four seasons in one day is layers" and cardigans, because "you can't hygge when you are cold" (Wiking 2016: 105). His final nod to Danish fashion culture is a nod to the Sarah Lund jumper, popularized by the Danish TV drama *The Killing* (discussed in Chapter 7), making the fisherman's inspired woollen sweater so popular that "the company producing it on the Faroe Islands couldn't keep up with demand" (Wiking 2016: 108). Based on his account, Danish fashion is tied to the pop cultural value and references of shows and products that have become successful international exports and have transcended the domestic market.

In contrast, an interesting outsider perspective on Danish fashion can be found in Kay Xander Mellish's book, *How to Live in Denmark: A Humorous Guide for Foreigners and Their Danish Friends* (2017). Mellish is a Copenhagen-based American consultant, author and podcaster specializing in helping expats who move to Denmark and Danish companies who want to work internationally. She has a podcast episode and a section of her book dedicated to Danish fashion, where she claimed that "Danes dress to match the Danish landscape. That means grey. And brown and green, and some blue. Maybe some beige for the adventurous. If you find yourself wearing purple or orange, or hot pink, you will stand out in Denmark" (Mellish 2017: 42). But Mellish did not distinguish between Copenhagen and the rest of Denmark. When writing about Danish fashion, she claimed that

> there is such a thing as Danish Fashion, and there is a Danish Fashion Week. Designers like Malene Birger, Bruuns Bazaar, and Day Birger et Mikkelsen have made a name for themselves internationally. But what they design is not what your average Dane wears. What the average Dane wears is outerwear. It's cold in Denmark, so people's wardrobes are heavy on sweaters, boots, and coats and jackets. [...] There's even a category of outerwear I never knew existed called "rain gear." Rain gear is like a plastic jogging suit, and it goes over your clothes and allows you to bicycle or walk around in the rain without getting wet.
>
> (Mellish 2017: 42)

Mellish's description of Danish fashion may be hyperbolic and exaggerated, but she hit a nerve with the rain gear and the distinction between what fashion influencers wear (or want to be seen wearing on their Instagram feeds) and what the average person wears in their daily life.

For example, the Copenhagen-based social media fashion influencer Pernille Teisbæk made a brand out of the concept of "Scandi Chic" while promoting Danish brands and designers and also profiting from paid partnerships with H&M and other Swedish and Scandinavian brands. Teisbæk's book *Dress Scandinavian: Style Your Life and Wardrobe the Danish Way* (2017) is available both in Danish and in English translation and purposefully blurs the lines between Danish and Scandinavian fashion, design, style and lifestyle in order to reach a wider audience and construct a more globally appealing lifestyle identity and brand. Teisbæk started as a fashion blogger with "Lookdeepernille" (2012–16), which led her to a career as a fashion stylist and then her own consulting company, Social Zoo, an agency she co-founded in Copenhagen with Hannah Løffler Schmidt. In the introduction to her book, Teisbæk noted that comfort, confidence and tranquillity are the main ingredients of what she described as "Scandinavian style," claiming that

> within the world of fashion, Scandinavian design obtained a rather remarkable position. It's a style that signals confidence and self-assurance – and rightfully so. In truth, most people are partial to comfortable clothes and Scandinavian fashion is quite simple and easy to wear. Comfort radiates confidence and strength.
> (Teisbæk 2017: 14)

She described the Scandinavian look as "casual and minimalistic" but "never accidental" because "comfort ranks highly," but every little detail has been "carefully considered" (Teisbæk 2017: 18). Later in the book, she described Scandinavian style as "quite androgynous" and "unisex" because sometimes "your entire outfit might belong to your partner, brother, father or male friend" (Teisbæk 2017: 56). Similar references and branding narratives about "Scandi Chic" permeate social media to attract followers and tourists to explore and consume a lifestyle mythology that is, on the one hand, placeless, but simultaneously relies on established understandings of tying the expectations of place imaginaries to values inherited from the legacies of "Scandinavian" design history and its cultural values. Moreover, Copenhagen's geographical proximity to Sweden, especially Malmö and Lund on the Swedish east coast, facilitates a commuter culture between Denmark and Sweden that thrives, thanks to the now world-renowned Øresund Bridge, popularized in the Danish-Swedish co-production of the Nordic noir crime series, *The Bridge* (2011–18), which encourages easier collaboration between Danish and Swedish fashion brands and industry professionals (as evident in the representations at Copenhagen Fashion Week and the fashion trade shows), all of which contributes to the continued interest in blending the locational demarcations of "Scandinavian" fashion and design.

Another coffee-table book on "Scandinavian" fashion that profiles Danish, Swedish and Finnish fashion designers is by Dorothea Gundtoft and entitled *Fashion Scandinavia: Contemporary Cool* (2013). Most of the Danish designers featured in this book are graduates of the Kolding Design School or the Royal Academy in Copenhagen (formerly known as the Danish Design Academy), who did additional schooling at fashion schools in London. It is also evident that most of the Danish designers and brands featured in this book were educated and launched their businesses after the 2005 Danish fashion policy. In her introduction, Gundtoft stated,

> Scandinavians have lived and breathed design every day, from their iconic furniture and gastro food to the functional clothing they wear, which fits in with the local architecture and designed environment. The Scandinavian look is mainly characterized by simplicity, minimalism, humanized function, and low-cost production.
>
> (Gundtoft 2013: 6)

She too made a connection between fashion and furniture design and used the term "Scandinavian" to make Danish design more international, claiming, "Scandinavian style attracted many consumers after *Time* magazine featured a cover image of a chair by Danish designer Hans J. Wegner in 1949" (Gundtoft 2013: 6). Gundtoft included the work of Danish fashion designer Anne Sofie Madsen, who graduated from the Royal Academy in Copenhagen and was chosen for the official opening show of Copenhagen Fashion Week in 2011, commenting on the contemporary value of Danish design education:

> It's obvious that you don't get as much press when you graduate from a Danish school as when you graduate from Central Saint Martins. I really enjoyed studying in Denmark, but, if I were to recommend anything for others, I would recommend Central Saint Martins as it would have made a lot of things easier. The brand value and reputation of the school give more opportunities, although I think people often believe that if you go to a famous design school then everything just comes automatically.
>
> (Anne Sofie Madsen quoted in Gundtoft 2013: 27)

This is a revealing testimony because, in only ten years, fashion education in Denmark has not only improved noticeably but gained a global reputation. Many international students who start their fashion education in London now come to Denmark because Copenhagen in particular has come to represent sustainable fashion design in the global fashion industry. The new generation of fashion design students specifically comments on how fashion design in the United

Kingdom is still centred on outdated business practices, while Danish design schools offer more circular design education opportunities.

The Danish brand Bruuns Bazaar was launched in 1994 by two brothers Teis and Bjørn Bruun and became the first Danish fashion brand to present at Paris Fashion Week. Its head designer, Rebekka Bay, formerly worked as the creative director at COS, graduated from Kolding Design School and moved to London to get more professional experience before returning to Copenhagen (Gundtoft 2013: 42–43). The Danish streetwear brand Wood Wood, established by Karl-Oskar Olsen and Brian Jensen, was asked if they represent "Danish style or Scandinavian style in general," to which they responded:

> We like to think of ourselves as global; we just happen to have a base in Copenhagen. I guess in some ways you can see or feel the Scandinavian way of thinking about design in terms of aesthetics, materials and structure, which is important, but we always mix our inspiration stories together quite chaotically, so they won't become too recognizably Danish or Scandinavian.
>
> (quoted in Gundtoft 2013: 244)

Not all the designers featured in Grundtoft's book are still part of the Danish fashion scene. But the book provided an important insight into the landscape of the Danish fashion industry, including fashion education, after the strategic investments into fashion began to transform the Danish fashion economy.

Conclusion

Despite the fact that technically speaking, there is no such thing as "Scandinavian" fashion or design because it is a branding construct, its persistence and usability in both fashion and design narratives remain important. The problem with homogenizing multiple cultures and identities under one common denominator of a branding umbrella like "Scandi Chic" is a perpetuation of vagueness, building on the surface value of concepts that have become devoid of meaning, history, location and culture. Moreover, the homogeneity of identity markers comes at a price: "this sameness is built upon control, exclusion and eradication of difference" (Fallan & Zetterlund 2016: 173). The reluctance to single out Denmark or Copenhagen as a fashion centre with a distinct fashion culture perhaps explains why there hasn't been a book on Copenhagen fashion until now.

Over the past decade, Copenhagen has rebranded itself as the centre of sustainable, or rather, circular fashion through organizations such as the Lifestyle & Design Cluster (discussed in Chapter 8), Copenhagen Fashion Week's sustainability agenda (discussed in Chapter 3), slow fashion brands, activists and influencers who educate consumers on ethical consumption practices, and many other efforts to meet the UN Sustainable Development Goals (SDGs) by 2030. The Copenhagen Business School (CBS) offers a free online course on sustainable fashion. Under the leadership of Else Skjold, the Royal Academy restructured its fashion design program around sustainability and hired Kate Fletcher as part-time faculty. However, the majority of the efforts directed towards making its fashion industry greener and less green-washed do not really define sustainability or provide a lasting definition of a fashion culture that goes beyond the economic value of fashion as a commodity culture. As elusive as this definition may be, in the remaining chapters of this book, we continue to chip away at what constitutes Copenhagen Chic.

REFERENCES

Center for Global Workers' Rights (CGWR). "Abandoned? The Impact of Covid-19 on Workers and Businesses at the Bottom of Global Garment Supply Chains." 27 Mar. 2020, www.workersrights.org/wp-content/uploads/2020/03/Abandoned-Penn-State-WRC-Report-March-27-2020.pdf. Accessed 21 Oct. 2022

Center for Global Workers' Rights (CGWR). "COVID-19 Tracker." Updated: 21 April 2021, www.workersrights.org/issues/covid-19/tracker/. Accessed 21 Oct. 2022.

Dahlgren, Anna, editor. *Fashioned in the North: Nordic Histories, Agents, and Images of Fashion Photography*. Lund: Nordic Academic Press, 2020.

Dahlgren, Anna. "Introduction." *Fashioned in the North: Nordic Histories, Agents, and Images of Fashion Photography*, edited by Anna Dahlgren. Lund: Nordic Academic Press, 2020, pp. 9–29.

Danhostel. *Wikipedia*, www.en.wikipedia.org/wiki/Danhostel_Copenhagen_City. Accessed 13 Mar. 2023.

Fallan, Kjetil, and Christina Zetterlund. "Altering a Homogenized Heritage: Articulating Heterogeneous Material Cultures in Norway and Sweden." *Designing Worlds: National Design Histories in an Age of Globalization*, edited by Kjetil Fallan and Grace Lees-Maffei. New York: Berghahn, 2016, pp. 172–187.

Gelfer-Jørgensen, Mirjam. "Scandinavianism – A Cultural Brand." *Scandinavian Design Beyond the Myth: Fifty Years of Scandinavian Design from the Nordic Countries*, edited by Widar Halén and Kerstin Wickman. Stockholm: Arvinius Förlag, 2006, pp. 17–25.

Guldberg, Jørn. "'Scandinavian Design' as Discourse: The Exhibition Design in Scandinavia, 1954–57." *Design Issues*, vol. 27, no. 2, 2011, pp. 41–58.

Gundtoft, Dorothea. *Fashion Scandinavia: Contemporary Cool*. London: Thames & Hudson, 2013.

Halén, Widar. "Fifty Years of Scandinavian Design – And After." *Scandinavian Design Beyond the Myth: Fifty Years of Scandinavian Design from the Nordic Countries*, edited by Widar Halén and Kerstin Wickman. Stockholm: Arvinius Förlag, 2006, pp. 7–13.

Halén, Widar and Kerstin Wickman, editors. *Scandinavian Design Beyond the Myth: Fifty Years of Scandinavian Design from the Nordic Countries*. Stockholm: Arvinius Förlag, 2006.

Huggan, Graham. *The Post-Colonial Exotic: Marketing the Margins*. London: Routledge, 2001, p. 13.

Julier, Guy, and Anders V. Munch. "Introducing Design Culture." *Design Culture: Objects and Approaches*, edited by Guy Julier, Mads Nygaard Folkmann, Niels Peter Skou, Hans-Christian Jensen, and Anders V. Munch. New York: Bloomsbury, 2019, pp. 1–9.

Kent, Sarah. "How Copenhagen Became Fashion's Sustainability Capital." *Business of Fashion*, 28 Jan. 2020.

Kingsley, Patrick. *How to Be Danish: From Lego to Lund, A Short Introduction to the State of Denmark*. Croydon: Short Books, 2012.

Krarup, Søren. "The History of Denmark Podcast." Episode 19: Christian IV Part I, www.podcasts.apple.com/dk/podcast/the-history-of-denmark/id1046277825. Accessed 21 Oct. 2022.

Lyngbye Pedersen, Birgit. "When Clothes Make People: The Clothing Industry Association and the Marketing of the Danish Clothing Industry From 1955 to 1960." *Dansk Mode/Danish Fashion: Research, Education, Application*, edited by Julie Sommerlund. Copenhagen: The Danish Design School Press, 2011, pp. 129–157.

Lyngbye Pedersen, Birgit. "Dressed Up for the International Market: A Study of the Danish Fashion Fair Promoting the Danish Fashion Industry, 1947–1970." *Nordic Fashion Studies*, edited by Peter McNeil and Louis Wallenberg. Stockholm: Axl Books, 2012, pp. 115–129.

Lynge-Jorlén, Ane. *Fashion Stylists: History, Meaning and Practice*. New York: Bloomsbury, 2020.

McNeil, Peter, and Louis Wallenberg, editors. *Nordic Fashion Studies*. Stockholm: Axl Books, 2012.

Melchior, Marie Riegels. "Denmark." *Berg Encyclopedia of World Dress and Fashion*, edited by Lise Skov. Vol. 8 – Western Europe, New York: Bloomsbury Fashion Central, 2010a, pp. 330–335.

Melchior, Marie Riegels. "'Doing' Danish Fashion: On National Identity and Design Practices of a Small Danish Fashion Company." *Fashion Practice*, vol. 2, no. 1, 2010b, pp. 13–40.

Melchior, Marie Riegels. "Catwalking the Nation: Challenges and Possibilities in the Case of the Danish Fashion Industry." *Culture Unbound*, vol. 3, 2011a, pp. 55–70.

Melchior, Marie Riegels. "From Design Nations to Fashion Nations? Unpacking Contemporary Scandinavian Fashion Dreams." *Fashion Theory*, vol. 15, no. 2, 2011b, pp. 177–200.

Melchior, Marie Riegels, Lise Skov, and Fabian Faurholt Csaba. "Translating Fashion into Danish." *Culture Unbound*, vol. 3, 2011c, pp. 209–228.

Melchior, Marie Riegels. "Fur – An Issue of Life and Death." *Fashion Theory*, vol. 19, no. 4, 2015, pp. 483–490.

Melchior, Marie Riegels. "COVER: Danish Fashion and Photography." *Fashioned in the North: Nordic Histories, Agents, and Images of Fashion Photography*, edited by Anna Dahlgren. Lund: Nordic Academic Press, 2020a, pp. 133–152.

Melchior, Marie Riegels. "In the Changing Room: A Study of the Act of Styling before 'Styling' in Danish Fashion, 1900–1965." *Fashion Stylists: History, Meaning and Practice*, edited by Ane Lynge-Jorlén. New York: Bloomsbury, 2020b, pp. 41–61.

Mellish, Kay Xander. *How to Live in Denmark: A Humorous Guide for Foreigners and Their Danish Friends*. Copenhagen BoD, 2017.

Munch, Anders V. "Throughout Any Scale: Design as Thinking in Totalities." *Design as Gesamtkunstwerk*. Rhodos: International Publisher, 2012, pp. 92–127.

Munch, Anders V. "On the Outskirts. Geography of Design and the Self-Exoticisation of Danish Design." *Journal of Design History*, vol. 30, no. 1, 2017, pp. 50–67.

Munch, Anders V. "Ideals of the Quotidian in Danish Design." *Everyday Design. Signs of Awareness*, edited by Kurosawa Hiromi. Kanazawa: 21st Century Museum of Contemporary Design, 2018, pp. 48–52.

Sark, Katrina. "Else Skjold and Kate Fletcher at Copenhagen Fashion Week." *Chic Podcast*, episode 2, 20 Aug. 2019. www.anchor.fm/chic-podcast/episodes/Episode-2—Else-Skjold-and-Kate-Fletcher-at-Copenhagen-Fashion-Week-e51dh0. Accessed 21 Oct. 2022.

Sark, Katrina. "Herning Textile Industry." *Chic Podcast*, episode 7, 1 Mar. 2020a. www.anchor.fm/chic-podcast/episodes/Episode-7—Herning-Textile-Industry-eb666g. Accessed 21 Oct. 2022.

Sark, Katrina. "Frederik Larsen on Making Copenhagen Fashion Week Sustainable." *Chic Podcast*, episode 10, 6 Apr. 2020b. www.anchor.fm/chic-podcast/episodes/Episode-10—Frederik-Larsen-on-Making-Copenhagen-Fashion-Week-Sustainable-ece6v6. Accessed 21 Oct. 2022.

Sark, Katrina. "Else Skjold and Sustainable Fashion Education." *Chic Podcast*, episode 18, 5 Aug. 2020c. www.anchor.fm/chic-podcast/episodes/Episode-18—Else-Skjold-and-Sustainable-Fashion-Education-ehnslo. Accessed 21 Oct. 2022.

Sark, Katrina and Sara Danièle Bélanger-Michaud. *Montréal Chic: A Locational History of Montréal Fashion*. Bristol: Intellect, 2016.

Skjold, Else. *Fashion Research at Design Schools*. Kolding: Designskolen Kolding, 2008.

Skjold, Else. "The Fashion Industry Is So Yesterday." *Politiken*, 9 Aug. 2020, www.kglakademi.dk/sites/default/files/downloads/news/feature_politiken_9.8.2020.pdf. Accessed 21 Oct. 2022.

Skou, Niels Peter, and Anders V. Munch "New Nordic and Scandinavian Retro: Reassessment of Values and Aesthetics in Contemporary Nordic Design." *Journal of Aesthetics & Culture*, vol. 8, 2016, pp. 1–12.

Sommerlund, Julie, editor. *Dansk Mode / Danish Fashion: Research, Education, Application*. Copenhagen: The Danish Design School Press, 2011.

Sommerlund, Julie. "Deological Design?" *Dansk Mode / Danish Fashion: Research, Education, Application*, edited by Julie Sommerlund. Copenhagen: The Danish Design School Press, 2011, pp. 165–178.

Spandet-Møller, Henrik. *Danish Fashion Going Global*. Hellerup: Henrik Spandet-Møller/HSMH Holding ApS, 2011.

Tanggaard, Lene. "Creativity with a Danish Edge." *The Palgrave Handbook of Creativity and Culture Research*, edited by V. P. Glăveanu. London: Palgrave Studies in Creativity and Culture, 2016.

Teilmann-Lock, Stina. "The Myth of Danish Design and the Implicit Claims of Labels." *Designing Worlds: National Design Histories in an Age of Globalization*, edited by Kjetil Fallan and Grace Lees-Maffei. New York: Berghahn, 2016, pp. 156–171.

Teisbaek, Pernille. *Dress Scandinavian: Style your Life and Wardrobe the Danish Way*. London: Ebury Press, 2017.

Urban Chic Book Series, www.urban-chic.net/. Accessed 13 Mar. 2023.

Wiking, Meik. *The Little Book of Hygge: The Danish Way to Live Well*. London: Penguin Life, 2016.

Wilson, Elizabeth. *Adorned in Dreams: Fashion and Modernity*. London: I.B. Tauris, 2013 (1985).

2

Copenhagen Fashion History

Marie Riegels Melchior

As the capital of Denmark and a major trading post, fashion has sailed into Copenhagen harbour from near and far for centuries in the form of new materials, outfits worn by seafarers and ideas brought from other ports and cities of ways to dress fashionably. Many of the city's buildings have served the industry's busy tailors, seamstresses, weavers and dyers and other hands needed to make a completed fashion product. An understanding of fashion as a collection of cultural and economic practices, such as the one expressed by business historian Regina Blaszczyk (2007), tightly knits the activities of a city like Copenhagen with the idea of fashion, from production to consumption, and even to the daily practice of getting dressed. As many other scholars have observed, fashion and the city have become increasingly interconnected since the urban, industrial and consumer revolutions of the late eighteenth and nineteenth centuries (Wilson 1985; Breward & Evans 2005; Gilbert & Casadei 2020).

When wandering the streets of Copenhagen, the historical layers of fashion are readily available for viewing, if one is not too distracted by the sight of hip contemporary fashions being modelled in the streets by the Copenhageners or displayed in the shops of the city centre and neighbourhood districts of Vesterbro, Nørrebro, Østerbro and Christianshavn. For instance, walking from the parliament building of Christiansborg towards the National Museum of Denmark, which contains the largest museum dress and fashion collection in the country, one passes the strikingly painted Thorvaldsen's Museum on Vindebrogade (Figures 2.1 and 2.2), which in 1848 became the first museum in Denmark to open to the public. With its featured artist and collector, Bertel Thorvaldsen (1770–1844), buried at its centre, the museum is a literal mausoleum. The outside walls of the building feature large frescoes depicting the Danes welcoming the internationally renowned artist upon his return from Italy in 1838, bringing both his own works and his significant art collection. Painted by Jørgen Sonne, the wall along Vindebrogade shows the rising Copenhagen bourgeoisie dressed in their latest fashions: the day suits of the men, and the long, elegant dresses of the women.

FIGURE 2.1: Thorvaldsen's Museum facing Vindebrogade, June 2021. The fashions of the Copenhagen bourgeoisie in the 1830s, when welcoming the artist Bertel Thorvaldsen (1770–1844) home, are illustrated on the museum's outer walls by the artist Jørgen Sonne (1801–90), photo by Marie Riegels Melchior.

Over the course of the nineteenth century, these were to become the primary and largest group of fashion consumers in Copenhagen, together with the elite of the royal court. From 1660 until 1849, Denmark was under an absolute monarchy. In that period, the royal court and the country's nobility were the main fashion influencers, and the local fashion industry worked mainly in their service (Andersen 1977). With the introduction of constitutional monarchy in the nineteenth century, however, the bourgeoisie along with its norms and values began to take the lead both in fashion and in the commercial industry fashion was becoming (Bech 1989).

After passing the Thorvaldsen's Museum, across the canal and around the right corner of the National Museum of Denmark is Rådhusstræde, then turning left across the small square called Vandkunsten, one arrives at Farvergade, or "Dyer Street." Here is where, at the time around 1560, under the reign of King Frederik II (1534–88), textile-dyeing workshops were located, serving the early fashion industry that would develop with inspiration from continental Europe during the Renaissance and the modern era. Walking east again across the old city centre, crossing the pedestrian street of Strøget, through the old *Klædebo-kvarteret* ("the cloth quarter," where during the Middle Ages merchants were selling cloth and clothing), and

FIGURE 2.2: Close-up of the painted motifs on the walls of Thorvaldsen's Museum, photo by Marie Riegels Melchior.

up along Købmagergade, where the main high street fashion shopping is located today, one passes Silkegade, or "Silk Street." The name refers to a time around 1620 when King Christian IV (1577–1648) took the initiative to invite German silk weavers who had fled the religious turmoil in their homeland between Lutherans and Catholics, in the hopes of establishing the luxury industry of silk weaving in Copenhagen. Unfortunately, the king's good intentions went unfulfilled, as the silk industry in Copenhagen never took off. Although woven materials made of wool, cotton and flax were produced in Copenhagen and nearby areas until the twentieth century, a luxury fashion industry never developed in the city. Despite a few exceptionally skilled tailors, Copenhagen was mostly at the receiving end of luxury fashion, importing goods from the great metropolises of Europe: Paris, London, Berlin, Vienna, Florence, Rome, etc.

Beyond the street names of Copenhagen, other layers of the city's relationship with fashion are revealed when looking at buildings (most built before 1970) that have played host to the fashion industry, its production and distribution. During the nineteenth and twentieth centuries, many courtyards in the city's centre and inner districts housed cramped seamstresses' workshops and ground-floor clothing shops. In order to supplement their earnings, women would also sit and sew in their small rental apartments, while keeping house and looking after their children. With Copenhagen's expansion during the industrialization of the late nineteenth and early twentieth centuries, buildings as high as five storeys were built to host novel department stores. Across from the Royal Theatre, the department store Magasin du Nord (Figure 2.3) was inaugurated in 1879. Along Strøget, department stores proliferated: Crome and Goldsmith (opened 1884, closed 1971), Jac. Olsen (opened 1884, closed 1972), Fonnesbech (opened 1847, moved in 1938 to

FIGURE 2.3: The department store Magasin du Nord built in Parisian Hôtel de Ville style by the architects Albert Jensen & Henri Glæsel and located close to Kongens Nytorv in the centre of Copenhagen. The photo is from 1918. Notice many automobiles parked in front of the building with the logo of the department store on the side. All over the city the Magasin du Nord brand and the ambience of fashion and luxury goods could be experienced. Photo by unknown photographer, Magasin du Nord Museum, with permission.

a new building that now houses the Copenhagen Stock Exchange, closed 1970) and Illum (opened 1899). Købmagergade featured Messen (opened 1885, closed 1972), while Vesterbrogade boasted Havemanns Magasin (opened 1919, moved in 1940 to a new, modern building, closed 1975) and on Østerbrogade the fashionable department store was Mode Palæet (opened in 1896). These large stores created new public spaces for consumption. Everyone could visit the department store, but the women of the bourgeoisie or elite class – *Københavnerinde* – were the main target audience. Just as it was fashionable to refer to the stereotype of the *Parisienne* or the *Berlinerin*, the *Københavnerinden* was featured in Danish fashion and women's magazines as an idealized, chic urban woman, a connoisseur of fashion, independent, elegant and stylish. In 1928, the painter and poet Emil Krause (1871–1945) published his take on the *Københavnerinde*:

Københavnerinden
Silkeben og franske Hæle, dunkelt sløret Glans i Øjet
Pagehaaret dækker Kinden. Halsen svaj og fremadbøjet
Tasken daskende i Haanden, slank og enkel, fix i Tøjet
Det er Københavnerinde, som ses paa Strøget.
    Trippende i Kjolestumpen, strammet yderlige af Vinden
    Danner hun en malerisk og plastisk Gruppe med Venninden
    Saa en Række hvide Tænder og et Smil paa Pudderkinden
    Ja, hun kender sine Vaaben, Københavnerinden.
                             (Emil Krause, På kryds og tværs. København i
                                   billeder og vers. Gyldendal 1928)

The Copenhagen Woman
A silk stockinged leg and French heels, a dimly blurred gloss in the eye.
A pageboy cut covers her cheek. Her neck is cricked and bent forward.
The bag swishing in her hand, slender and simple, fashionably dressed,
It is the Copenhagen woman who is seen on Strøget.
    Tripping in a short dress, tightened further by the wind,
    She forms a picturesque and fleshed-out grouping with her girlfriend,
    A row of white teeth and a smile on her powdered cheek.
    Yes, she knows her weapons, the Copenhagen woman.
                                 (English translation by Marie Riegels Melchior)

Københavnerinden came to the department stores' fashion salons to buy her bespoke, fashionable clothing or frequented independent fashion salons. Beginning around 1913, she was invited to the fashion shows hosted by department stores, just a few years after the first mannequin show in Paris (Evans 2013).

Even a retirement home in the centre of Copenhagen, east of the Royal Gardens at Rosengade 1, bears the mark of the fashion industry, as it was built in 1978 with the support of the Association of Dress and Fashion Retailers in Copenhagen to house elderly people who had worked in the industry. There are many more examples of fashion's history in the city, which I will continue to unpack, albeit with a narrower historical scope, from the latter half of the twentieth century to the present day. With this framing, I emphasize how the visibility of fashion in Copenhagen was transformed during this period. For one thing, fashion production, in the sense of actual clothing manufacturing, more or less left the city. Instead, the industry's visibility in Copenhagen is mainly manifested in fashion consumption, fashion marketing and branding, as well as fashion's institutionalization.

From museums to trade organizations, Copenhagen promotes fashion as a vehicle for growth, whether in the city's urban development, its creative industries (including fashion design) or its visibility as a tourist destination. It seems that fashion has become an important part of the answer to the question posed by national and municipal governments, as well as by developers, as to how to transform Copenhagen into a cosmopolitan hub geared towards what urban studies theorist Richard Florida called the creative class, whose members seek to work and live in a dynamic and creative urban environment (Florida 2005). However, this answer may not prove wholly unproblematic for cities like Copenhagen, as fashion is causing climate and environmental challenges worldwide. This is true not only in locations where garment production is actually taking place but just as much where fashion consumption is concentrated, raising a question about how completely Copenhagen ought to yoke its future to fashion, which I will address in the conclusion of this chapter.

My point of departure for this chapter is interdisciplinary. I am informed mainly by cultural history, design and fashion studies. The sources I have consulted for the chapter are a combination of secondary sources, such as books about the history of Danish fashion and Copenhagen; primary sources, such as trade journals, newspapers and fashion magazines; and interviews I have conducted with fashion professionals in Copenhagen since commencing my study of twentieth century and contemporary Danish fashion history.

Wonderful Copenhagen: 1950s and 1960s

In a popular 1952 Hollywood film about the writer and poet Hans Christian Andersen, Danny Kaye gave voice to the song "Wonderful Copenhagen." Almost instantly this highly romanticized song title became a favoured slogan of tourist campaigns, appearing on iconic posters like the one showing a smiling policeman holding back a crowd of just-as-smiling drivers, cyclists and pedestrians to help a duck and her brood of ducklings cross the street. What a wonderful city, populated by happy, caring and well-dressed people, where authorities derive pleasure from protecting the city's wildlife (Figure 2.4)! This image of Copenhagen persists, not least due to annual rankings in the World Happiness Reports, generated by the United Nations Sustainable Development Solutions Network since 2012. Danes have consistently ranked as the happiest and second-happiest people, while Copenhagen has ranked as the fifth-happiest city in the world, as well as the second-most liveable city in Europe (Copcap).

From the perspective of Danish fashion history, the "Wonderful Copenhagen" claim matched the energy and industrial progress that established the foundation of the modern Danish welfare state after the Second World War. People were in general optimistic and forward-looking, expecting to experience improvement after five years of Nazi–German collaboration and occupation. Denmark received aid via the Marshall Plan and in due course invested in its industrial infrastructure to facilitate mass production, suggesting a future of progress, jobs for both men and women, improved personal finances for most citizens, and a national economy experiencing accelerating growth through the 1960s (Danmarkshistorien.dk). This also included the development of the mass production of clothing. If clothing had previously been a limited resource for those who could afford it, the full-blown industrialization of clothing production, together with the improved quality of mass-produced products, made clothing accessible, with plenty of ready-to-wear clothing for sale by the end of the 1950s. Consequently, the industry needed to develop ways of selling its products so that the time spent on the store shelf or rack did not outlast consumer taste for the designs. In other words, the industry was eager to transform users into regular and continuous consumers. Following the trend in other western countries to adopt an American-style belief in the market's ability to secure a prosperous future for the many and not only a few, fashion became the marketing solution for the clothing industry. Thinking in terms of fashion led the industry to structure itself via collections, with the continuous production of newness facilitated by the industrialized organization of clothing production. Gradually, professionally trained fashion designers began collaborating with clothing manufacturers, and with that, the clothing industry became the fashion industry, both structurally and in the way the industry presented itself.

A Danish ready-to-wear fashion system developed with biannual trade shows, fashion weeks presenting forward-looking styles, fashion designers' shows and fresh press coverage every season with the launch of new collections. At the time, these fashion designers trained in Copenhagen at the *Kunsthåndværkerskolen* (the "School of Arts and Crafts," or what today is known as the Royal Danish Academy of Fine Arts, School of Design) or at *Margrethe-Skolen*, a preparatory school mainly for young women who wanted to learn sewing and aesthetics, skills valued in life

FIGURE 2.4: In 1959, the artist Viggo Vagnby (1896–1966) drew the poster for the Tourist Association of Copenhagen, which would become iconic for Danes as well as visitors to Copenhagen as it caught the atmosphere of the capital city: happy, cozy and caring. ©Viggo Vagnby, with permission.

as a married woman and mother (renamed the Scandinavian Academy of Fashion Design in 2017). Parisian haute couture fashion houses were already demonstrating how to market clothing as fashion to stimulate consumption among their prime target groups: the upper-middle-class and elites. These sales technologies had been adopted by the Danish fashion salons by the early twentieth century, particularly fashion shows and collaboration with the press to promote each new season's collection. With its expansion into mass production, the scale of fashion grew along with its visibility and accessibility to Danes.

The project of making the Danish consumer into a fashion consumer was undertaken by a joint initiative of fashion retailers and manufacturers, establishing the Danish Men's Wear Council in 1958 and the Danish Women's Wear Council one year later. Both organizations initiated campaigns targeting the end user of Danish fashion, which at the time was primarily the Danish consumer. The first campaign from the Men's Wear Council preached that Danish men needed to change outfits more often, particularly when interacting in different contexts. "*Skal De ud, så Klæd Dem om*" ("If you're going out, change clothes") declared advertisements in national newspapers. The two Councils established the Danish industry's first Fashion Week (women's wear) and Men's Fashion Fair (men's wear) in Copenhagen in 1958. The first events addressed Danish consumers, encouraging them to visit the many companies presenting their collections at the fairs. Just one year later, however, the fashion week events began to take on a business-to-business focus, and eventually, the main ambition of the events became the promotion of Danish fashion abroad. The industrialization of clothing production required both investment and, in the case of the Copenhagen-based companies, new locations to secure sufficient space for machinery and production along assembly lines. Wherever possible, previous sewing facilities were abandoned, and new ones were established. This transformed the city of Copenhagen, as its busy workshops gradually disappeared. The tailors, assistants and salespersons crossing streets with meters of fabric under their arms, or delivery bikes loaded with completed outfits dispatched to customers, became rare sights as the 1960s progressed.

Many within the industry could see that its strategic focus on fashion would not save it forever and that sooner or later it would have to outsource production to compete on price, especially with respect to the cost of labour. Still, not all were able to see these changes coming, or anticipate how quickly they would transform the industry. Instead, they invested in locally based development, building what they believed would be sufficient manufacturing capacity on the outskirts of Copenhagen. The area around Lersøpark Allé to the northwest of Copenhagen was given over to the clothing industry in 1947, and by 1957, seven clothing and textile manufacturers had established new facilities here in an open, green space surrounded by new, modern homes. All the factory buildings were made of red brick, lending the area a homogeneous look, and the new concentration of clothing factories caused the area to be dubbed *Konfektionsbyen* (ready-to-wear village). At its peak, the area employed 1200 people (Hovedstadhistorie.dk). By the 1970s, however, the factories had either closed down or moved even further away from the city, chasing government subsidies that supported the creation of new jobs in rural areas where agricultural workers were being made redundant through the increasing mechanization of Danish farming practices.

By the 1970s, Copenhagen was a run-down capital city, as industrial buildings in the city centre were abandoned, along with the many downtown courtyards that had previously hosted smaller-scale clothing and textile production. The population of the city centre was also falling, as people with means preferred to move to new housing developments in the suburbs. Gradually, however, the Copenhagen city centre was transformed once again with the restoration and renovation of valuable historical buildings, and the crowded courtyard buildings were demolished to sanitize surrounding living quarters. By the 1990s, population trends had reversed, and people were moving back into a city centre that was being developed and gentrified according to the high-end needs of the more affluent members of society.

Strøget (Figure 2.5), which has been the high street in the city centre since the 1880s, was converted into a pedestrian street in 1962, with 1.1 kilometres worth of shops lining the popular shopping route and making Copenhagen an ever more attractive destination. Along this new pedestrian mall, a handful of fashion shops targeting teenagers emerged during the 1950s and 1960s and attracted not only young Copenhageners but also young Danes living outside the city. In 1956, the boutique *Deres* opened, offering local as well as international youth fashion. In 1958, another boutique for young people opened, *Nørgaard paa Strøget* (Figure 2.6), converted by the visionary son of its previous owner from a shop specializing in mourning clothes into a fashion boutique modelled after those appearing at the same time along Kings Road in London. It sold fashion designs by British Mary Quant and French Cacharel, Danish brands like Dranella, Bent Visti and Mugge Kølpin, as well as their own designs. During the 1960s, even more fashion boutiques arrived, such as *Boutique Bistro*, which opened in 1967 and featured the owner's own label, "Margit Brandt Design." Together, these shops gave a youthful feeling to the Copenhagen city centre.

As mentioned, the main department stores were located along the pedestrian mall Strøget: Magasin du Nord, Illum, Fonnesbech, Jac. Olsen and Crome & Goldsmith. During the 1950s, their fashion departments were the destination of choice if buyers wanted "a bite of Paris," as Erik Mortensen (1926–98), who later became the head of fashion design at the haute couture house Pierre Balmain, explained (Mortensen 1988). Here, elegant women's fashions were sold, made to measure

FIGURE 2.5: Just converted into a pedestrian street – Strøget, the main shopping street of Copenhagen, is crowded with people on their shopping sprees or between appointments. The photo is from 1963 when the fashions dictated suits for men, two-piece suits for women or a knee-long everyday dress. Photo by Aage Sørensen, Scanpix Denmark, with permission.

to ensure their exquisite elegance. Among the most prestigious independent fashion salons providing this service for the affluent, style-conscious fashion consumer were Holger Blom, Uffe Brydegaard and Preben Birch. Holger Blom was located just around the corner from the Royal Theater on Holmens Kanal, where he also dressed many of the leading actresses at the theatre; this allowed him to promote his fashion designs from the stage as if at a fashion show (Verge 2017).

As the fashion boutiques for young people emerged, the fashion salons gradually disappeared, as did a number of department stores. Accompanying the movement of people away from apartments in the city was the emergence of new shopping facilities in the suburbs, favoured by many for their convenience. In other words, fashion was a participant in the changes in Copenhagen in the post-war and industrialization eras. Ready-to-wear fashion went on to become the dominant variety of fashion in Copenhagen, whether it arose from the local manufacturing industry, the ready-to-wear industry or from the new, modern experiences of young shoppers frequenting artistically decorated boutiques bursting with youthful energy.

FIGURE 2.6: Nørgaard på Strøget. One of the first shops in Copenhagen to embrace the youth fashion of the late 1950s and early 1960s was *Nørgaard paa Strøget*, which opened in 1958. The photo is from 1978, portraying a display of group photos of the employees. Photo by Susanne Mertz, with permission by VISDA.

Copenhagen – Paris of the North: 1970s

> The awareness of the international ready-to-wear industry is being directed towards Copenhagen as the Paris of the North. The reason for this? – For the second time, Copenhagen has been chosen as the venue for two international Fashion Fairs, the Scandinavian Fashion Week and the Copenhagen Fashion Fair.
> (*Klæder skaber folk* 1968: 30)

This was the text of an announcement in the clothing manufacturers' trade journal *Klæder skaber folk* in 1968. In the twenty years following the Second World War, the Danish clothing industry developed from an industry focused on the domestic market to an export industry selling Danish fashion designs abroad. After years of negotiations between the two main clothing production clusters in Denmark – the region including the towns of Brande, Herning and Ikast in central Jutland and the Copenhagen area – Copenhagen had emerged as the main centre for promoting clothing primarily made and designed in Denmark. From a pragmatic point of view, this made sense due to the city's proximity to the country's main international airport, supply of hotels to host national and international buyers during the biannual fashion week, as well as its restaurants and other cultural offerings to entertain them during their stay. These advantages were not persuasive to everyone in the industry, as many in Jutland wanted to do things differently than in Copenhagen. But despite these differences, the Scandinavian Fashion Week remained in Copenhagen, where since 1958 *Dansk modeuge* had presented Danish women's wear, alongside the *Dansk Herremode Messe*, the Danish Men's Fashion Fair. The firms in Jutland, on the other hand, had promoted their products via the *Dansk Textil Messe* ("Danish Textile Fair") since 1947. By choosing the name Scandinavian Fashion Week, the industry sought to attract companies from neighbouring countries and establish Copenhagen as an international hub for fashion. Most importantly, they hoped to tempt international buyers to make significant purchases of fashion design from companies based in Denmark and other Nordic countries.

Copenhagen had to dress up, so to speak, to achieve the Danish clothing industry's ambition to become *the* fashion centre in Scandinavia. In this case, "dressing up" meant being able to support the industry's required infrastructure, including hosting both the biannual fashion week and local companies' own fashion shows; nourishing an ecosystem of modelling agencies, fashion photographers and stylists; and sustaining its identity as a year-round, everyday fashion hub for the industry. This meant that Copenhagen needed a permanent trade centre. In 1970, the Scandinavian Trade Centre for Fashion opened, featuring 13,000 square meters of floor space with 150 permanent showrooms, adjacent to the new high-rise Imperial Hotel at Sct. Jørgenssø (the lake to the west of the old city, located today just behind the Imperial cinema). The vanguard of Danish fashion design – the smaller independent design companies mostly buying their products from local clothing manufacturers, or in some cases manufacturing their own clothing – began to use unusual and surprising venues for their fashion shows in the late 1960s, as they knew it would require creativity to meet the expectations of the international buyers of that era. These buyers would expect that the local fashion scene could bear comparison with Paris or London, offering spectacular fashion shows followed by chic parties. The Margit Brandt Design company understood this well and pioneered the use of fashion show locations that highlighted not only their own designs but Copenhagen itself. For one show in 1970, they converted the Hofteateret, an old court theatre, next to Christiansborg Palace, into a catwalk, where models, some on roller skates, exhibited the company's "71 Brazil Brandt" collection. Other companies banded together to make a film to promote their collections, using this unusual tactic to attract the necessary attention. The liberal atmosphere of Copenhagen in the early 1970s following the legalization of porn production in 1969 didn't hurt the Danish fashion industry either. Margit Brandt Design did not disappoint guests in this respect when, at its 1971 fashion show at the Glyptotek Museum amidst art from ancient Greece, Rome and Egypt, underwear models began spontaneously dancing topless down the catwalk.

In 1967, fashion designer Trice Tomsen (b.1945) opened the first modelling agency in Copenhagen, joining forces in 1987 with Elite International Management. Models such as Lotte Freddie (who later became a fashion journalist), Grethe Caspersen and Aase Daily were the faces of Copenhagen fashion long before Helena Christensen came to prominence; later, she remained identified with Copenhagen fashion despite her international career as one of the legendary supermodels. Whether or not Copenhagen could claim to be the Paris of the North, it was certainly the undisputed capital of Danish fashion by 1970. The Danish clothing industry was transforming into a fashion industry, and this transformation took place in Copenhagen. Fashion gave the otherwise rundown city a lively kick, lending it the youthful energy of an industry eager to succeed as an international export powerhouse with a home base in Copenhagen.

Crisis, copies and uncertainty for Copenhagen fashion: 1980s and 1990s

After the energetic 1960s and early 1970s, an economic crisis struck Denmark. The 1972 referendum in favour of joining the European Common Market led to both new trade regulations, as well as increased competition from imported ready-to-wear products from other member states. Meanwhile, the energy crisis of the period challenged the household budgets of most Danes dependent on oil for home heating and personal vehicles. Copenhagen felt the crisis as keenly as the rest of the country, but the fashion industry maintained its base there as its gateway to both the export and domestic markets. A new location for trade shows opened just south of the city in 1975, called *Bella Centeret*. Offering plenty of space as well as new and modern surroundings, it suited the fashion industry to be part of the new, if difficult, reality. Outsourcing of manufacturing to low-wage countries in southern Europe was on the rise, while production in Asia, mainly Hong Kong, was beginning as well. The industry's labour unions pleaded with Danish consumers to be loyal to local workers by buying Danish fashion and other consumer goods. Manufacturers were willing to support the initiative by supplying small Danish flags with which to tag their products, but in the late 1980s, the trade journal *Textile* concluded that Danes did not really care whether their clothing was made in Denmark or not (*Textile* 1988: 8).

Scandinavian collaboration around maintaining Copenhagen as the locus for the Scandinavian Fashion Fair also lost momentum in the 1980s. The other Scandinavian countries started their own fashion fairs in Stockholm, Helsinki, and Oslo since the crisis brought on by the gradual conversion to a global industry meant that local manufacturers were mainly selling to their respective domestic markets. This was also the case among Danish manufacturers. By the early 1990s, the Scandinavian collaboration had ended, and a new organization established the Copenhagen International Fashion Fair in 1993 (*Textile*, nr. 8, 4 August 1993). A year later, a group of investors seeking to restore Copenhagen's reputation as the "Scandinavian fashion mecca" opened *Scandinavian Fashion House* in a former harbour area, hosting showrooms for companies in an attempt to recall the city's fashion heyday in the 1960s and early 1970s (*Textile*, nr. 2, 2 February 1994).

In the difficult decade of the 1980s, the Danish fashion industry was no longer focused on independent fashion design as its primary competitive advantage. Instead, companies sought to be their consumers' first choice by making products of the best quality for the best price. Following international trends in design that profiled products less by a named fashion designer and more by a brand name, Danish fashion obtained a reputation among domestic consumers for selling knock-off designs. Only a few fashion brands maintained their focus on original design, and thus became known for more avant-garde looks, notably Ivan Grundahl, Mads Nørgaard Copenhagen, Noa Noa, Grith & Graumann and Bitte Kai Rand. These brands, based in Copenhagen, were fashion design companies first and foremost, and rarely if ever owned their own manufacturing facilities. They sometimes made their production orders at factories at home in Denmark, but more often abroad, in Belgium, Italy, Portugal or Spain. After the collapse of the Soviet Union, Poland became another preferred site for clothing production. Importantly, however, these companies maintained their own fashion boutiques in the city centre, which both contributed to Copenhagen's atmosphere as a somewhat fashionable city and catered to Danes coming from the suburbs or farther afield as well as to tourists visiting the Danish capital.

During the 1990s, the co-branding of Copenhagen and Danish fashion was seen as a lucrative business. The two entities needed each other. Copenhagen needed to revive and maintain its trendsetting identity, and the fashion industry in Denmark, now transformed more or less into brand houses, needed to boost its fashionable and urban connotations. The Copenhagen fashion brands initiated a consumer-oriented fashion festival in the early 1990s to attract the attention of both locals and visitors. The festival program included fashion shows and talks accessible to the ordinary consumer. Those interested in fashion, and particularly in fashion as a cultural and economic phenomenon, as I am, remember these exciting events as communicating a sense of urban chic. During the same period, a variety of fashion prizes were introduced to highlight for consumers the presumed talent and quality in the field of Danish fashion design. The women's magazine *ALT for damerne* introduced its *Guldknappen* (Golden Button) prize in 1985; the Holger Blom Prize was awarded for a few years beginning in 1988, and later the women's magazine *IN* introduced a prize in 2003.

Neither these initiatives nor the work undertaken to rebrand Copenhagen as the home of Danish fashion did much to slow the globalization of the fashion industry or its consequences. The Multifibre Arrangement, established in the 1970s between the so-called developed and developing countries, regulated the import of textiles and clothing from developing countries, essentially offsetting their competitive advantages of low production costs, cheap labour, etc. This agreement regulated the fashion industry between 1974 and 1994. Until 2005, when the agreement was abandoned completely, it was possible to maintain local clothing manufacturing in Denmark, but after that point, outsourcing was the dominant reality. Faced with this, the singular focus of the fashion industry in Denmark became branding, since its design and marketing were what was based in Denmark; therefore, developing the fashion culture in Denmark could mean local fashion industry jobs, boosting interest in Copenhagen as a stimulating and fashionable urban atmosphere, and a creative city. Fashioning Copenhagen, fashioning the Danes, through highlighting local fashion brands made sense, since it comported with the relatively high standard of living enjoyed by Danes due to the Danish welfare state and the distribution of income through its taxation system. The middle-class Danish way of life – being fashionably dressed, living in tidy houses and apartments, being well-educated through the taxpayer-financed public school and university system – created a dream-like image of Denmark that proved invaluable in branding the Danish fashion industry, while it adjusted to the changing market conditions of a global industry based on complex transnational supply chains and in need of constant media exposure to ensure consumer awareness. In reality, the fashion market is well-served even if those around the globe who cannot afford to buy brand-name clothing are fashionably dressed.

Fashioning Copenhagen as a Global Fashion City: 2000s

Copenhagen, like other cities at the turn of the new millennium, received renewed attention from not only the Danish fashion industry but also the Danish public sector, including the Ministry of Industry, Business and Financial Affairs, the municipality of Copenhagen, the national tourism bureau and various cultural institutions (see Breward & Gilbert 2006; Rogerson 2006; Martinez 2007; Larner et al. 2007; Skov & Melchior 2011; Wubs et al. 2020). The new attention towards Copenhagen revolved around the idea of repositioning Copenhagen as "the fifth global fashion cluster," as articulated in a report by the Ministry of Industry, Business and Financial Affairs on the future of the Danish fashion industry in 2005 (FORA 2005). It was an ambitious plan, woven into a broader business development policy focusing on the post-industrial economy, innovation (particularly so-called "user-driven innovation") and creative industries (Melchior 2013). The ambitious vision was inspired by studies of how the city of Antwerp had become a fashion capital by cultivating itself as a hub for avant-garde fashion culture (FORA 2003). This development occurred over the course of the 1990s and was tightly intertwined with the success of three institutions: a fashion school, a specialized fashion museum and a branding network organization, all sharing a building named *ModeNatie* in the centre of Antwerp. The Danish fashion industry had never been on the receiving end of such focused and interventionist policy from the government as in 2005; previous policies affecting the industry had been characterized only by formulating framework conditions. This meant radical changes to the industry, specifically, a boost to the role of the city of Copenhagen in developing the future of the Danish fashion industry. Copenhagen was needed as the location, the spot on the world fashion map, to attract the international attention necessary to strengthen the industry. Ideally, this would lead to a greater number of jobs directly connected to the fashion industry, increasing the export of Danish fashion design, a boost in the creativity of Danish fashion designers and fashion shopping in Copenhagen, and thereby also elevating Copenhagen as a tourist destination for fashion and design-conscious visitors.

In 2005, the network organization Danish Fashion Institute (renamed Global Fashion Agenda in 2018) was established with the mandate of the industry and the government to cast Copenhagen as a fashion capital and Danish fashion as a locational, overarching brand. Within the industry, a reorganization of the existing framework for trade and fashion shows took place. One of the first initiatives of the Institute was to rename its main event Copenhagen Fashion Week (Figure 2.7) after years of marketing it under the name of Copenhagen Fashion Days. The Institute increased the level of coordination between fashion week activities and developed its PR and marketing strategies, perhaps most significantly by transmitting the week's fashion shows live on big screens at several locations in the city centre. Not since the fashion week emerged in Copenhagen in the late 1950s had the event addressed the people of Copenhagen in such a direct way. Fashion shows and the clothing modelled there had been closed affairs, only revealed to consumers when the new fashions arrived in the shops months later, or through reports in news media and fashion magazines. *Dansk Daily*, a free newspaper distributed in cafés and public transit stations, was another initiative

FIGURE 2.7: Live transmission from Copenhagen Fashion Week in February 2007. On a big screen placed directly in front of the Copenhagen City Hall, fashion is shouted out loud as part of the city experience during the biannual, commercial fashion week, photo by Marie Riegels Melchior.

that directly offered Copenhageners the latest fashion news every day of fashion week. Cultural institutions such as the Design Museum Denmark and the Danish Design Centre also took an active role in promoting fashion. In particular, the Design Museum sought to build an understanding of Danish fashion by changing its collection policy to focus more specifically on Danish fashion design, which was implemented in 2013, and by curating special exhibitions that articulated a Danish fashion heritage. My own Ph.D. dissertation on Danish fashion, defended in 2009, was part of this development, and was initiated by the Design Museum Denmark in collaboration with Denmark's Design School (today the Royal Danish Academy of Fine Arts, School of Design).

The last twenty years of positioning Copenhagen as an international fashion city have not resulted in the naming of streets after influential industry leaders, at least not yet. However, its impact is evident in the continuous presence of fashion activities in the city. From the industry's perspective, Copenhagen Fashion Week and the Global Fashion Summit – initiated in 2009 in order to focus the global fashion industry's attention on its impact on climate change – are the most prominent events taking place here. The fashion design schools, the small designer shops in the city centre and inner districts, as well as the mainstream fashion shops in the city all affirm the role of fashion in Copenhagen. And we must not forget its well-dressed residents, fashioning Copenhagen while riding their bikes, sitting in cafes, visiting cultural institutions and just living in the city. With fashion so completely disseminated in everyday life due to the ready-to-wear industry and the relatively strong Danish economy, Copenhagen's relationship with fashion continues to be vibrant and lively.

Conclusion

Recent scholarly work on fashion cities by the geographers David Gilbert and Patrizia Casadei (2018) asks whether the era of fashion cities is over. Since the middle of the twentieth century, it has been the ambition of industry and political leaders alike to make Copenhagen a fashion city. In view of pressing concerns regarding the fashion industry's role in climate change, particular initiatives promoting fashion are contested, including the fashion city. Gilbert and Casadai imagine a different future:

> The end of the fashion city, an epoch that started in the urban, industrial and consumer revolutions of the late-eighteenth and nineteenth centuries, is as much about the nature of twenty-first century urbanism as specific changes in the relationship with fashion. As we have become an urban species on an urban planet, the nature of cities and urbanism has been changing profoundly, and perhaps the experiences and influence of the great modern metropolis far less significant.
> (Gilbert & Casadai 2018: 404)

As more and more people live with fashion in urban contexts, the ability to claim status as a fashion city may have lost its value. Yet, fashion is part of a Copenhagener's daily life, and is expected to remain so even as production, distribution and consumption of fashion may change over time, and even as fashion may someday be regulated by governments and international organizations in order to meet goals related to sustainability and climate change. Perhaps in the future, aspirations for Copenhagen chic will be replaced by aspirations for planetary chic.

REFERENCES

Andersen, Ellen. *Danske dragter. Moden i 1700-årene*. Copenhagen: Nationalmuseet and Nyt Nordisk Forlag Arnold Busck, 1977.

Bech, Viben. *Danske dragter. Moden 1840–1890*. Copenhagen: Nationalmuseet and Nyt Nordisk Forlag Arnold Busck, 1989.

Blaszczyk, Regina. *Producing Fashion: Commerce, Culture, and Consumers*. Philadelphia: University of Pennsylvania Press, 2007.

Breward, Christopher, and Caroline Evans, editors. *Fashion & Modernity*. Oxford: Berg, 2005.

Breward, Christopher, and David Gilbert, editors. *Fashion's World Cities*. Oxford: Berg, 2006.

Copcap, www.copcap.com/news/danes-are-the-second-happiest-peoplein-the-world. Accessed 13 Mar. 2023.

Danmarkshistorien, www.danmarkshistorien.dk. Accessed 13 Mar. 2023.

Evans, Caroline. *The Mechanical Smile: Modernism and the First Fashion Shows in France and America, 1900–1929*. New Haven: Yale University Press, 2013.

Florida, Richard. *Den kreative klasse*. Århus: Klim, 2005.

FORA. *Sammenligning af danske og udenlandske rammebetingelser og innovationssystemer inden for modebranchen*. København: Økonomi-og Erhvervsministeriets enhed for erhvervsøkonomisk forskning og analyse, 2003.

FORA. *Brugerdreven innovation i dansk mode – den 5. globale modeklynge*. København: Økonomi-og Erhvervsministeriets enhed for erhvervsøkonomisk forskning og analyse, 2005.

Gilbert, David, and Patrizia Casadei. "The Hunting of the Fashion City: Rethinking the Relationship Between Fashion and the Urban in the Twenty-First Century." *Fashion Theory: Journal of Dress, Body and Culture*, vol. 24, no. 3, 2018, pp. 393–408.

Hovedstadshistorie, www.hovedstadshistorie.dk/emdrup/lersoe-parkalle-emdrup/. Accessed 13 Mar. 2023.

Klæder skaber folk. Trade Journal. Number 8, 1968.

Krause, Emil. *På kryds og tværs. København i billeder og vers*. Copenhagen: Gyldendal, 1928.

Larner, Wendy, Maureen Molloy, and Alison Goodrum. "Globalization, Cultural Economy and Not-So-Global Cities: The New Zealand Designer Fashion Industry." *Environment and Planning D: Society and Space*, vol. 25, no. 3, 2007, pp. 381–400.

Martinez, Javier Gimeno. "Selling Avant-Garde: How Antwerp Became a Fashion Capital (1990–2002)." *Urban Studies*, vol. 44, no. 12, 2007, pp. 2449–2464.

Melchior, Marie Riegels. *Dansk på Mode! Fortællinger om design, identitet og historie i og omkring dansk modeindustri*. Copenhagen: Museum Tusculanums Forlag, 2013.

Rogerson, C. M. "Developing the Fashion Industry in Africa: The Case of Johannesburg." *Urban Forum*, vol. 17, no. 3, 2006, pp. 215–240.

Skov, Lise, and Marie Riegels Melchior. "Dreams of Small Nations in a Polycentric Fashion World." *Special issue of Fashion Theory: Journal of Dress, Body and Culture*, vol. 15, no. 2, 2011.

Textile. *Trade Journal*. Number 17, 2 December 1988.

Textile. *Trade Journal*. Number 8, 4 August 1993.

Textile. *Trade Journal*. Number 2, 2 February 1994.

Trap.lex. www.trap.lex.dk/Konfektionsbyen. Accessed 13 Mar. 2023.

Verge, Marianne. *Modekongen Holger Blom*. København: Gyldendal, 2017.

Wilson, Elizabeth. *Adorned in Dreams: Fashion and Modernity*. New Brunswick: Rutgers University Press, 1985.

3

Fashioning Sustainability

Else Skjold and Frederik Larsen

Over the last decade, Denmark has become widely renowned for promoting the agenda of sustainable fashion – not least because of the Copenhagen Fashion Summit (CFS) now led by Global Fashion Agenda (GFA), and recently the 2023 sustainability strategy of the Copenhagen Fashion Week (CFW) was launched in January 2020. The challenges the fashion industry is beginning to address have global implications, but what is the historical development leading up to these initiatives, and how have perceptions and practices of fashion sustainability developed in Denmark? This chapter examines the current history of sustainability in fashion in Copenhagen and presents the organizational shifts that have influenced this development. The role of Copenhagen is central to other cultural currents in the creative industries that have drawn attention to Denmark since the 1990s, with innovative cultural movements such as the New Nordic cuisine and the Dogme films, and our research reveals how institutionalizing fashion sustainability in Denmark has been interlinked with them. Our chapter frames this development in an economic-experiential context, thus also highlighting how various sustainability perceptions and practices came to be left out, under-researched and under-valued, and why the Danish fashion sector currently finds itself in a deep crisis.

Our chapter presents aspects of the global and local developments that have shaped the relationship between fashion, culture and sustainability. As such, it is not a comprehensive history, but a grounded view of the institutional and cultural changes that have influenced the perceptions of sustainable fashion and Copenhagen's cultural landscape. Insights in the chapter are based on more than ten years of research and engagement by both authors in developing new knowledge and practices for green transition in Danish fashion. Being involved in the Danish fashion industry and fashion education has allowed the authors privileged insight into the process of shaping sustainability in Denmark. We acknowledge, however, that that proximity also creates a partial perspective, and so the following chapter presents our narration of the history of sustainability in fashion in Copenhagen.

How Danish fashion entered the experience economy

On 27 April 2020, in the middle of the global COVID-19 pandemic lockdowns, representatives of the Danish fashion industry posted a public letter to the Danish government with an appeal for help, as massive amounts of unsold clothing were piling up in warehouses with new seasonal collections arriving weekly. The letter, signed by the *Dansk Mode og Textil* ("DM&T – Danish Fashion and Textile") organization that has been mandated to promote the Danish fashion sector since 1991, stated the following (in our translation from Danish):

> Dear Member of Parliament,
> In only one and a half months' time, retail, and its suppliers, whether it includes fashion, textile, sports or interior companies, have been shaken so seriously in their existence that the consequences are catastrophic. We are facing massive bankruptcies and shop closings among suppliers and retailers. We have already seen the first. More will follow. If we do not act now, we face a reality so difficult that it massively overshadows the financial crisis [of 2008]. Small and larger retail warehouses lie empty. Forced to shut down and close, without customers, employees, or turnover.
>
> In the shops, the products of the season are on the hangers and on the shelves, ready to be sold. The lifestyle companies' products are ready in the warehouses. And products already commissioned and paid for are on their way to Denmark. If these products are not sold immediately, they will lose all value. This is how it is in a sector driven by seasonal change. There will be fatal consequences for the thousands of employees that have been sent home on compensated salaries. If things don't change, when the compensation plan runs out, we fear a tsunami of layoffs. A sad but inevitable consequence.
>
> So, dear Member of Parliament – if we are to avoid this, we need to act now [...] Time is short. We cannot wait any longer, so let us together do what it takes to save thousands of Danish workplaces.
>
> (DM&T 2020)

The letter is very telling both regarding the way the Danish fashion sector has increasingly engaged with the experience economy and the very short lifespans of (fast) fashion products. It also shows how this has affected the sector's ability (or lack thereof) to navigate in the green transition – even in a pandemic. The letter describes the struggles of an industry with supply chains spread globally, and an increasingly vulnerable sector, as demands for transparency, corporate social responsibility (CSR) and climate action are rising. All in a sector where products are increasingly short-lived and business logic is based on a constant lowering of prices. One of the results of the letter was a twenty million DKK investment by the Danish Ministry of Industry, Business and Financial Affairs in the work of the so-called "Taskforce" for green transition in the Danish fashion sector in 2021, which consisted of researchers, non-governmental organizations (NGOs), companies and trade organization members, but was chaired by the sustainability representative of the Danish fast fashion conglomerate Bestseller. As a result, 48 Danish fashion companies had an intense counselling period of three months on how to move forward with their green transition work.

The Danish industry is not alone in this. A similar development has taken place in other European countries, such as Britain (as described by McRobbie 2000). Like these countries, Denmark outsourced almost 100 per cent of its clothing production in the late 1980s focusing from then on either on design-led fashion brands typically located in and around Copenhagen or market-led (fast fashion) brands typically located in Jutland (Melchior 2013). As this book is dedicated to the city of Copenhagen, the authors will primarily focus on the design-led brands but will first offer comments on the general development of the sector.

As has been elaborately described by Marie Riegels Melchior, the hype surrounding Danish design-led fashion brands took off during the 2000s, with brands such as Day, Birger & Mikkelsen, Bruus Bazar, Munthe+Simonsen, Rützow and others. To help brand these designers as celebrity art workers, Copenhagen Fashion Week (CFW) was initiated in 2006 as a platform hosting bi-annual catwalk schedules, as a supplement to various existing fairs. The initiative of the CFW was embedded in the founding of the Danish Fashion Institute (later the Global Fashion Agenda, GFA), initially led by the then CEO Eva Kruse and publicly funded with recommendations from the FORA #8 Innovation Report of 2005, commissioned by the Danish Ministry of Commerce (FORA 2005). In this respect, the Danish fashion scene responded to the development of Eurocentric fashion as an experience economy, where branding is key and the materiality of production less important (as described by Pine & Gilmore 1999). In a Danish context, Tran (2008) describes the structure and challenges for Danish fashion as an experience economy as the focus shifted towards creative output and away from production.

The heightened focus on design, branding and marketing characterizes an experience economy, particularly in and around a creative industry like fashion. As in other creative industries, events such as fairs and festivals have significant influence on fashion. They help gather the industry through the development of trends, establishing industry hierarchies, awarding praise and defining boundaries, by accepting some and rejecting others (Moeran & Strandgaard 2010). In the film industry, festivals have been central, but in fashion, no other event has been more significant than the fashion week format. Fashion weeks are part of the institutional layer that governs the industry, practically and symbolically.

Traditionally, fashion weeks in Paris, Milan, London, Tokyo and New York have been gatekeepers for designers and brands. Practically, they have facilitated the presentation of designers' new collections to buyers and the press, while symbolically, they have established and maintained hierarchies of styles, trends, brands and designers. Over the latter half of the twentieth century, the importance of the fashion week format grew, and by the early 2000s fashion weeks became both regional and national fixtures globally (Skov 2006). With the proliferation of fashion weeks, the competition among them grew. Although few fashion weeks threatened the top tier of Paris, Milan, New York and London, in the Danish fashion industry, ambitions to position CFW near the top of the hierarchy in terms of cultural influence and economic activities prompted the concept of a "fifth fashion cluster." These ambitions were eventually abandoned, but the efforts to bolster CFW led to a heightened focus locally on the event and its position in city branding, as new events were introduced to allow the wider public into the usually closed-off world of fashion. One such event was the "world's longest catwalk" in 2010 in the centre of Copenhagen.

The importance of fashion weeks as marketing and sales platforms diminished during the 2010s. Although fashion companies have been surprisingly late in accepting and adopting online platforms and opportunities in marketing, branding and selling, online connectivity has had an immense impact on the fashion industry, as well as on fashion weeks. The ability to sell directly to customers and the opportunity to reach a large global audience have diversified the relations between actors, making designers and brands less dependent on fashion weeks as the gateway to publicity and sales. These changes have meant that the institutions of fashion – the fashion show, the collection, fashion magazines and fashion weeks – have been challenged. Nevertheless, the prevailing idea of fashion as an established part of the experience economy driven by branding and somewhat detached from the material, societal and global consequences of industry structures has to a large extent intensified since the turn of the millennium.

To a great extent, the same tendency was seen in the gradual acceleration of fashion research in Denmark in the early 2000s, when there was a great interest in defining, understanding and contextualizing the DNA of Danish fashion. Marie Riegels Melchior was one of the first Ph.D.s in the field of fashion and design in Denmark, and as such her early work was part of the academization process for all design education in the European Union. Simultaneous with her work, the Danish Fashion Consortium (MOKO) was established as an attempt to bridge and develop fashion as a research area across other institutions (Skjold 2008). As part of this development, the Copenhagen Business School (CBS) launched the research program ©reative encounters in 2008 with a strand on fashion research led by then Associate Professor Lise Skov. The program's agenda was to develop an understanding of the position of Danish fashion from a global perspective and in an experience economy context. These research strands were primarily positioned between cultural studies and business anthropology. Fashion was largely defined, with a few exceptions such as the development of wardrobe research (Fletcher & Klepp 2017), as a cultural phenomenon detached from the material objects of clothing, and as an interlinked system of stakeholders constituting ideas of fashion and fashion practices, as stated by Kawamura (2005).

The development of the Danish fashion scene – primarily the design-led scene in the Copenhagen area – did not happen in isolation. The same period produced the Dogme films initiated by, among others, Lars von Trier and Thomas Vinterberg, who were celebrated worldwide for their ground-breaking new aesthetics and provocative ideas of filmmaking (discussed in Chapter 6). The New Nordic Cuisine movement with the restaurant NOMA and chefs Claus Meyer and René Redzepi also placed attention on what was going on in Copenhagen, as they went back to local Danish produce, flavours and cooking traditions and elevated them to the gourmet level. In this respect, branding and researching Danish fashion as something particular and locally flavoured was in tune with its time and the general societal, economic and cultural currents of the period. Although the principles of local production and techniques were not widely adapted in the fashion industry, heightening experiences and cultural value lent themselves well to the ambition of defining a Danish or Nordic fashion identity.

The globalization of Danish fashion

In a paradoxical way these efforts to understand the essence and historical constructions of what constitutes Danish fashion came in the aftermath of the almost 100 per cent outsourcing of Danish clothing manufacture, something that has still not returned. Before the 1990s, most garment manufacturing in Denmark was located in Jutland, with the cities of Herning and Ikast as epicentres. The evolution of the garment and textile industries especially in Herning from the early to the late twentieth century is often described as "the miracle on the heath," referring to the area's flat landscape, but also to the rise in emerging workplaces in the many small- and semi-small manufacturing and textile factories. In the aftermath of the Second World War, in 1951 and 1952, a delegation of Danish ministerial and trade organization representatives visited the United States, funded by the Marshall Plan, to study the so-called rationalization processes of garment manufacture, which led to an increase in standardized work processes but also standardized garment products. The variety of products was reduced with the effect of more affordable prices, which fundamentally meant that more Danes could afford to buy more new garments – a concept and business model that has since been mobilized very successfully by the global fast fashion industry. Furthermore, the Danes were good at making garments for their own population and their neighbouring countries (Holm-Jensen 2018). However, the economic crisis of the 1970s and 1980s hit the fashion and textiles sector particularly hard. The 1970s brought various attempts at protectionist regulation and campaigns for Danes to buy Danish products. This development is described in an open letter to the Danish government of December 1976, written by the leaders of the two dominating unions at the time for the fashion and textiles industries, *Beklædningsarbejderforbundet* and *Textilarbejderforbundet* (in our translation from Danish):

> Dear Politicians,
> No sector has so often read its own obituary as the garment and textile sector. During the debate in the 1960s about new markets and changing framing conditions the sector was often highlighted as one that could be easily transferred to other regions of Europe. But since the post-war years it has turned out – not least in the recent years – that product development, rationalization, quality assessment, design, marketing, and many other things have made this "dying" sector more vibrant than ever. The number of members in our respective unions has been relatively stable throughout the 1970s. The unemployment rate has shown radical fluctuation, but here we share the destiny of other sectors.
>
> We write to you not to ask for help to keep an industry alive that has no future. But we hope that you will make use of your influence to change the public procurement schemes so that Danish garment and textile products are favoured when purchasing for hospitals, care homes, city halls, and public institutions in general, so that the general unemployment challenges of Danish society are addressed and acted upon.

This letter was printed in 1985, a publication of the two unions, where outsourcing of production to Asia is mentioned as a possible direction for the sector – but not at all at the scale it actually took place only a few years later (*Dansk Beklædnings- og Textilarbejderforbund* 1985). Jensen (2013) describes how globalization in the sector resulted in a massive outsourcing of workplaces to Asia over only a few years, from the end of the 1980s to the early 1990s; how the general development towards competition on price and (fast) delivery increased the focus on seasonal trends rather than other parameters; and how Denmark in just a few years exported or simply lost its know-how in textile and garment production.

The configuration of fashion sustainability in the new millennium

It is in this context that the particular history of fashion and sustainability in Copenhagen should be examined. Similar to other European countries, the outsourcing of production meant the loss of technical skills. But it also created physical distance between the designing, manufacturing and everyday wearing of fashion products. In the same period, the de-regulation of the textile trade through the abolition of the Multi-Fibre Arrangement (MFA) increased the import of textile products from China, Bangladesh and Turkey, among others (Dicken 2007). The growing global attention to social responsibility, sustainability and particularly the climate crisis has become increasingly visible in the fashion industry over the last decade. This attention has also influenced and shaped the Danish fashion industry, design approaches, marketing and organizational actors.

In the rest of this chapter, we explore the understanding of fashion in Denmark as an experience economy and focus mainly on industry actors. Designers and brands have experimented with different ways of challenging the unsustainability of the industry, but societal changes and changing dress practices are significant factors in need of change, as well as the specific ways sustainability has become part of the branding of fashion in Copenhagen.

In the early 2000s, the interest in sustainability on the part of fashion buyers and the budding demand from consumers saw the establishment of a sustainability fair with a particular outsider perspective on the industry and consumer cultures. The "Un-fair" began as an alternative to the established fairs and grew into its own event. The fair's outsider view was part of a critique of the fashion system (Csaba & Larsen 2011). A few pioneer brands started venturing away from the CFW, such as the brand Noir, established in 2005. Attempting a luxury approach to sustainability, founder Peter Ingversen created a design-led profile for the brand and catered to a clientele not usually associated with sustainability. However, in the blazing years of aspiring to be recognized as a fashion city internationally, initiatives such as this were rather isolated. 2010 marked the establishment of the Copenhagen Fashion Summit led by Eva Kruse, who was also CEO of the Danish Fashion Institute and thereby the Copenhagen Fashion Week. The Copenhagen Fashion Summit represented the significance of sustainability to the management of global fashion companies, which is a stark contrast to the outsider perspective represented by events such as the "Un-fair" fair.

From the late 2000s until the late 2010s, two institutions were remarkably active in regard to growing research on fashion sustainability in Denmark. First, Design School Kolding (DSKD) was a pioneer in developing both research and education on sustainability work not least because of Emerita Associate Professor and textiles designer Vibeke Riisberg, who conducted some of the earliest work in the area, going back to the 1980s, and who has mentored a long line of both educators and researchers in sustainability work since then. Second, the *Creative encounters* program and its fostering of wardrobe research (Fletcher & Klepp 2017), and later the Swedish MISTRA program, developed an extensive body of research knowledge about sustainable consumer behaviour and secondary market drivers (sharing and circular economy, resale, etc.). After this, educational development for sustainability work was implemented by KEA Design School in Copenhagen and VIA University College in Herning and Aarhus – both contributing to educational formats, knowledge development and research build-up. Only the Royal Danish Academy lagged behind. There, the UN Sustainable Development Goals (SDGs) were installed as a strategic focus for the school in 2016, but it was not until the late 2010s that sustainability work was implemented thoroughly in both education and research. Finally, in 2015 the University of Southern Denmark (SDU) added a fashion studies stream to its design culture and economics program. But it was not until 2019 that the fashion stream was re-developed to include sustainability, ethics and decoloniality in all fashion courses (Niessen interview with Sark 2020).

Thus, the Danish fashion scene never really entered the knowledge economy, as industry initiatives and research initiatives never really engaged each other – despite the recommendations of the FORA #8 report. A few pioneer brands investigated new ways of operating, but largely there remains an immense knowledge gap, which hinders the average fashion small and medium-sized enterprise (SME) in participating in the green transition. They do not have the skills to operate strategically in the growing field of sustainability approaches and in the global supply chains, as the push for linear growth conflicts with their ability to perform (DM&T 2020). Furthermore, discrepancies between the sustainability work of the Global Fashion Agenda, on the one side, and the research environments, on the other, resulted in an open clash with the launch of the "Global Fashion Research Agenda" conference held in Copenhagen in May 2019, in the buildup to the CFS. The conference was closely coordinated with the formation of the international Union of Concerned Researchers in Fashion (UCRF) as a response to the lack of critical and research-based guidance in the global fashion industry, as well as the accusation of increased greenwashing at the CFS.

Despite the recommendations of the FORA #8 report of 2005 for a knowledge centre for all stakeholders, which had originally underpinned the political investigation in DAFI and later the CFS, neither Danish nor international researchers in fashion sustainability had until then been included in the Summit or in the reports conducted by DAFI and later the GFA. As such, the Copenhagen Fashion Summit was symptomatic of an industry that had entered the experience economy in the 1990s but had never really entered the knowledge economy. Thus, many promising initiatives that placed Denmark and Copenhagen centrally in the development of fashion sustainability work were never coordinated and by the end of the 2010s left the various Danish stakeholders in the area divided. However, the institutions of the Danish fashion industry, as well as in other countries, have gradually reacted to the growing political and societal pressure for the industry to assume responsibility and take action. With the appointment of a new CEO, Cecilie Thorsmark, in 2018, CFW took steps to bring social and environmental responsibility to the centre of its activities and redefined the role of the fashion week as an industry actor. By the end of the 2010s, Danish brands such as Carcel, Artikel, Sur Le Chemin and Maja Brix offered new ways of designing and producing clothing, while challenging the conventional fashion industry model.

2020: A pivotal year for fashion sustainability

The year 2020 marked a turning point in the Danish context in regard to the further development and coordinated effort of gathering stakeholders for collaboration. First, the social democratic government led by Mette Frederiksen began playing a very active part. It was elected in what was publicly named "the climate election" of 5 June 2019, indicating that the climate has now become a general concern for Danes. Announcing the ambition of a 70 per cent CO_2 reduction strategy by 2030, it installed thirteen so-called climate partnerships in a variety of industry sectors to be developed together with ministerial staff, trade organizations, leading industry players, public–private entities and researchers. Of special interest here are the circular economy partnership and the partnership for trade and textiles. What is key in both are the recommendations of cross-disciplinary research, in close combination with the green transition of the sector through industry-research collaborations, and educational schemes for all Danes for furthering circular practices in society (IM4 2021). These partnerships became the foundation of the first ever political investigation into a green transition in the fashion and textile sectors in Denmark, with the call of the Danish Innovation Fund, on 10 March 2021, for a vision for how to reach climate goals, how to build green workplaces, how to reduce emissions by a minimum of 70 per cent by 2030 and generally how to implement the goals of the climate partnerships in fashion and textiles. Out of this came the document *Circular Economy with a Focus on Plastics and Textiles. A 2030 & 2050 Roadmap*. This is not a "sustainability roadmap" per se, but rather focuses primarily on resource use and circularity. The document will most likely shape the development of the sector – research environments included – for the next decade or longer, and the first research projects were initiated in September 2022. What is defining about the roadmap are the recommendations for reshoring product development and manufacture to as great an extent as possible through automation and technology coupled with smart and systemic design strategies and consumer insights research. According to the roadmap ambitions, this will secure a circular economy fuelled by fewer and better-developed products with the capacity for entering secondary markets, and for providing high-quality resources in what is currently named the textiles waste sector – which could be the source of new designs for repurposing, new markets and maximized resource uptake. All this is to be installed in a Danish fashion industry configured by a few large umbrella brands and mostly SMEs (small and medium-sized enterprises) through knowledge-sharing schemes inspired by the cooperative business model of COOP or Copenhagen Fur. A central player in this body of work is the innovation network Lifestyle & Design Cluster financed by the Danish Ministry of Higher Education and Science, which has managed to bring together various stakeholders such as ministries, researchers, educators, brands, trade organizations, NGOs and more.

The year 2020 also saw the delivery of a status report on sustainability work in the Danish fashion and textiles sector. Based on a large industry survey conducted by the Royal Danish Academy together with the Copenhagen Business School and Denmark's largest trade organization, Danish Fashion and Textiles (DM&T), it was concluded that Danish fashion brands struggle with defining, navigating and overcoming the hurdles that prevent sustainability and green transition work. The main focus is placed on ensuring certification schemes for supply chains, but there is great uncertainty regarding which certification to trust and follow, and global supply chains make it very difficult to be sure whether regulations are followed in terms of good working conditions and environmental impact. The report also clearly indicates that the pressure is increasing for creating transparency, and the main stakeholders in this are the retailers who are increasingly demanding certifications to be implemented and documented. However, there is very little demand for sustainability performance from Danish consumers, who furthermore are presented as unknowledgeable about the companies participating in the survey. The average Dane has not caught up with the transition to sustainability, and Denmark is increasingly faced with massive overconsumption, which in 2018 amounted to about 15 kg of consumed textile products, whereas other European citizens bought 12.3 kg (Watson et al. 2018). There is very little value gained from discarded garments in the use phase, in secondary markets or at municipal waste plants. On that basis, the report suggests that Danish fashion and textiles brands are not very aware of state-of-the-art research on green transition, in which various strategies are suggested, such as more use-led design development for better product attachment and longevity, more revenue streams redirected to secondary markets in the shape of resale and services and strategic collection work for sustainability directed at the actual market rather than seasonal trends – just to mention a few of the report's recommendations (DM&T 2020).

Similarly, 2020 saw the launch of a new framework for the CFW sustainability strategy of 2023 co-developed by In futurum. The framework presents a holistic approach to sustainability and is part minimum requirements and part point system where, by 2023, brands need to deliver points in six categories and score points to be allowed on the CFW runways. By 2021, the framework was also adopted (to be later implemented) at the largest Danish fashion trade fair, the Copenhagen International Fashion Fair (CIFF), and by the Danish Business Authority as a framework for a public program facilitating sustainability development in Danish fashion companies. Most recently, the framework was acknowledged internationally when two major Norwegian fashion organizations announced that they will also be implementing the sustainability framework (Figure 3.1).

FIGURE 3.1: CEO Cecilie Thorsmark presenting the CFW "Sustainability Action Plan" in January 2020. Photo by Frederik Valdemar Kjeldgaard, with permission.

What is particular about the framework is that it is agile and adaptable to many levels and ways of working towards a more environmentally sustainable and socially responsible fashion company. Additionally, it covers not only supply and materials but also such parameters as user understanding, design and circular business models. By centring on small and medium-sized companies, the framework is aimed at the majority of Danish fashion companies and attempts to make sustainability choices accessible to them. The framework builds on developments in sustainability research in fashion over the last decades. Knowledge from design research, development studies, management, sociology and technical sciences has been activated to create a comprehensive and usable framework. Representatives from the industry were consulted in the development process to make sure the topics addressed in the requirements and scoring system corresponded with concerns in the industry. Importantly, experts across a range of fields, from critical fashion research and activism to human rights and climate research, offered feedback. The ambition of the framework was essentially to introduce a regulatory structure (albeit originally only a requirement for brands wanting to participate in Fashion Week) that simultaneously offers guidance and education. At the beginning of 2020, the framework was tested with eleven companies in an effort to understand how they interacted with the requirements and to help establish a scoring structure. The feedback from the companies was then used to create guidelines and adjust questions.

Rolling out the framework and securing support are ongoing, and the effect will be visible once the requirement and scoring system is activated in 2023. But the impact of the commitment from a major fashion institution like CFW is already changing the way companies, brands, designers and institutions engage with sustainability. Levering their position to push sustainability to the centre of the industry represents a significant change for an event traditionally associated with the front-facing glamour of fashion, catwalks, parties and new trends: namely, including the backstage realities of producing, selling and consuming fashion products (Figures 3.2 and 3.3).

Finally, 2020 also marked the year the Royal Danish Academy launched a new MA program, entitled *New Landscapes for Change: Fashion, Clothing and Textiles*, at the Royal Academy in Copenhagen, in which the principles of wardrobe research and the general perception of fashion are key. As a counterpoint to the efforts in defining and conceptualizing what is particularly "Danish," which was a primary focus of much of the research taking place throughout the 2000s, this program rests on the idea of "Daning" as a verb, thereby enhancing the legacy of Danish designers as inclusive, broadly understood – inclusive of multiple clothing and fashion cultures globally in terms of race, age, gender and others; of embedding education in a broader eco-centric movement that is earth-centred

FIGURE 3.2: Circular Fashion Days exhibition organized by the Lifestyle & Design Cluster at CIFF during CFW 2021, photo by K. Sark.

FIGURE 3.3: Circular Fashion Days exhibition organized by the Lifestyle & Design Cluster at CIFF during CFW 2021, photo by K. Sark.

rather than growth-centred (see Fletcher & Tham 2019), and of addressing sensitivity towards the damaging effects of the fast fashion mindset and drivers both socially and environmentally, particularly in the Global South and East. As such, the program is inscribed in overall efforts to decolonize perceptions of fashion as western, as detached from the material aspects of production and consumption, and as driven by an experience economy that is colonial in itself, as it fuels exploitation of species, people and the planet to provide cheap and short-lived products, ideas that are well expressed in the Union of Concerned Researchers in Fashion (UCRF) led by leading international scholars of fashion sustainability and including fashion researchers and educators from all over the world. As such, the Royal Academy in Copenhagen is now part of a broad and thriving network of sustainability research and practice at Danish design schools, including Design School Kolding, VIA University College and KEA Design School, as well as the University of Southern Denmark in Kolding (Figure 3.4).

FIGURE 3.4: MANIFESTO: student exhibition at the program New Landscapes for Change, Fashion, Clothing & Textiles, displayed at the 70 per cent Less CO_2 exhibition at the Royal Danish Academy, from 7 October 2021 to 14 January 2022, photo by the Royal Danish Academy, with permission.

Conclusion: What's next? Sustainability at the core of industry, research and education

Presenting an image of Copenhagen as a centre for sustainable fashion is at the same time fitting and highly problematic. Even without presenting the devastating impact the fashion industry has on the climate crisis, land degradation, biodiversity loss, inequality and human rights globally, the local context itself offers a sobering context. The consumption and waste of fashion products continue to rise, and the industry is still broadly focused on growth and cheap products. Within the frame of the experience economy, sustainability has become a branding mechanism with the potential to create awareness and the risk of misleading consumers (through greenwashing). At the same time, the development of sustainability in Copenhagen fashion and in the industry over the last decades has seen innovation in design practices, in research, and in new events and frameworks with global reach. By way of ending this chapter, we offer our reflections on what sustainability in fashion could mean for Copenhagen in the future.

The severity of these issues is beginning to be recognized, and few fashion brands can escape acknowledging how sustainability affects their business. But as the letter presented at the beginning of the chapter makes clear, marketing (fast) fashion products in an experience economy exposes a disconnect between cultural value and material reality. In order to move towards a more ethical fashion culture, a deeper engagement with the production of fashion products, their material value and their social lives beyond sales, as well as their afterlives, is desperately needed. As we have addressed, establishing Danish fashion as an experience economy took place after the almost complete outsourcing of production and loss of manufacturing jobs. A thorough examination of the realities of global fashion production and its injustices is therefore crucial. Lastly, the cultural value that fashion marketing relies on still perpetuates elitist and discriminating European ideals, usually under the guise of so-called "democratic" (fast) fashion. With the implementation of new frameworks for the industry based on the creation of new research and knowledge, we may see a change emerge. But the future of Copenhagen as an influential site for sustainability in fashion will have to involve fundamentally challenging existing industrial structures and a revaluation of the culture of fashion.

REFERENCES

Csaba, Fabian, and Frederik Larsen. "The Role of Fairs in the Development and Division of Fields CPH Kids and Danish Children's Fashion." *Conference Paper, Creative Encounters*, 2011.

Dansk Beklædnings- og Textilarbejderforbund. *Textil og Skotøj i 100 år*. Edited by Christensen, Jacob, Jensen, Tommy and Weiss, Ove. Printed in Denmark, 1985.

Dicken, Peter. *Global Shift: Mapping the Changing Contours of the World Economy*. London: Sage, 2007.

DM&T. *Bæredygtighed i den danske mode- og tekstilbranche.* Report commissioned and co-authored by Danish Fashion and Textiles, Skjold, Else & Pedersen, Esben Gjerdrum, 2020.

DM&T. "Hjælp os med at redde tusindvis af arbejdspladser." Open letter to the DK Goverment published 27th of April, as found 1 November 2020, www.dmogt.dk/branchenyt/aabent-brev-til-folketinget-covid-19. Accessed 13. Mar. 2023.

Fletcher, Kate, and Ingun Klepp, editors. *Opening Up the Wardrobe: A Methods Book.* Sofiemyr: Novus Forlag, 2017.

Fletcher, Kate, and Mathilda Tham. *Earth Logic: Fashion Action Research Plan.* Report commissioned by JJ Charitable Trust, 2019.

FORA #8. *Brugerdreven innovation i dansk mode – den 5. globale modeklynge?* Edited by Stine Hedegaard Jørgensen and Rasmus Bech Hansen. Report commissioned by the Danish Ministry of Commerce/Department for Industry Economics, Research and Analysis, 2005. As found 1 Nov. 2020, www.rosted.nu/attachments/File/2005/BDI_i_dansk_mode_20050308.pdf. Accessed 13. Mar. 2023.

Holm-Jensen, Kristine. *ULD. Historien om den midtjyske tekstilindustri i det 20. århundrede.* Copenhagen: Forlaget Stout, 2018.

IM4. *Circular Economy With a Focus on Plastics and Textiles: A 2030 & 2050 Roadmap.* Commissioned by the Danish Innovation Fund for InnoMission4; plastics and textiles and conducted by the CØ-PT partnership, 2021.

Jensen, Kristoffer. *Beklædningsindustriens møde med industrialiseringen. Brancheorganisationer og individuelle virksomheder under pres, perioden 1960–2000.* Odense: ©Author and Syddansk Universitetsforlag, 2013.

Kawamura, Yunija. *Fashion-ology: An Introduction to Fashion Studies.* Oxford: Berg/Oxford, 2005.

Melchior, Marie Riegels. *Dansk på Mode! Fortællinger om design, identitet og historie i og omkring den danske modeindustri.* Copenhagen: Museum Tusculums Forlag, 2013.

Moeran, Brian, and Jesper Strandgaard Pedersen, editors. *Negotiating Values in the Creative Industries: Fairs, Festivals and Competitive Events.* Cambridge: Cambridge University Press, 2011.

Niessen, Sandra. "Decolonizing the Fashion Curriculum in Denmark and Beyond: Interview with Kat Sark." *Fashion Theory, Special Issue on Decoloniality and Fashion*, vol. 24, no. 6, 2020, pp. 971–974.

Pine, Joseph, and James H. Gilmore. *The Experience Economy: Work Is Theatre and Every Business a Stage.* Boston: Harvard Business Press, 1999.

Skjold, Else. *Fashion Research at Design Schools.* Unpublished report commissioned by Design School Kolding. Kolding: ©Design School Kolding and MOKO, 2008.

Skov, Lise, Else Skjold, Brian Moeran, Frederik Larsen, and Fabian Csaba. *The Fashion Show as an Art Form*. Copenhagen: Department of Intercultural Communication and Management, Copenhagen Business School, 2009.

Tran, Yan. *Fashion in Danish Experience Economy: Challenges for Growth*. Copenhagen: Samfundlitteratur, 2008.

Watson, David. *Kortlægning af tekstilflows i Danmark*. Odense: Miljøstyrelsen, 2018.

4

Fashioning Functionality

Trine Brun Petersen and Maria Mackinney-Valentin

Scandinavian culture and lifestyle have enjoyed increased international attention, boosted in part by the popularity of New Nordic Cuisine and Nordic Noir entertainment. This interest has given rise to several books that explain Danish culture to outsiders, such as *The Little Book of Hygge: The Danish Way to Live Well* (Wiking 2016), *The Year of Living Danishly* (Russell 2015) and *The Danish Way of Parenting* (Alexander 2016). This coverage of Danish culture has also led to increased interest in Danish fashion, which is often described as being "down-to-earth and honest" (Conlon 2021), but very little has been written about Copenhagen fashion. In this chapter, we explore the concept of Copenhagen fashion through an analysis of contemporary consumer practices, trends and brands based in Copenhagen. The study builds on existing scholarship on Danish fashion and uses it as a launching pad for an analysis of how Copenhagen fashion and style are materially and discursively constructed. This frames our analysis of brands and consumer culture in Copenhagen, which is based on the companies' branding and design, as well as media representations. Historically, Danish fashion has been celebrated for its functionality and usability, and the chapter explores how selected Copenhagen brands and style trends position themselves in relation to this narrative. It also looks at functionality as a leading value in Danish and, by implication, Copenhagen fashion.

Copenhagen as a fashion city

Denmark was rated number one in the UN World Happiness Report in 2012, 2013 and 2016 (Wiking 2016: 273) due to the high level of social security and a generally high level of freedom and trust among citizens. Denmark is well known for its political system and welfare state, which offers a range of social services, such as free education, health care and pensions to all citizens. This secures an unprecedented degree of income redistribution among its citizens, and Denmark is counted among the most economically and socially equal countries in the world. Thanks to affordable childcare, heavily subsidized by taxes, Denmark has one of the highest proportions of working mothers, and, at least in principle, women and men equally share responsibility for supporting the family and caring for the children. It is, however, disputed whether this has in fact resulted in an equal sharing of domestic chores, or rather in women taking on the double role of breadwinner and housekeeper (Boddum 2018). Nonetheless, equal opportunity is considered a core value that permeates the political system, social institutions and social norms. This is, among other things, reflected in the so-called *Jante law*, from the 1933 novel *En flygtning krydser sit spor* (*A Fugitive Crosses His Tracks*) by Aksel Sandemose. The essence of *Jante law* is that one shall not believe that one is better than others, and this is commonly referred to as a constitutive trait of Danish society.

In the last two decades, Copenhagen has been through a radical process of transformation from a run-down city with considerable social problems to the spacious, green and gentrified capital it is today (Stensgaard 2005). Among other things, this development has focused on preserving and developing Copenhagen's biking culture, which is supported by a meticulous system of biking lanes, including the so-called "super-biking lanes" designed to promote commuting by bike. For most Copenhageners, the bicycle is an essential means of transportation and is used in all sorts of weather. Extensive urban renewal schemes have made Copenhagen a highly attractive city to live in and, as a result, housing prices have soared. For historical reasons, however, profits from housing sales are excluded from taxes, and this has created a new class of affluent "housing millionaires," particularly in the Copenhagen area (Thomsen 2021). The combination of uneven value increase in the housing market accelerated by a tax system that rewards property investment has sparked considerable debate (Rhode 2021) and has added to the national narrative of the "privileged" capital as opposed to the "diligent" provinces.

Historically, Copenhagen has been a key location for the Danish fashion scene, and the city has traditionally been regarded as the epicentre for new movements and trends. Copenhagen established itself as the centre for fashion communication and retailing, whereas central Jutland has traditionally been regarded as the centre for the production of textiles and clothing. The Danish fashion and textile industry constitutes the fourth largest sector in the country, but the domestic market is relatively small, so most of the output is exported. The trade organization *Dansk Mode & Textil* (Danish Fashion and Textiles) assessed that approximately 33 per cent of Danish fashion is sold domestically. This means that most Danish fashion companies are oriented towards a global rather than national market, which makes it difficult to establish any direct link between what is being designed in Denmark and what Copenhageners actually wear. The apparent paradox of exploring Copenhagen fashion through globally oriented brands is solved by focusing on brands that profile themselves via their Copenhagen origins and combining this with an analysis of style trends in Copenhagen.

Danish fashion as pragmatic

To our knowledge, no specific accounts of what constitutes Copenhagen fashion have been published until now. There is, however, a small body of literature committed to describing and characterizing Danish fashion. This chapter builds on two of these: fashion historian Marie Riegel Melchior's work on the Danish fashion industry and fashion scholar Julie Sommerlund's work on the welfare state as a formative factor in Danish fashion and dressing norms. In her work, Melchior has explored the rise, development and national identity of the Danish fashion industry (Melchior 2010, 2011, 2013). In a chapter from 2011, Melchior explores the concept of Danish fashion as not characterized by a common style or aesthetic, but rather by a particularly pragmatic approach to fashion. In the same vein, Sommerlund views Danish fashion as intertwined with and shaped by the welfare state, particularly in terms of how everyday life in Denmark conditions sartorial practices (Sommerlund 2011). Denmark has a large public sector, which is financed by progressive taxes as well as by relatively high wages. This, she argues, conditions everyday life in Denmark and hence influences social and dress norms. She finds it particularly important that Danish women have one of the highest workplace participation rates in the world, but still maintain a higher fertility rate than most other countries. At the same time, the relatively small differences in income among Danish wage-earners combined with a high and progressing tax burden means that very few families can afford domestic help. This lack of domestic help means that Danish women have a strong incentive to prefer garments that are easy to care for and simple, shunning the labour-intensive practice of ironing in particular. This streamlining of everyday life is not without its challenges, and many women find themselves divided between traditional notions of femininity and their demanding lives as full-time professionals and caregivers. This social structure entails that Danish women must handle a multitude of professional and domestic tasks during the day. At the same time, Denmark is generally a very informal society and there is little tradition of dressing "up" for social occasions and "down" for practical chores. Most Danes wear the same clothes throughout the day, and therefore their outfits must be able to adapt to a wide range of professional, representational and practical activities. Sommerlund argues that this configuration of use has led to a preference for garments that are practical yet presentable and that can be maintained with a minimum of effort. According to Sommerlund, Danish fashion is not characterized by a specific "look" but rather by its common sense and cost-effective approach. The socio-economic conditions in the welfare state have resulted in a particular Danish "meta-aesthetic," which is based on values of accessibility rather than social competition and demonstration of class superiority, even though social differences do exist in Denmark and are to a certain extent communicated sartorially. In the following, we will draw on this notion of Danish fashion as functional and accessible in exploring leading fashion brands from Copenhagen and how they interact with urban style trends.

Danish fashion as functional

Historically, Danish fashion has been represented as functional, practical and sensible. In 1969, *The New York Times* published a feature on Danish design under the heading "For Scandinavian Designers, Function is Key," in which they praised Danish fashion for its "free" and "functional" character, as well for the accessible pricing (quoted in Melchior 2006). In the late 1990s, this picture of Danish fashion as functional, practical and cost-conscious was challenged by the rise of the bohemian aesthetic (or "boho" style), represented by designers such as Munthe plus Simonsen, Bruuns Bazaar, Rützou and Day Birger et Mikkelsen. This look was colourful, with patterned fabrics, flowing silhouettes and ample use of decorative details, such as embroidery, pearls and sequins. This seemed to be a passing trend, however, and in the noughties (2000–09), Danish fashion was again represented as characterized by functionality, practicality and accessibility. In 2006, the Danish Fashion Institute published a report that was intended to serve as a foundation for the institute's branding of Danish fashion internally and externally (Melchior & Olsen-Rule 2006). The report mapped the history, network and style narratives of Danish fashion. This led the authors, Marie Riegels Melchior and Nikolina Olsen-Rule, to conclude that Danish fashion is characterized by its affordability and usability, which they condensed into the notion that Danish fashion is above all accessible in terms of aesthetics.

In an article in the Danish newspaper *Information*, Pia Friis Laneth, who is an expert on women's history, linked Danish fashion and style to the functionalist movement: "the Danish beauty ideal is very much focused on practicality. It is almost a tribute to the plain and industrious. The Functionalist movement has not only left its mark on architecture and furniture but also on the beauty ideal" (Tholl 2010: n.p., translated by the authors). In later years, this representation of Danish fashion has shifted slightly and has come to include more of a focus on creating a structured, minimalist look. As fashion blogger Marie Jedig puts it in a feature in *The Observer*, "it is all about quality rather than quantity – we like simple things that last forever," and later she added,

> almost all of my friends have a "does this come in black?" policy, which really sums up the Danish mentality around style [...] Instead, there's more of a focus on design,

shape, tailoring and texture because decisions about colour are taken out of the equation. Plus, monochrome means that everything goes with everything.

(Jedig cited in Russell 2015: n.p.)

As a whole, the feature paints a picture of Danish fashion as down-to-earth and restrained, and Danes are represented as having a relaxed attitude to fashion (Russell 2015). This representation of Danish fashion and styles forms the backdrop for the following sections, which explore Copenhagen brands and style trends.

Nørgaard paa Strøget

One of the most important actors in Copenhagen's fashion history is the company Nørgaard paa Strøget, which was founded in 1958 by businessman Jørgen Nørgaard. The company produced their own garments in a factory in Jutland but is primarily known for innovative retailing, as well as for its politically tinted approach to fashion. The shop was prominently located on Strøget, the exclusive shopping street in Copenhagen. The brand name combined the name of the founder with the name of the location. The name made use of both the Danish special letter ø and the outdated spelling norm of using two a's instead of å, which signalled the company's Copenhagen heritage, as well as their decision to limit themselves to the Danish market (paraphrased by Dam in Dam 2008).

The shop represented a break with traditional bourgeois shopping culture and quickly became known for its youthful selection and artistic vibe. It carried a range of self-produced basic "wardrobe essentials" alongside more trendy items, designed by contemporary fashion designers. From quite early on, the company aligned itself with the dominant social movements of the time, particularly the youth rebellion and the women's liberation movement. Jørgen Nørgaard became a well-known interpreter of international fashion trends in the Danish press. In this capacity, he championed the idea of fashion as a "cultural seismograph," which was able to record new social movements and provide them with a distinct visual identity. Nowhere was this more evident than in relation to the modern, liberated women. The Nørgaard family with their four children was highlighted as a prime example of gender equality and shared parental responsibility (Barfod 2008), while the independent, sexually liberated woman was discursively constructed as the company's core customer. In a dialogue with the Danish second-wave feminists – "The Red Stockings" – who saw fashion as an exploitation of women, Jørgen Nørgaard argued that

> liberated women are more fun – both to be with and to be married to. And to create clothing for. Perhaps because no woman gets her independence as a gift but becomes

courageous and at best also sexually liberated by taking up other battles as well. The fight to be seen as more than just lovely, the fight to be heard, to avoid dominating and disrespectful boyfriends and other men, for obtaining equal pay and a place in the job market, which corresponds to the effort, the education, and the professionalism [...] An equal partner who expresses her emancipation through her clothing. She has said goodbye to being the hunted and has become the hunter herself.
(paraphrased by Dam in Dam 2008: 45–47, translated by the authors)

This focus on the modern woman as strong, independent and sexually liberated was corroborated by the company's often daring selection of fashion items, such as tight-fitting jeans, then strongly associated with working-class ideals and America, or the brand staple, the 101-shirt, whose tight fit accentuated the bosom. Nørgaard is also credited with being the first to introduce "hotpants" in Denmark (Dam 2008: 42), a garment that signalled a more liberated approach to female sexuality. The Nørgaard brand and retail space can be seen as an early example of Danish fashion being discursively constructed as fundamentally practical and sensible without entirely renouncing playfulness and sensuality. In recent years, the fashion company Ganni has given this aesthetic an innovative twist.

Ganni

Ganni was founded at the beginning of the noughties, but it was not until the couple Nicolaj and Ditte Reffstrup took over in 2009 that its transformation into a leading fashion brand really began. The Reffstrups have been featured in numerous articles in the Danish and international press, and their family life functions as an important demonstration of Ganni's core values and the associated lifestyle. The company branded itself as representing the middle ground between traditional Scandinavian functionalism and the colourful "boho style" of the 1990s. As Ditte Reffstrup stated in an interview in the Danish business newspaper *Børsen*,

> I had a feeling that something was missing in what was coming out of Copenhagen. That what the world had seen was either bohemian or androgynous, but that there also existed a woman who dressed colourfully, in dresses and a pair of sneakers or worn-out cowboy boots, and who wasn't represented on the fashion scene.
> (cited in Dam 2020: 18, translated by the authors)

In line with this agenda, Ganni's style is quite far from the stereotype of Danish fashion as being monochrome and toned-down. Instead, Ganni markets garments that are frilly and frivolous, such as dresses with colourful patterns or idiosyncratic prints, as with the fruit T-shirt, which became a massive hit in 2016. The key to the brand's look is, however, primarily in the styling, where colourful, flowery dresses are combined with sporty accessories such as sneakers, which allows for a distinctively feminine look without compromising freedom of movement (Figure 4.2).

The profile is visually conspicuous in its pattern and style clashes, but at the same time, the company focuses on crafting a brand look that is laidback, comfortable and easy to wear. The brand positions itself as being inclusive, both in terms of pricing and style, and prides itself on being able to embrace young girls, as well as more mature, settled women (Dam 2020). In establishing this focus on accessibility and useability, Ganni draws heavily on its Danish heritage, and Ditte Reffstrup's humble upbringing in the fishing town Hirtshals in Northern Jutland is used to illustrate her grounding and feel for what women like to wear in their everyday lives (Skarum 2016). At the same time, however, the couple associates themselves strongly with the urban atmosphere of Copenhagen, which they contrast with the suburbs: "Not just as a family, but as a business we connect with the city centre of Covpenhagen" (Conlon 2021: n.p.). In this quote, the urban vibe of Copenhagen is presented as central to the couple's creative energy and inspiration. The

FIGURE 4.1: Nørgaard paa Strøget store front in Copenhagen 2022, photo by Trine Brun Petersen.

FIGURE 4.2: "Ganni Girls" in frilly dresses and practical footwear. Collection "GANNI × Selfridges: Let's Go Outside," photo by Clare Shilland, with permission from Ganni.

importance of Copenhagen and its lifestyle for Ganni's brand identity is underlined in a feature in *Børsen*, which outlined Ganni's development from a little-known company to one of Denmark's most hyped fashion brands. In this, Nicolaj Reffstrup delineates the essential "Ganni Girl" and links her to the welfare state and Copenhagen's infrastructure more specifically:

> To me, Ganni is still the essence of this biking woman, who is self-reliant [...] this also has to do with the fact that she lives in Copenhagen, where it is safe and secure,

you have faith in other people, and you are sure to get an education and a job. And even if you don't, everything will still be all right.

(cited in Dam 2020: 18, translated by the authors)

In this quote, the Ganni Girl is constructed as a versatile, carefree and privileged woman, who bikes around Copenhagen in all sorts of weather. This air of existential lightness is repeated in an article in *The Guardian*, which featured the Ganni couple and their new home in the affluent Copenhagen district Østerbro. The feature described the family's bohemian lifestyle, including how they until recently lived in collective housing with their three children, as well as how their home is crammed with designer furniture, which they bought cheap without realizing its value, as well as art made by their close friends. In the feature, an intimate link is established between the brand identity of Ganni and the new home, and the couple's success is represented as being the result of a lucky coincidence rather than determination and hard work (Conlon 2021). Such media narratives link Ganni closely to the Copenhagen fashion scene by constructing the desire for a particular Copenhagen lifestyle that signals a locational and symbolic sense of belonging.

Copenhagen comfort

Another common perception of style in contemporary Copenhagen is one of comfort because "when it comes to fashion, the city excels at a playful blend of bicycle-friendly comfort and Scandinavian chic" (Ahmed 2018: n.p.). The following section explores the narrative of Copenhagen comfort dressing in relation to how it relates to international fashion styles that celebrate a seemingly relaxed aesthetic, such as normcore and athleisure. It also explores the Danish phenomenon of *hygge* that became an international trend only to perhaps loop back to Copenhagen, where it made the dress culture even more casual. In the 2010s, the subversive style of looking "normal" rose to the international fashion forefront under the heading of "normcore" – the apparently hardcore idea of looking deliberately ordinary. This idea was performed in a subtle way of sticking out by looking inconspicuous. This translated into putting effort into looking boring as a paradoxical strategy of social distinction – sticking out by fitting in, so to speak. Some described this "new normal" (Williams 2014) as coming out of Scandinavian style generally understood as casual, functional and subtle to a degree that Scandinavian style could be seen as the origin of normcore: "it was the advent of normcore" (Sykes 2016: n.p.).

Linked to and equally disruptive of dress conventions was the 2010s dress style of "athleisure" that also pointed in the direction of more relaxed attire. Athleisure merged athletic- and leisurewear, challenging the convention of dressing for specific occasions. With athleisure, sweatpants and yoga pants became acceptable to wear both to the gym, a party, work and straight to bed. The tendency was described as "stylish comfort" (Robin 2015) and "sofa dressing" (Cochrane 2018). There seemed to be a shift from dressing for others to an emphasis on well-being and comfort. This was seen by some as a sign of the end of dressing etiquette: "The dress code is dead, having been slowly starved of oxygen by the ubiquity of informality" (Cartner-Morley 2016: n.p.).

The COVID-19 lockdowns brought new meaning to the idea of dressing down without any apparent sense of decorum. No longer reserved for holidays and lazy Sundays, working from home relaxed dress practices all over the world. The shift was described as "practical" and "comfortable," not unlike the general narrative of Scandi-style in general and Copenhagen style in particular. A number of dress items were put on furlough: "bras, high-heeled shoes, hard waistbands" (Marriott 2021: n.p.), which in fact was not far off from the general vibe of existing Copenhagen dress culture. However, dressing down during the lockdown was for many an expression of the stress and sheer monotony of the situation and a need for "cocooning" (Marriott 2021). Quarantine dressing has been described as "'comfort-blanket' clothing including pyjamas, hoodies and, of course, jogging bottoms" (Elan 2021: n.p.). The notion that clothes are not only something that we use to communicate social belonging and personal style narratives but may also be a sort of sartorial self-care seems in line with the insistence on well-being, comfort and freedom to be your own person in Copenhagen fashion culture. This emphasis on dressing to provide protection or as an expression of poor mental states differs from the emphasis on independence and functionality often associated with the Copenhagen style. So, while the lockdowns may visually have echoed what is often perceived to be Copenhagen's dress norms, the two are not identical. Yet, the lockdown with its extreme relaxation of decorum and emphasis on comfort may still have brought something to Copenhagen fashion. Pyjamas, in particular, became a quarantine staple. The nighttime favourite was already on the fashion radar before COVID, as fashion journalists contemplated whether one could go to a party in pyjamas (Cartner-Morley 2016). The style moved into high gear when faced with the lockdown reality of being "permanently in our pajamas" (Marriott 2021). One Copenhagen-based brand that was already tuned into the 24-hour pyjama cycle is headed by Emilie Helmstedt. She has mastered a chic balance of Copenhagen comfort in the shape of silky pyjamas with vibrant, playful prints that bring to mind childhood memories of strawberry fields and re-enactments of the Hans Christian Andersen fairy tale "Princess on the Pea." Helmstedt's mix of everyday practicality and whimsical individuality may just be showing the way for Copenhagen style preferences. She has at least struck an international chord with her play with illusion and reality being included in *Forbes*' "30 under 30" for 2021 for European art and culture.

Hygge and knitting

The Danish word *hygge* is described by Oxford Dictionaries as "a quality of cosiness and comfortable conviviality that engenders a feeling of contentment or well-being (regarded as a defining characteristic of Danish culture)" (2021). It is considered to have grown out of the establishment of the welfare state when people no longer had to work as much and therefore could spend more time with their families (Kvittingen 2018). In recent years, the word has been popularized internationally as related to Danish fashion, in that "clothes of sturdy simplicity are summoning up the spirit of "hygge," the Danish candidate for word of the year which translates as warm conviviality in a cold climate" (Ferrier 2016) quoted in *The Little Book of Hygge: The Danish Way to Live Well* (Wiking 2016: 264). Meik Wiking takes the term towards more marketable qualities, such as candlelight, comfort food and, above all, knitting. Denmark and the Nordic region in general have a long history of knitting as a way of creating garments suitable for the weather in a craft and material widely accessible regardless of social standing and geographical context. Especially sailor and fisherman's knits are an integral part of the Nordic dress heritage.

One of the most prominent young Copenhagen-based knit designers in recent years is Lærke Bagger. Her 144,000 followers on Instagram love her free and playful approach to knitwear. Knitting is also easy to create in any size, making it inclusive. A self-described hoarder, Bagger collected loose yarn ends as a poor student and that is how her first "Leftover sweater" was made, which has since become a staple of her brand. The sweater is both unique because no two sweaters are alike and waste-conscious in using mainly pieces of discarded yarn and breathing new life into something that would otherwise have been considered waste. Her way of celebrating the often overlooked or disregarded, such as scraps of yarn, is part of a more general material turn towards embracing mistakes as unique. This particularly resonates with hand knitting, which is often irregular. As *The New York Times* article on hand knitting phrased it, "cherish the wonkiness" (Atherley 2020). Knitting has been increasingly popular in Denmark in recent years, most prominently with the famous Sara Lund sweater from the TV series *The Killing* (discussed in Chapter 6). This development echoes both the tradition of the craft in the country, as well as a global boom in crafting, especially in Europe and Northern America. During the COVID pandemic, Danish online yarn stores experienced a 200 per cent rise in sales, some describing the dramatic rise in the interest in knitting as "out of control" (Grundahl 2021). The suggestion is that in times of crisis we go back to traditional crafts, such as knitting (Grundahl 2021).

During the first lockdown in Denmark in the spring of 2020, Bagger launched her recipe for the "Alone Together Sweater," which joined knitting enthusiasts around the world. With more than 4000 sweaters under the hashtag #alonetogethersweater, the endeavour became a testament to how knitting can form the basis of belonging across barriers of age, ability and life situation. This confirms related studies that knitting groups provide supportive communities both online and in real life. The stress of modern life and especially the challenges of lockdowns have perhaps contributed to the benefits of knitting beyond the fashionable output. Knitting is meditative, a monotonous process with a smooth rhythm that can bring you into a state of flow. This is in line with the link between mental health and knitting explored in emerging fields such as craft psychology. When knitting, your heart rate and blood pressure are reduced, which in turn offers health benefits. Knitting may contribute to reducing symptoms of stress, anxiety and depression. In addition, knitting may help manage chronic pain, improve cognitive function and increase happiness (Højmark 2016). In this sense, the idea of Copenhagen fashion culture is widened from broader societal and social mechanisms to the more private sphere of mental health and well-being (Figure 4.3).

FIGURE 4.3: Knit-designer Lærke Bagger's knitted dress 2021, on display at the Design Museum in Copenhagen in 2022, photo by K. Sark.

Freedom of visual expression

While the most prominent narratives of dressing like a Copenhagener are concerned with a sense of practical, comfortable and comforting clothing, there are also designers working towards freedom of visual expression as a different expression of fashion. A pioneer in Copenhagen's avant-garde fashion scene for over twenty years, Henrik Vibskov refuses to settle into one category, embracing instead the cross-disciplinary magic of being a fashion designer, visual artist and musician. *The New York Times* called him "Fashion's Renaissance Man" (Corcoran 2014). He has shown his artwork at PS1/Moma in New York and Palais de Tokyo in Paris. He is a member of the esteemed Parisian Chambre Syndicale, and he has played at the famous Roskilde Music Festival as a drummer. Based in Copenhagen, but still quite different from the standard narrative of style, Vibskov has a declared mission of pushing Copenhageners to communicate more through their clothes, explaining that "clothes are important – it is how we read each other. It is how we show who we are" (Skarum 2013: n.p.). So, rather than protecting us through cocooning, Vibskov encourages us to break out of the shell and share with the world our true selves with all the colours of the rainbow, proving that dressing loudly does not mean you cannot still ride your bike to work in the rain (Figures 4.4 and 4.5).

Other newcomers to the Copenhagen scene and proponents of a louder fashion aesthetic are the design-duo Saks Potts, founded by Barbara Potts and Catherine Saks in 2014 in Copenhagen. The childhood friends share an affinity for great coats as a necessity for anyone living through cold Danish winters – and sometimes summers too. Their brand took off with their coats, and they have since moved into full collections and accessories. They encourage Copenhagen women to dare to stand out. *The New York Times* described the brand as "keen to distance themselves from Danish hygge and minimalism" (Ahmed 2018: n.p.). Their coats are known for being brightly coloured and whimsical in design, joining craft and artistic playfulness. Even though the brand is rooted and inspired by Copenhagen, its fans include Beyoncé, Rihanna, Lady Gaga and Gigi Hadid. Saks Potts represent a position on the Copenhagen fashion scene where freedom of expression is demonstrated through visual exuberance without losing sight of the ideal of practicality and functionality, including the preference for getting around by bike.

Conclusion

The discourse of Danish and Copenhagen fashion has varied over the years, but the dominant narrative foregrounds functionality, practicality and accessibility.

FIGURE 4.4: Henrik Vibskov store in Copenhagen, 2022, photo by Trine Brun Petersen.

FIGURE 4.5: Henrik Vibskov store front in Copenhagen, 2022, photo by Trine Brun Petersen.

Our study corroborates Melchior's and Sommerlund's findings that Danish and, by implication, Copenhagen fashion cannot be identified with a specific look or style. As demonstrated in this chapter, Danish fashion has both a minimalistic and a more frivolous stream. The represented brands range from the simple garments of Nørgaard paa Strøget to the artistic, quirky look of Henrik Vibskov. Several of the brands we have analyzed are characterized by ample use of colours, patterns and detailing. This visual profile sets them apart from the dominant narrative of Danish fashion as being minimalist and understated. Despite this, the garments are still designed to be rational in use and handling, and most are made to be machine-washable and to support an active lifestyle. In this sense, the garments are adapted to Copenhagen's informal lifestyle. This means relatively simple, but versatile garments, which can easily accommodate biking in the rain and other practical chores, without sacrificing presentability.

Like Melchior and Sommerlund, we have linked Copenhagen fashion and style to the Danish welfare state and its emphasis on economic and social equality. This political-economic system conditions everyday life in Copenhagen. In our material, the welfare state has emerged as a constitutive factor for Copenhagen fashion in three regards. First, this social model creates a society with a high participation rate, without enabling people to pay for domestic help or services. This means that most people must perform a multitude of roles during the day, which is reflected in everyday dress. This promotes a specific configuration of use that privileges functional garments and affords freedom of movement. Second, the safety net of the welfare state is addressed as a central prerequisite for choosing an unconventional lifestyle and for being willing to take risks. In the case of Ganni, the economic security of the welfare state is presented as a key condition for developing an improvised, unconcerned lifestyle. Finally, we identified freedom as a key concept in Copenhagen fashion because the right to express yourself without fearing reprisal is a central tenet of Copenhagen fashion culture. This is a particularly salient point in relation to Henrik Vibskov, whose unconventional designs and styling celebrate creativity and individual expression. Moreover, style trends such as normcore, athleisure and comfort dressing all privilege a casual attitude to fashion, which seems to negate fashion as a means of demonstrating social superiority.

The Copenhagen fashion brands, trends and style practices analyzed in this chapter vary considerably in their look and styling and promote style trends that revolve around casual living, the maximization of comfort, and the right to participate without dressing up or engaging in time-consuming and costly grooming regimes. This has led to a rather subtle fashion culture dominated by comfortable, casual dress practices, in which function and fashion are superposed and intertwined. Our analysis demonstrates the close connection between fashion, lifestyle and social identities. While the commercial, global fashion system may be instrumental in creating the material prerequisites, the specific meaning of these fashioned identities is dependent on local fashion culture and its stylistic expressions.

REFERENCES

Ahmed, Osman. "Three Independent Danish Brands to Know." *New York Times*, 6 Feb. 2018, www.nytimes.com/2018/02/06/t-magazine/fashion/danish-clothing-brands-cecilie-bahnsen-saks-potts.html. Accessed 21 Oct. 2022.

Alexander, Jessica Joelle. *The Danish Way of Parenting: What the Happiest People in the World Know about Raising Confident, Capable Kids.* New York: Penguin Audio, 2016.

Atherley, Kate. "Pick Up the Knitting Needles for a Mood Booster." *New York Times*, 19 Dec. 2020, www.nytimes.com/2020/12/19/at-home/knitting-mood-booster.html. Accessed 21 Oct. 2022.

Barfod, Niels. "Jørgen." *Nørgaard paa Strøget*, edited by Bodil Busk Laursen. Copenhagen: Gyldendal, 2008, pp. 14–23.

Boddum, Dorte Ipsen. "Arbejdsgivere: Manglende ligestilling derhjemme står i vejen for lederjob og bestyrelsesposter til kvinder." *Finans*, 8 Mar. 2018, www.finans.dk/politik/ECE10390459/arbejdsgivere-manglende-ligestilling-derhjemme-staar-i-vejen-for-lederjob-og-bestyrelsesposter-til-kvinder/?ctxref=ext. Accessed 21 Oct. 2022.

Brugge, Mathilde. "Nordjysk bager fik et chok, da han hørte, hvad en fastelavnsbolle kan koste i København: 'Folk ville dø af grin, hvis vi gjorde det'." *Danmarks Radio*, 12 Feb. 2021, www.dr.dk/nyheder/indland/nordjysk-bager-fik-et-chok-da-han-hoerte-hvad-en-fastelavnsbolle-kan-koste-i. Accessed 21 Oct. 2022.

Cartner-Morley, Jess. "Can You Really Wear Pyjamas to a Party?" *The Guardian*, 12 Mar. 2016, www.theguardian.com/fashion/2016/mar/12/fashion-can-you-wear-pyjamas-party-lingerie-jess-cartner-morley. Accessed 21 Oct. 2022.

Cochrane, Lauren. "Get Comfy! How Curling Up on the Sofa Became the Height of Fashion." *The Guardian*, 7 Nov. 2018, www.theguardian.com/fashion/2018/nov/07/get-comfy-sleepleisure-how-curling-up-on-the-sofa-became-the-height-of-fashion. Accessed 21 Oct. 2022.

Conlon, Scarlett. "Stylish at Home in Copenhagen." *The Guardian*, 14 Mar. 2021, www.theguardian.com/lifeandstyle/2021/mar/14/stylishly-at-home-in-copenhagen-with-the-husband-and-wife-team-behind-ganni-label. Accessed 21 Oct. 2022.

Corcoran, Heather. "Henrik Vibskov, Fashion's Renaissance Man, Showcases His Fine Art." *New York Times Magazine*, 5 Jun. 2014, www.tmagazine.blogs.nytimes.com/2014/06/05/henrik-vibskov-designs-for-bjork-and-has-art-show-at-ruttkowski-68/. Accessed 21 Oct. 2022.

Dam, Hanne. "Funktion og forførelse." *Nørgaard paa Strøget*, edited by Bodil Busk Laursen. Copenhagen: Gyldendal, 2008, pp. 36–59.

Dam, Rikke Agnete. "Da Ganni gik fra at være et lille dansk tøjmærke til et stort internationalt brand." *Børsen*, 6 Feb. 2020.

Elan, Priya. "'Hate-Wear' and 'Sadwear': Fashion's New Names for Lockdown Dressing." *The Guardian*, 17 Jan. 2021, www.theguardian.com/fashion/2021/jan/17/hate-wear-and-sadwear-fashion-new-names-for-covid-lockdown-dressing. Accessed 21 Oct. 2022.

Ferrier, Morwenna. "From Nordic Noir to Hygge Hype – How Scandi Style Took over the High Street." *The Guardian*, 6 Nov. 2016, www.theguardian.com/lifeandstyle/2016/nov/06/scandinavian-style-takes-over-uk-fashion-retailing. Accessed 21 Oct. 2022.

Fletcher, Kate. "Durability, Fashion, Sustainability: The Processes and Practices of Use." *Fashion Practice*, vol. 4, no. 2, 2012, pp. 221–238.

Grundahl, Søren Pors. "Strikkegarn i lange baner: 2020 har været det vildeste år." *TVS*, 27 Jan. 2021, www.tvsyd.dk/syd-og-soenderjylland/strikkegarn-i-lange-baner-2020-har-vaeret-det-vildeste-aar. Accessed 21 Oct. 2022.

Højmark, Louise. "Når håndarbejde heler sjælen." *Kristeligt dagblad*, 16 Jul. 2016, www.kristeligt-dagblad.dk/kultur/alle-tanker-forsvinder-naar-man-haekler. Accessed 21 Oct. 2022.

Holst, Katrine. "Dansk mode hitter i New York." *DR*, 11 Aug. 2010, www.dr.dk/nyheder/kultur/dansk-mode-hitter-i-new-york. Accessed 21 Oct. 2022.

Kvittingen, Ida. "Derfor er ordet hygge så særligt for os." *Videnskab.dk*, 6 Jan. 2018, www.videnskab.dk/kultur-samfund/hygge-er-en-sproglig-kulturbombe. Accessed 21 Oct. 2022.

Marriot, Hannah. "Permanent PJs and Pivoting Designers: How the Pandemic Hit the Fashion World." *The Guardian*, 24 Jan. 2021, www.theguardian.com/membership/2021/jan/24/pandemic-fashion-covid-clothing. Accessed 21 Oct. 2022.

Melchior, Marie Riegels. "Hvad er dansk mode? – tre fortællinger gennem et halvt århundrede." *Dansk Mode. Historie Design Identitet*, edited by Thomas Schødt Rasmussen. Copenhagen: MOKO, 2006, pp. 33–48.

Melchior, Marie Riegels. "'Doing' Danish Fashion: On National Identity and Design Practices of a Small Danish Fashion Company." *Fashion Practice*, vol. 2, no. 1, 2010, pp. 13–40.

Melchior, Marie Riegels. "Dansk modetøj er demokratisk mode." *Klædt på til skindet. Modens kultur og æstetik*, edited by Lars Dybdal and Ida Engholm. Copenhagen: Vandkunsten, 2011, pp. 108–121.

Melchior, Marie Riegels. *Dansk på mode! Fortællinger om design, identitet og historie i og omkring dansk modeindustri*. Copenhagen: Museum Tusculanum, 2013.

Melchior, Marie Riegels, and Nikolina Olsen-Rule. "Conclusion." *Dansk Mode: Historie Design Identitet*, edited by Thomas Schødt Rasmussen. Copenhagen: MOKO, 2006, pp. 33–48.

Rhode, Thomas Søgaard. "Hummelgaard klandrede Østerbros 'absolut øvre middelklasse' for arbejdsforholdene hos Nemlig.com – men firmaet har flere kunder i socialdemokratisk højborg." *Berlingske*, 21 Apr. 2021, www.berlingske.dk/politik/hummelgaard-klandre-de-oesterbros-absolut-oevre-middelklasse-for. Accessed 21 Oct. 2022.

Robin, Marci. "No Spanx." *The Guardian*, 3 May 2015, www.theguardian.com/fashion/2015/may/31/spanx-granny-panties-millennial-comfort-fashion. Accessed 21 Oct. 2022.

Russell, Helen. "Danish Fashion Takes Centre Stage – And with Hardly a Wooly Jumper in Sight." *The Observer*, 1 Feb. 2015, www.theguardian.com/world/2015/feb/01/danish-fashion-design-clothing-copenhagen. Accessed 21 Oct. 2022.

Russell, Helen. *The Year of Living Danishly: Uncovering the Secrets of the World's Happiest Country*. London: Icon Books, 2015.

Rytter, Thea. "Lærke Baggers striktrøje gik verden rundt: Den skal bringe folk sammen." *Femina*, 25 Jan. 2021, www.femina.dk/stil/mode/laerke-baggers-striktroeje-gik-verden-rundt-den-skal-bringe-folk-sammen. Accessed 21 Oct. 2022.

Sandemose, Aksel. *En flygtning krydser sit spor*. Copenhagen: Ti danske forlæggeres bogklub, 1961.

Skarum, Sarah. "Henrik Vibskov: Meget mere end en gøgler." *Berlingske*, 9 Jun. 2013, www.berlingske.dk/design/henrik-vibskov-meget-mere-end-en-goegler. Accessed 21 Oct. 2022.

Skarum, Sarah. "Nogle tager på yogaretreat. Jeg tager til Hirtshals." *Berlingske*. 1 May 2016: n.pag.

Sommerlund, Julie. "Ideologisk design?" *Dansk mode. Forskning. Uddannelse. Praksis*, edited by Julie Sommerlund. Copenhagen: The Danish Design School Press, 2011, pp. 165–185.

Stensgaard, Pernille. *København – folk og kvarterer*. Copenhagen: Gyldendal, 2005.

Sykes, Pandora. "Meet the New Wave of Scandi Style." *The Times*, 7 Aug. 2016, www.thetimes.co.uk/article/the-danish-girls-fq5vgv7qm. Accessed 21 Oct. 2022.

Tholl, Sofie. "Skønhed er ingen skam at stræbe efter." *Information*, 6 Nov. 2010, www.information.dk/moti/2010/11/skoenhed-ingen-skam-straebe. Accessed 21 Oct. 2022.

Thomsen, Kåre Holm. "Den pinefulde friværdi." *Weekendavisen*, 12 May 2021, www.weekendavisen.dk/2021-19/ideer/den-pinefulde-frivaerdi. Accessed 21 Oct. 2022.

Wiking, Meik. *Little Book of Hygge: The Danish Way to Live Well*. London: Penguin, 2016.

Williams, Alex. "The New Normal." *New York Times*, 2 Apr. 2014, www.nytimes.com/2014/04/03/fashion/normcore-fashion-movement-or-massive-in-joke.html. Accessed 21 Oct. 2022.

5

The Bearded Queens of Copenhagen

Anders Larsen and Maria Mackinney-Valentin

Jack (he/him) is a 34-year-old cisgendered man, who lives in the Copenhagen neighbourhood Valby with his Italian boyfriend. He describes himself as of mixed heritage: English, Italian, Palestinian and Israeli. Jack is about average height, broad, has a shaved head and a thick black beard. He works at Irma, an upscale local supermarket, during the week. On weekends, Jack spends hours applying heavy make-up and strapping his hairy torso into a tight corset. During this transformation, he becomes Jaxie (she/her), a celebrity drag queen known for her prominent beard.

> I love to take as many references and fragments as possible and put them into a bag and shake them before I pour them out on the table and decide what to do with them. Take my Hello Kitty Mega Man Robot-situation. I don't think that many people think about what would happen if a video game character was into Hello Kitty, and if he was a robot who was a drag queen. I even made a Hello Kitty bomb so that my drag character would have weapons. That is good drag to me.
> (Jack/Jaxie, Copenhagen, 2021)

Jaxie mainly performs at the gay bar GAY and the pop-up event Drag House. She starred in a Danish TV drag make-over competition and has a strong online presence with more than 10,000 followers. Jaxie is one of several bearded queens in Copenhagen (Figure 5.1). The bearded queens are an integrated part of the various drag scenes, and, at the same time, a disruption of the norms that govern drag.

This chapter examines queer fashion practices in Copenhagen. Fashion is here understood as being about more than clothes, encompassing elements such as make-up and facial hair as aspects of getting dressed. The chapter does not attempt to write about LGBTQ+ fashion as that would be reductive and ignore that the spectrum includes diverse and at times conflicting approaches to fashion and dress. Instead, it looks at queer sartorial practices through the cases of

FIGURE 5.1: Jaxie in her Hello Kitty Mega Man costume, which is one of her favourite ensembles, Copenhagen, 2018, photo by Jack Ashley Benn, with permission.

three bearded drag performers aged 25–34: Brynhildr the Viqueen, Maj Mokaj and Jaxie. The performers were selected based on their shared preference for bearded drag, while also representing a varied approach to the aesthetic and intended impact of drag as a subversive art form, including issues of ethnicity and cultural belonging. Drag is inextricably connected with queer culture. It is most often associated with the simulation of and play on the notion of gender through the use of costuming and make-up, but it covers a broader phenomenon of queer play with social roles, even play with roles that most people take for granted – for example, using the term boy drag for a cisman dressed in menswear (Brennan 2017). Drag thus simulates social categories such as gender roles and thereby brings attention to the constructed nature of not just the cultural category "woman" but also race, ethnicity and social class (Johnson & Larsen 2020). A central theme of the present chapter is how the beard enables the wearer to play with several social identities and perform in a way that either adheres to the context or subverts it. The chapter thus broadens the scope of the literature on facial hair in contemporary Copenhagen from being a way to perform social categories such as masculinity and age (Petersen & Mackinney-Valentin 2016) to holding the potential for destabilizing the binary gender system and shifting between standing out and fitting in. In order to contextualize the interpretations of the findings presented in the chapter, it is necessary to briefly introduce the queer history of fashion in Copenhagen. This will be followed by an introduction to the field, methods employed and findings.

Queering the fashion history of Copenhagen

Noah (he/him/they/them) is 29 years old, with a Turkish background, and identifies as non-binary, even though he immediately adds that everyone sees him as male. He lives in the neighbourhood of Vesterbro in a flat he shares with a DJ from the gay community. He is average height, has olive skin, big brown eyes and a thick black beard. Noah was unemployed at the time of the interview but has previously worked in retail. Noah often performs as Maj Mokaj (she/her) at the bars in Copenhagen's Meatpacking District and is also active on social media but with a smaller following of around 800. "It is different in Copenhagen. There are more people like me in Copenhagen," Noah/Maj explained in our 2021 interview. For Noah and other queer people, Copenhagen has been a safer space than the rest of Denmark. But charting a queer history of sartorial practices in Copenhagen is complex.

Copenhagen is marketed as a beacon of light for queer people and was named the most LGBTQ+ friendly city by Lonely Planet in 2019. The lobby work that secured World Pride in Copenhagen in the summer of 2021 drew on this image and stressed that Denmark has been at the forefront of LGBTQ+ rights, from the decriminalization of homosexuality in 1933 to the introduction of same-sex partnerships in 1989. The official website of the event even claimed that it is in the Danish DNA to recognize gay rights as human rights. This narrative is publicly accepted in Denmark, to the point that even the right-wing sees supporting gay rights as a national value, and at times uses it as a manner of separating "real" Danes from outsiders (Nebeling & Andersson 2018). The capital has historically offered a critical mass, in which queer people could find likeminded souls and, at the same time, disappear in the crowds (Beck 1988). To this date, it hosts the largest queer community in the country. Male homosexuality was criminalized in Denmark up until 1933, and female sexuality was barely recognized. This means that standing out as queer used to come with serious ramifications. The police statute of Copenhagen furthermore criminalized male crossdressing in 1913. Historians mainly have access to sources dealing with queer men of the past through criminal records. These were produced when men were prosecuted for having or pursuing same-sex relations, and they rarely mention what the delinquents were wearing. Some documents do mention details, such as two people dressed as men dancing or that men were wearing women's clothing. The latter was the case when the police raided the association Nekkab in March of 1923 (Mchangama & Stjernfeldt 2016). However, such mentions are rare.

Apart from criminal records, we have accounts of a few notable individuals who were more or less openly queer. These include artists, such as the couple Marie Luplau and Emilie Mundt, the painter Kristian Zahrtmann, the author Herman

Bang and the painter Lilly Elbe, also known in popular culture as the Danish Girl (discussed in Chapter 6). The latter attracted much attention both during her life but also in more recent years due to her gender transition, which according to the accepted myth started with her modelling in female clothes for her wife, artist Gerda Wegener. The Copenhagen-based designer Holger Blom is said to have worn silk trousers, and one gets the sense from the sources that we are dealing with a euphemism for his homosexuality. It was a public secret that Blom was a homosexual, and while it was suggested in both gossip magazines and in pop culture at the time, including the 1957 film *Kispus* (discussed in Chapter 6), it was never explicitly disclosed (Verge 2017).

We can assume that queer men historically have employed dress in order to blend into the straight world, but little is known regarding whether they also used "secret" sartorial codes that would have revealed them to other men who practiced "the love that did not dare speak its name." An example is when the Federation of 1948, which was the national federation for homophiles, produced discrete finger rings, pins and the like with their logo in the early 1950s (Svalebølle 2021). A similar argument has been raised about the gay scenes in New York and San Francisco by the American scholar Hal Fischer in his now iconic book *Gay Semiotics*, where he examines the meaning of everyday objects recontextualized by queer men (Fischer 1977). As with queer history overall, the history of transgressing gendered codes in sartorial practices is woefully lacking in the Danish context. Gender bending is better documented in Anglo-Saxon research, both as a practice in Shakespearean theatre and in the Molly Houses of eighteenth-century London, where men would wear dresses and be assigned female so-called "molly names" (Conaway 2004). In the Danish context, it appears that crossdressing was practiced in the nineteenth century at the all-male student union at the University of Copenhagen in connection with plays (Henriksen & Al Arab 2021). Whereas the use of female garments by men in heterosexual spaces was deemed comedic and safe, the bending of gender expression by homosexuals in queer spaces was seen as immoral and harmful to society. This is evident from the police banning male crossdressing in 1913. Male crossdressing was most likely associated with male sex work, which was seen as a major societal problem, as healthy men faced the risk of being lured into perversion and potentially contaminated with homosexuality. For example, the Danish Supreme Court abolished the Nekkab association in 1924 with clear references to the immoral nature of crossdressing that took place at their parties (Henriksen & Al Arab 2021).

Male homosexuality was reclassified as a result of the social reforms of 1930. It became a mental illness and could thus not be sanctioned legally. This resulted in the decriminalization of homosexuality in 1933. It needs to be made clear that the decriminalization in no way resulted in acceptance. In public opinion, homosexuality remained immoral and problematic for public health, and gay men thus had to remain inconspicuous. The emerging gay rights movement that followed in the wake of the Second World War aimed at normalizing homosexuality by showcasing queer individuals as respectable citizens. This included not standing out, as men who dressed flamboyantly or women who dressed in a masculine manner did. This changed in the 1970s. The momentum created by the Stonewall Movement and the revolutionary discourse that grew out of the youth rebellion of the late 1960s inspired the formation of the Gay Liberation Front in Copenhagen in 1971. The Gay Liberation Front campaigned through activist zaps that on several occasions included activists posing as drum majorettes in skirts and big beards (Edelberg 2014). A former activist from the Gay Liberation Front explained that the first time he experienced the impact of crossdressing used as a political statement was during a visit to *Homosexuelle Aktion Westberlin* in the German capital in the summer of 1971 (Petersen & Kongsdal 2020). The practice was soon adopted by the Copenhagen-based activists and was used for happenings around the city and later on stage at the gay community centre Bøssehuset in Christiania. The practice continues to this date at the Theatre of Bøssehuset. It includes ill-fitting, second-hand dresses, facial hair, exaggerated makeup and the adaptation of (most often) female activist names. The Gay Liberation Front marked the first generation of queer men who deliberately aimed to be seen as gay by the mainstream. This caused controversy, not just in relation to the establishment, but also internally in the Danish Association of Gays and Lesbians, where the older generation saw the new language and sartorial practices as inflammatory and damaging for the cause.

Alongside the Gay Liberation Front, Copenhagen had a thriving drag scene in the 1980s and early 1990s. The drag scene did not stand in opposition to life around Bøssehuset, and there were several instances of activists attending mainstream drag bars as well as established drag performers participating in beauty pageants arranged by Bøssehuset (Henriksen & Al Arab 2021). A performance collective by the name of DUNST emerged at the beginning of the new millennium. Their performances were in many ways an extension of the activism of Bøssehuset and the Gay Liberation Front. They used the term *trash drag* to describe their aesthetic. DUNST was informed by queer theory and a punk aesthetic, and their performers mainly came from the electronic underground scene and the community around the squatter house *Ungdomshuset*. Their performances were a constant play on abjection and taboo and often included faecal matter, urine and anal penetration, and performers would often have beards that were either home-grown or drawn on (Danbolt 2011). Whereas performers at Bøssehuset and the mainstream drag scene had been men dressing as more or less convincing women, DUNST performers were of all genders and did not limit their drag to a binary understanding of gender. Neither did they necessarily comment on the heteronormative gender binary by simulating sartorial practices. Just as the mainstream drag scene had a certain overlap with the performers at Bøssehuset, DUNST was also housed at Bøssehuset for a while, but was later excluded as their performances were considered too provocative. DUNST stopped performing as a group due to a combination of internal conflicts and some performers moving to Berlin, but several of their Copenhagen-based performers continued in different constellations: some around the queer performance space Warehouse 9, others at Bøssehuset in Christiania and a number of other venues. Several of these performers continue to employ facial hair in their costuming to this day.

Apart from the radical performers of DUNST, Copenhagen also hosted a number of other events that incorporated genderbending, most noteworthy the beauty pageant Frøken Verden beginning in the 1980s (Nissen & Paulsen 2000). The latest wave of gender bending in Copenhagen was sparked by the advent of the American reality show *RuPaul's Drag Race*, which has been credited with "shifting the visibility of drag culture" (Niall & Gudelunas 2017). The show aired in 2009 and slowly started getting the attention of Copenhagen queers. It led to the emergence of a group of young performers who, independently of the existing drag scene, started performing in an idiom highly inspired by the show. Other than the shows at Draghouse (which opened for performances in 2013) and GAY (which opened in 2014), a ballroom scene has emerged in the past decade. The two idioms partially overlap and share a series of references that double as queer and American (Johnson & Larsen 2020). In addition to the performances on stage and at queer political demonstrations, drag performers have also become present on mainstream media platforms, such as the radio show *Er du sunshine?* (Radio 24syv 2017–19) and television shows such as *Far med Fjerboa* (Danmarks Radio 2020) and *Sommeren der ændrede mit liv* (Danmarks Radio 2020).

Methodology

Jaxie uses her beard to play with notions of femininity, noting, "oversized lips, batting lashes, but then add a big black beard to it" (Jack/Jaxie 2021). Jaxie, as well as Brynhildr and Maj, differ from the mainstream drag scene. The vast majority of Copenhagen drag queens shave before getting into drag, but a few are known for getting on stage with facial hair. A survey of the drag scenes in Copenhagen revealed a total of seven drag queens and two drag kings who use facial hair as part of their drag costuming. Apart from the use of facial hair, little unites them. The three informants were selected based on age and biological sex, and the fact that they have beards both in and out of drag. The three informants are under the age of 35 and were assigned male at birth. None of them have been active at Bøssehuset, and the interviews revealed that they had little or no knowledge of the Gay Liberation Front and DUNST. Two of the remaining performers are also under 40, but one only has a moustache and often shaves it off when performing, and the other one rarely performs. The last two performers are former members of DUNST, are in their late 40s and rarely perform. While the three selected informants do not capture the full diversity of queer life in Copenhagen, their practices serve to illustrate strategies employed by queer individuals when negotiating (and performing) social identities – in relation to the hegemonic heteronormative society they find themselves in, as well as dominant norms in various queer spaces.

The authors conducted a series of semi-structured interviews with the drag performers in their homes. Informants were asked to select a photo of themselves that summed up the essence of their drag character prior to the interview. All three informants referred to their social media presence and how Instagram plays a central role in the construction of their image. The chosen Instagram posts served as an opener for a conversation about how the informants do drag. After the interview, the informants showed the authors where they store their clothes. This served as an opener for practices surrounding storing clothing and how this reflects the management of social identities through the separation between their "civilian identity" and their drag persona, as well as considerations the informants make regarding their well-being and safety when getting dressed.

Drag – To be and to do

A central finding in the interviews is that drag is more than just the costuming. One is not simply a drag queen – drag is rather something that is done. It is the act of deconstructing and representing gendered identities through embodied practices of mimicry and hyperbole, as well as the person who does it (Litwiller 2020). The performativity of drag is thus double. It is both performative as it exemplifies the observations on gender made by Judith Butler (1990) but also performative in the sense that it is performed by artists who require spectators, either in real life or mediated through a platform such as Instagram. As with other performances, there is an unstated contract between the performer and the audience. It is make-believe, and yet the audience is seduced by the spectacle. The suspense of disbelief is evident in the case of Bearded Queens, as the deliberate use of facial hair disrupts the conventions of female fashion, as well as classic drag. It furthermore suggests that both spectators and performers are aware of a hegemonic system of gendered signifiers but are willing to suspend their belief in them – either for the sake of diversion or as a deliberate attempt to renegotiate gendered identities.

"It is my lady beard," explained Fru Bryn/Brynhildr in the interview (2021). Fru Bryn (she/her/they/them) is 25 years old, ethnically Danish and identifies as non-binary. She lives alone in an apartment in Amager. She is taller than average, heavy set, bald and has a big strawberry blond beard. Fru Bryn is a student and works part time at a retirement home. She also often performs under the name Brynhildr the Viqueen (she/her) at GAY. Brynhildr is very active on social media and has more than 4500 followers. She has also been the host of a podcast *Dragedronningerne* that revolved around the drag scene in Copenhagen. One may wonder what the term "lady beard" entails. The existing Danish research on beards suggests that men in Copenhagen use facial hair as a way of performing primordial masculinity, virility and authority. The beard is a fashionable accessory, an extension of the body and a form of dress, while also being a convenient choice for many (Petersen & MacKinney-Valentin 2016). The tension of the masculine beard against feminine dress found in bearded drag is bound to generate a number of meanings (Figure 5.2).

All three informants talked about the beard as something that adds to their looks and makes them attractive, in and out of drag. But the meaning of good-looking

FIGURE 5.2: Fru Bryn in her basement, where she stores Brynhildr's costumes and wigs, Copenhagen 2021, photo by Anders Larsen.

is vastly different for their two manifestations. Fru Bryn explained that the beard becomes a way of reconfiguring notions of femininity. Inspiration was taken from cisgendered women with beards on social media that allowed her to claim a femininity that makes sense to her. Apart from the intimate meaning the beard holds for her, she also understands that the beard also inscribes itself into a heteronormative binary and thus conceals femininity. This is evident when Fru Bryn refers to the beard as a central attribute in her appearance when looking for partners on the hook-up app Grindr (Fru Bryn/Brynhildr 2021). All three informants see the beard as something that adds definition to their face, like home-grown makeup. Noah used the term "beard contouring" (Noah/Maj 2021) in a reference to a common make-up technique used by drag performers, and Jack admitted that his partner finds him more attractive when he wears his beard (Jack/Jaxie 2021). Apart from having aesthetic qualities, the beard also serves as a marker of masculine aggression, simplified by Noah explaining that the beard makes it look like he can defend himself (Noah/Maj 2021). When performing in drag, the beard is recontextualized and becomes a marker of resistance to both the heteronormative mainstream and mainstream drag. Traditional drag works in a binary where cismen perform as women, and ciswomen perform as men. The aim is to perform a hyperreal version of the opposite gender. This binary is increasingly blurred, and this chapter argues that the Bearded Queens contribute to the diffusion of categories. It is, however, also noteworthy that the subversive meaning of the beard is contextual, and only has that meaning when the informants are in drag.

Fashioning drag, fashioning the drag scene

There are various groupings in Copenhagen ranging from the mainstream template – drag influenced by the reality-show *RuPaul's Drag Race* in terms of how queens perform and look – to the underground scene that is described as "unpredictable and crazy" by Jaxie, who noted that

> if you go to their shows, they will most likely just sing a lullaby and roll around on the stage or trip on each other's dresses. It is all super weird, but it is magical, and it feels so new, and it is something that you can't find on television.
> (Jack/Jaxie 2021)

It appears that *RuPaul's Drag Race* is a major factor in shaping the drag scene of Copenhagen, as well as a language around classifications of drag performers. All three informants work with a mental map of the Copenhagen drag scene that they based on specific venues, as well as the people who attend them. The venues vary from the Concert Hall Vega, where Drag House takes place, to the mainstream gay bar GAY, to the edgy bars in the Meatpacking District and the underground venues at the Freetown Christiania. The informants see the mainstream as being made up of *template queens*, who mainly find their inspiration in *RuPaul's Drag Race*. These performers are characterized as "generic but talented" (Jack/Jaxie 2021). Their make-up is based on online tutorials, and they shave their faces and bodies before they mould them into a desirable shape with the use of padding and cinching. Brynhildr and Jaxie both frequently perform at mainstream events but see themselves as very different from the other performers. While they don't live up to the beauty standards that appear to dominate the mainstream, they both consider their drag as having a competitive edge because it is unique, which also implies authentic in their opinion. Maj Mokaj tends to perform at bars in the Meatpacking District and often goes online on Instagram where she poses as a social media influencer (Figure 5.3).

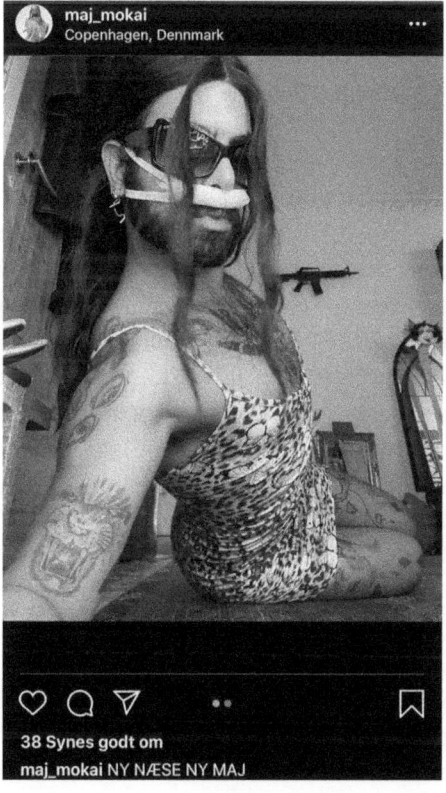

FIGURE 5.3: Maj, Copenhagen 2021, photo by Noah Kaber, with permission. "Maj always wears sunglasses. I think that it makes her mysterious. You never know if you have eye contact with her and that leaves you wondering if she is looking at you at the moment. Is she looking at me or is she oblivious to my existence? I usually say that everything revolves around Maj. That is her Motto" (Noah/Maj 2021).

Copenhagen as the catalyst

All three informants grew up in lower middle-class families in provincial Demark. They all see the move to Copenhagen as central in the formation of their queer identities and the way they dress. When describing Copenhagen style all three informants characterize the mainstream Copenhagener as someone who prefers outfits in muted colours such as black, grey and navy. Moving to Copenhagen did not mean that they gained freedom to express themselves by conforming to the way that most Copenhageners dress, but rather that they gained the freedom of anonymity. Noah explained that he felt that he had to perform in a manner acceptable to his brothers when growing up, noting that

> when I moved away, I felt like I could relax. I no longer had to fear that I would bump into someone who knew me. I got away and I could start experimenting with things I did not dare to experiment with in Aarhus. I still consider Aarhus as very conservative – bordering on hostile – towards people who dress in a more flamboyant manner.
> (Noah/Maj 2021)

He understood that he would fall victim to physical violence if he strayed from performing masculine, even after he came out as gay. Copenhagen has also served as a catalyst in the development of his drag persona. In fact, all three informants started doing drag after they moved to Copenhagen, and this was where they met other performers and became part of a community. It appears that Copenhagen creates a space for queer people to explore their identities through clothing as the city is big enough for them to find likeminded people but also because the city offers the option of disappearing in the crowd even though your clothing stands out from the mainstream. It also appears that Copenhagen continues to offer queer people a safe space where they have the option of fitting in and standing out while remaining safe.

Drag as identity play

Apart from the negotiation of privilege, the informants also use the play with identities as a strategy in the creation of their drag personas. Their identity play shifts between mimicry, social commentary and deliberate performance-slips. "I spell Maj with a J because that is the way it is spelled in Denmark. When you see the name, you tell yourself 'this is a Danish citizen.' I am the girl with the potatoes," Noah/Maj explained. Not only do they participate in gender drag but they also drag other aspects of their performance; for instance, we see all three perform cultural drag (Johnson & Larsen 2020). Jaxie engages in what can be termed species drag that includes performing as an alien, as well as cultural drag when she is a German Easter bunny by the name Heidi and a French cat called Chantilly. Maj, who bases her character on somewhat unsuccessfully mimicking influencers on Instagram, will often fluctuate between being hyper-effeminate, then deliberately slip and burp or perform a similar un-ladylike act (Noah/Maj 2021). Maj also plays with norms around Danishness. She ironically plays with the title "The Little Match Girl," which is seen as canonical in Danish literature, and merges the title with potatoes, a term used as slang when positioning "pearls" (i.e., immigrants) against potatoes (i.e., ethnic Danes) (Noah/Maj 2021). Similarly, Brynhildr moves between nationalities, and it is not uncommon that she delivers phrases or sentences in Americanized English (Fru Bryn/Brynhildr 2021). Finally, our informants ironically argue that they are authentic because their beard reveals that they are performing when in drag.

Boy drag and the negotiation of (cultural) identities

All three informants are very aware of how they present in and out of drag, and they manage their image and monitor the reception thereof. When dressed in "boy drag," they all work with aspects of their appearance and either amp those up or tone them down in order to gain situational privileges.

> If I am dressed neutrally for instance at work, people often think that I am an Arab security guard, and if I am out and about in a colourful tank top or button down with floral print or a shirt with a cat on it, they see me as a queer – or a freak.
> (Jack/Jaxie 2021)

Both Jack and Noah identify as immigrants. They both described how they are caught in a binary between two extremes and can manage their look in order to lean towards one or the other. At the one end, they are queer, white and safe looking; on the other end of the spectrum, they are Muslim, masculine and dangerous. The beard is not only something that marginalizes them but is also a way of looking tough. Noah explained that it makes him look like he can defend himself and be attractive (Noah/Maj 2021). All three informants talked about their beards as a way of looking more attractive to their partners. The beard helps sculp the face into a desirable shape and provides a tactility that connotes rough masculinity. Fru Bryn explained how she can trade erotic capital (Hakim 2011) with subcultural capital (Thornton 1995). She compared the reception she usually receives at her regular nightclub in drag with how she is received when she shows up "dressed as a civilian" (Fru Bryn/Brynhildr 2021). Then she receives fewer compliments, and people are less likely to laugh at her jokes. The other informants also shared the experience of being received differently when in and out of drag, most often as comic relief. In Brynhildr's experience, she is less desirable on dating and hook-up apps when she looks too effeminate; therefore, she employs the strategy of getting into "boy drag" in order to attract partners. This is achieved by toning down her makeup and putting on a hairpiece. When chatting on hook-up apps, she often changed her demeanour and answered with short replies and no emojis in order to come across as more "masculine" (Fru Bryn/Brynhildr 2021). All three informants thought of these switches in representation as being as equally performative as their drag personas, so we can see these as another version of their drag.

Bearded drag as double resistance

Traditional subcultural studies suggest a one-dimensional hierarchy of mainstream and subculture; however, we observed that queer people operate in a multidimensional space where social distinction is a function of place, social space and various other factors. The American socio-linguist Barret Rusty found that queer subcultures are an intermediate type of culture that is distinct from hegemonic culture but also contains its own subcultures (Barret 2017). All three informants operate in a drag mainstream and place themselves either in the periphery of it or in direct opposition to it.

> Drag is, for me, not about being beautiful or a woman for that matter. It is about playing with gender expression more than it is about becoming a specific gender. I hate that we limit femininity to being about beauty. It is about much more. We also need to accept that there is more than one way of looking good. When people ask me if Jaxie is good looking, I am like 100 percent. Jaxie is mega hot.
>
> (Jack/Jaxie 2021)

Jack does not see having a beard as standing in opposition to being a good drag queen or being beautiful. He shares these views with the two other informants. They all see themselves as standing in opposition to the *RuGirls*, who work in the idiom popularized by *RuPaul's Drag Race*, and yet they follow the show, use the terminology popularized in it, and admit having been inspired by performers who have been on the show. The three informants see their beards and body hair as a determining factor in distinguishing them from the *RuGirls*, or as one informant calls them, *the template queens* (Jack/Jaxie 2021). The mainstream performers shave their faces and bodies in order to emulate cis women, and they cinch their waists and pad their chest and hips in order to mould their bodies into an hourglass shape. The Bearded Queens, on the contrary, blur hyperbolic femininity by subverting the conventions of mainstream drag. At the same time, they also see themselves as standing in opposition to the "masc-for-masc" gays, as well as heteronormative straight society, all of which they refer to as mainstream (Figures 5.4 and 5.5).

FIGURE 5.4: A glimpse of Brynhildr's wigs and head pieces. Brynhildr will often adorn her bald head with a scarf. On other occasions, she will use wigs in various materials such as nylon, human hair, foam and chicken wire decorated with plastic flowers, Copenhagen 2021, photo by Anders Larsen.

FIGURE 5.5: Brynhildr, Copenhagen, 2021, photo by Fru Bryn, with permission. "Well, the make-up wasn't good that day if we look at the technique, but my skin was extra clean that day and my breasts looked amazing, and my beard has the perfect length and there were many things that made it all come together [...] I looked amazing that night!" (Fry Bryn/Brynhildr 2021).

Co-habitation – In the actual closet

Garments are performed within specific spaces and in varying forms of assemblage. The same dress may work as both an in- and out-of-drag item depending on whether or not there is a wig involved. Nevertheless, a central finding for the authors is that all three informants had a clear distinction between two wardrobes – spatially, as well as conceptually. They all distinguished between their wardrobes in and out of drag, and the practices surrounding wearing, styling, storing, washing, altering and maintaining these two wardrobes differ. All three informants stored their drag costumes away from what two of the informants, independently of each other, referred to as their "civilian clothing." The everyday "civilian" wardrobe was in all three cases either kept on hangers or folded neatly in drawers and sorted according to clothing items. Two informants kept their clothing in closets in their bedrooms, the third informant kept his clothes in a walk-in closet that he shared with his roommate. Whereas the "civilian" clothing was newly washed, sorted and folded, it appeared that there were few or no governing principles for the storing of the drag wardrobe. Brynhildr's costumes were kept in IKEA bags in a basement storage room; most of Jaxie's costumes were crammed into a broom cabinet; and Maj Mokaj's costumes were kept in a box shaped like a big Rubik's cube. All three informants reported that it was possible to "borrow" from one wardrobe and add it to the other one. This required either that the clothing item was altered or that it was styled differently from its usual use. This shows that the informants negotiate masculine and feminine signifiers when performing in and out of drag. "I have a dress that I wore the other day with socks and trainers. I had to change into Maj later that day and all I had to do was to pop on my wig and heels" (Noah/Maj 2021). It is, in some cases, possible for the wearer to wear the same item in and out of drag. Noah explained that he can wear the same dress as Noah as when he performs Maj, but that this requires that he "breaks up" the look with jeans when wearing it out of drag. Similarly, the dress needs to be contextualized by a wig and heels in order to transition from "civilian wear" to drag (Figures 5.6 and 5.7).

FIGURE 5.6: Jack showing where he keeps Jaxie's wigs, Copenhagen, 2021, photo by Anders Larsen.

FIGURE 5.7: Noah in his walk-in closet that he shares with his roommate, Copenhagen, 2021, photo by Anders Larsen.

Conclusion

The act of bending social markers questions norms around phenomena such as gender and sex and allows individuals to celebrate identities that otherwise are censured in the straight world and the gay mainstream. When examining Copenhagen, it appears that there is not one drag subculture, but rather a complex network of venues that drag performers appear in, both physical and virtual. There is not a clear overlap between performers and venues. Instead, it seems that performers can be found at all venues, but that their subcultural capital changes depending on where they perform, how they perform and who their audience is. For the informants, it is not determining whether their audience is gay or straight, but rather if the audience is perceived as conforming or edgy. All three informants talked about "polished" gays who perform in a masculine manner and seek masculine partners as something they wish to distance themselves from. Bearded drag becomes one of several strategies that reinforce this social distinction. Performing as a Bearded Queen makes our informants less palatable for mainstream consumers, and thus gives them a unique subcultural edge. All three informants have clear concepts of mainstreams in heteronormative society, the gay community and the drag community. Rather than constantly and conspicuously standing in opposition, the informants make contextual considerations about how to dress for a specific occasion to either blend in or to stand out. At the same time, it may also reflect more practical and personal considerations, such as looking attractive to a partner or the convenience of not shaving or the ability to sculpt the face with facial hair. One informant talked about making the decision to "camp up" a look when dressing as a "civilian" in order to avoid racism. The other informants used similar language and disclosed that the "camping up" could serve several purposes, from providing an affective reaction of well-being or empowerment in the wearer, through gaining subcultural status within the queer community, to distancing oneself from either mainstream gays or mainstream heterosexuals.

This chapter argues that the beard inscribes the wearer into a cis-heteronormative discourse about masculinity. This may come with the privilege of blending in, being seen as authoritative or sexually attractive, or as someone who can stand up for themselves. At the same time, the beard distinguishes our informants from other drag performers. This act of social distinction marks the wearer of the beard as someone who is different from the straight mainstream as well as the gay mainstream. The act of wearing a beard as a drag queen in Copenhagen is thus dual, and it creates a subculture with its own logic within a subculture.

REFERENCES

Bech, Henning. *Når Mænd Mødes: Homoseksualiteten og de homoseksuelle*. Gyldendal, 1988.

Brennan, Nial. "Contradictions between the Subversive and the Mainstream: Drag Cultures and *RuPaul's Drag Race*." *RuPaul's Drag Race and the Shifting Visibility of Drag Culture*, edited by Niall Brennan and David Gudelunas. London: Palgrave, 2017.

Brennan, Niall, and David Gudelunas. "Drag Culture, Global Participation and RuPaul's Drag Race." *RuPaul's Drag Race and the Shifting Visibility of Drag Culture*, edited by Niall Brennan and David Gudelunas. London: Palgrave, 2017.

Butler, Judith. *Gender Trouble*. Abington: Routledge, 1990.

Conaway, Charles. "Shakespeare, Molly House-Culture, and Eighteenth-Century Stage." *Comparative Drama*, vol. 38, no. 4, Winter, 2004–2005, pp. 401–423.

Danbolt, Mathias. "This Performance Stinks. Dunst and the Politics of Arrested Development." *Dance Theatre Journal*, vol. 24, no. 3, 2011, pp. 6–10.

Edelberg, Peter. "The Queer Road to Frisind: Copenhagen 1945–2012." *Queer Cities. Queer Cultures: Europe Since 1945*, edited by Jennifer Evans and Matt Cook. London: Bloomsbury Academic, 2014, pp. 55–74.

Fischer, Hal. *The Gay Seventies*, Gallery 16 Editions, 2019.

Hakim, Catherine. *Erotic Capital: The Power of Attraction in the Boardroom and the Bedroom*. New York: Basic Books, 2011.

Henriksen, Lars, and Chantal Al Arab. "Lars Henriksen og Chantal al Arab fortæller fra Bøssernes." *Danmarkshistorie. 1900–2020*, Copenhagen: Forlaget 28B, 2021.

Johnson, Martha, and Anders Larsen. "Exploring the Potential of Cultural Drag." *Frontiers: The Interdisciplinary Journal of Study Abroad*, vol. 32, no. 3, 2020, pp. 51–71.

Litwiller, Fenton. "Normative Drag Culture and the Making of Precarity." *Leisure Studies*, vol. 39, no. 4, 2020, pp. 600–612.

Mchangama, Jacob, and Frederik Stjernfeldt. "MEN." *Ytringsfrihedens Historie i Danmark*. Copenhagen: Gyldendal, 2016.

Nebeling Petersen, Michael, and A. B. Andersson. "Homo-Nationalism: Internal and External Boundary Drawing." *The Universal: Human Rights Review*, vol. 2, 2018, pp. 63–69.

Nissen, Vibeke, and Inge-Lise Paulsen. "Handling gi'r forvandling. Klip af homobevægelsens historie I Danmark." *Lambda Nordica*, vol. 6, nos. 2–3, 2000, pp. 9–41.

Petersen, Kristian Toftegaard, and Ole Kongsdal Jensen. *Erindringer om Bøssernes Befrielses Front. Et Aktivistliv*. Forlaget Karius, 2020.

Petersen, Trine Brun, and Maria Mackinney-Valentin. "Det Moderne Fuldskæg. Fra kønsflag til alders-camouflage." *À la mode: mode mellan konst, kultur och kommers*. Copenhagen: Museum Tusculanums Forlag, 2016.

Rusty, Barret. *From Drag Queens to Leathermen: Language, Gender, and Gay Male Subcultures*. Oxford: Oxford University Press, 2017.

Svalebølle, Bert. "Navneskifte til 'Forbundet af 1948.'" 1949, www.outandabout.dk/navneskifte-til-forbundet-af-1948-1949/#:~:text=F%C3%B8rst%20efter%20at%20foreningen%20i,optaget%20i%20et%20statsligt%20foreningsregister. Accessed 20 Oct. 2022.

Thornton, Sarah. *Club Cultures: Music, Media and Subcultural Capital*. London: Polity Press, 1995.

Verge, Marianne. *Modekongen Holger Blom: En livshistorie*. Copenhagen: Gyldendal, 2017.

6

Fashion in Film

Katrina Sark
With research contributions by Bjørn Utoft Sørensen,
Emilie Thomsen and Izabella Andersen

In this chapter, we focus on the history of Copenhagen film, paying close attention to the ways the city and its fashion have been represented through this medium. Because a comprehensive study of Copenhagen cinema does not yet exist, we have reviewed, compiled and analyzed several examples of historical and contemporary Danish and international films that have a special relationship with the city and its fashion. We examine the ways in which the city is mediated in historical and contemporary films, and how various film genres (ranging from social realism to costume dramas) inform the representations of the city. We also consider the differences between insiders' and outsiders' perspectives, such as the tourist gaze, and how it differs from Copenhageners' self-representation and self-fashioning in film.

Our methodology is based on film and media analysis, fashion history and cultural history, with a particular attention to the cultural, political and urban transformations in Copenhagen over time, and the role fashion plays in the city's culture. We specifically arranged our discussion of these films in chronological order according to the historical periods portrayed (rather than in order of the release dates) to reflect on the depictions of fashion history in this urban context. Our close readings of these films, the cultural–historical contexts in which they have been produced, and the historical settings they portray help us understand mediated fashion cultures and how they are constructed cinematically and historically. Because not enough research on Copenhagen film, media and fashion exists (especially in English), we begin the chapter with a brief overview of the history of Danish cinema and its ties to Copenhagen, primarily relying on the work compiled by film historian Peter Schepelern for the *Det Danske Filminstitut* ("Danish Film Institute") website in Danish. As no English sources are available on Copenhagen film with a focus on its fashion, we hope that our chapter will inspire more work in this field.

Fashion presented in film either influences contemporary styles or is influenced by them. We have examined a large corpus of Copenhagen-based Danish and international films and selected the following films for analysis: *Kispus* (dir. Erik Balling, 1956), *Olsen Banden* (dir. Eric Balling, 1968–98), *Lille Spejl* (*Mirror Mirror*, dir. Edward Fleming, 1978), *Unge Andersen* (*Young Andersen*, dir. Rumle Hammerich, 2005), *En kongelig affære* (*A Royal Affair*, dir. Nikolaj Arcel, 2012), *The Danish Girl* (dir. Tom Hooper, 2015), *The Model* (dir. Mads Matthiesen, 2016), *In the Blood* (dir. Rasmus Heisterberg, 2016), *Darkland* (dir. Fenar Ahmad, 2017), *Lykke-Per* (*A Fortunate Man*, dir. Bille August, 2018) and *Druk* (*Another Round*, dir. Thomas Vinterberg, 2020).

Together these films provide a glimpse into Copenhagen lifestyles, but they are by no means a comprehensive or complete study of Danish film set in Copenhagen. We selected these films because they help us understand how fashion has been represented at different points in the city's history, how it has evolved over time and how the city is represented today. While *Young Andersen*, *A Royal Affair*, *A Fortunate Man* and *The Danish Girl* are historical costume films and engage with the history of fashion, *Darkland* is an example of the Nordic Noir crime genre, which illuminates a harsh, urban, underground view of Copenhagen with a distinct urban fashion culture and what we describe as the dark side of hygge in terms of social exclusions. *Mirror Mirror* provides a glimpse into the queer and drag culture of the late 1970s. *The Model* and *In the Blood* reflect contemporary Danish lifestyles through young people's challenges in situations where life gets out of control. *Druk* provides a glimpse into contemporary Danish society, everyday life and the dark side of hygge through addiction. All the films selected here also engage with significant moments in Danish history. Fashion in these films is often used to express social and cultural dichotomies, identity negotiations and conflicts. It provides a visual language for underlying landscapes of personal and cultural struggles.

Cinematic Copenhagen: A brief historical overview

Copenhagen is a cinematic city, as well as a cultural and media hub. It is the home of the Danish Film Institute (DFI), founded in 1972 to provide state subsidies, to support the development, production and distribution of select Danish films, to maintain the national film archives, and since 1984 to award the annual Danish film prize, Robert Award – the Danish equivalent of the American Oscars or the British BAFTAs (named after the statuette's creator, the Danish painter and sculptor Robert Jacobsen) presented by the members of the Danish Film Academy. It is also where in 1906 the Copenhagen filmmaker Ole Olsen established his production company Nordisk Film (originally named Ole Olsen Filmfabrik), which was responsible for the making of many silent films and later popular entertainment films such as the *Olsen Banden* collection. It is the fourth-oldest film studio in the world, after the Gaumont, Pathé and Titanus, and the oldest studio to be continuously active. Since its merger with Egmont media group in 1992, it is the largest producer and distributor of electronic entertainment in the Nordic region. Copenhagen also hosts several important annual film festivals, including the Copenhagen Film Festival (originally 2003–08, and again since 2017). Copenhagen International Film Festival existed between 2003 and 2008, and then merged with the Natfilm Festival to become known as CPH:PIX. Then there are also the CPH DOX – Documentary Film Festival (since 2003), the Short Film Festival (since 2012) and even the Copenhagen Fashion Film Festival (since 2015).

Danish cinema has a long and vibrant history thanks to early filmmakers such as Carl Theodor Dreyer (1889–1968), international film stars such as Asta Nielsen (1881–1972), who was born in Copenhagen but made 70 of her 74 films in Berlin, where she founded her own film studio and was known simply as *Die Asta* (the Asta). She became famous in part due to the popular *Konfektionskomödien* (fashion comedies), such as *Roslowsky's Mistress* (dir. Felix Basch, 1921). Cinema has always been a medium for fashion, and even early cinema manufactured desires for fashion in collaborations with fashion and entertainment magazines. As Mila Ganeva found in her research on Weimar fashion, in a 1919 interview for *Elegante Welt*, Asta Nielsen, who had just resumed filmmaking in Germany after the First World War, declared her conscious involvement in the promotion of clothes and trendy appearances, stating: "a well-made film must have the effect of a good fashion magazine" (quoted in Ganeva 2008: 114). Nielsen was an early fashion influencer, as many women tried to imitate her hair styles, shawls, tight dresses and hats, and according to director Rudolf Meinert, she had an acute sense of how colours, lines and fabrics appeared on screen and could be maximized for effect (Ganeva 2008: 114). Nielsen's contemporary, Bodil Ipsen (1889–1964), was an actress and film director, and is considered one of the greatest stars of Danish cinematic history. The Bodil Awards established in 1948, one of the oldest film prizes in Europe awarded annually by the Danish Film Critics Association in Copenhagen, are named after two of the most important actresses in Danish cinema, Bodil Ipsen and Bodil Kjer (Figure 6.1).

In the aftermath of the Second World War, Erik Balling (1924–2005) became one of the most beloved Danish filmmakers, creating iconic films such as *Olsen Banden* (1968–98) and television epics such as *Huset på Christianshavn* (1970–77), which was made into the film, *Ballade på Christianshavn* (1971) and *Matador* (1978–82). In the 1950s and 1960s, Balling filmed several romantic comedies that

FIGURE 6.1: Asta Nielsen exhibition at the Brandts Museum, Odense, 2020, photo by K. Sark.

were set in Copenhagen, including *Kispus* (1956) – the first Danish film in colour – which portrayed the city's vibrant fashion milieu. The 1960s witnessed a rapid spread of television and subsequent state financial support for the Danish film industry, which produced the Danish new wave of art films, inspired by the French New Wave. The Danish Film School was established in Copenhagen in 1966, followed by the introduction of Film Studies at the University of Copenhagen in 1967. Writing about the mod youth quake style of the 1960s, Marie Riegels Melchior described Danish fashion of that time as "casual, with simple and clean lines" and corresponding to "Danish furniture design at the time, which had already by then gained international recognition" and was known as Danish Modern (Melchior 2010). The understated and minimalist simplicity of clothing and fashion is prevalent in most Danish films from this period.

The 1970s, 1980s and 1990s were characterized by social realism. Moreover, following the legalization of pornography in Denmark in 1969 and the general lessening of film censorship, a new genre of films emerged that was known as the "sexual folk comedy," with more or less explicitly erotic content. For a short time, it created a sensation around Danish film and is the reason why in many countries "Danish films" became slang for porn. The 1990s were marked by a generational shift in Danish filmmaking. Film censorship (established in 1907) was largely abolished and transformed into labelling according to age appropriateness. The Dogme 95 Manifesto, written by Lars von Trier and Thomas Vinterberg and presented in Paris on 20 March 1995, broke with the high production values of Hollywood films to foreground more experimental film realism, which included the use of authentic locations, simultaneous recording of sound and image, handheld camera without lighting, and the rejection of any digitally enhanced post-production editing (Schepelern). *Festen* (*The Celebration* 1998) directed by Thomas Vinterberg, was the first Dogme 95 film. It launched a new avant-garde film aesthetic from Denmark and received international acclaim for its innovative auteur perspective. This dark comedy-drama won the Jury Prize at the Cannes Film Festival in 1998 and launched Vinterberg's international career. By the mid 1990s, the grunge style in music, film and fashion had evolved into "boho chic" – with the bohemian *fin de siècle* sentimentality reworked into a "hippy idiom to create a disordered appearance" (Wilson 2013: 250). The 2000s were marked by what are known as "Euro Pudding" productions (Schepelern), following the internationalization of Danish-produced, English-language films made as European co-productions with British, Swedish and German actors, as well as collaborations between different European production companies and film foundations. But the decade also produced many crime films, as well as dramas about middle-class families in suburbia, and many romantic comedies of varying quality.

Contemporary Danish cinema is known internationally, primarily through the work of innovative filmmakers such as Lars von Trier (born in Kongens Lyngby, north of Copenhagen in 1956), Susanne Bier (born in Copenhagen in 1960) and Thomas Vinterberg (born in Frederiksberg in 1969), all of whom started out as independent *auteurs* and now work both in Denmark and in Hollywood. Ironically, their Dogme 95 artistic rebellion against Hollywood aesthetics secured them successful international careers. Thomas Vinterberg was nominated for Best Director at the 2021 Academy Awards for his film *Druk* (*Another Round*, 2020), which won in the Best Foreign Film category. His lead actor Mads Mikkelsen, born in Copenhagen in 1965, who became known in Denmark for his role in Nicolas Winding Refn's *Pusher* crime trilogy (1996–2005), had his Hollywood breakthrough after being cast in *Casino Royale* (2006, dir. Martin Campbell) and *Coco Chanel & Igor Stravinsky* (2008, dir. Jan Kounen). Vinterberg is currently developing his first television project, a six-episode climate crisis series, *Families Like Ours*, which explores a near-future Denmark when the country is gradually evacuated due to rising sea levels. Prior to 2021, only three Danish films had won Academy Awards for Best Foreign Films: Gabriel Axel's *Babette's Feast* (1988), Bille August's *Pelle the Conqueror* (1989) and Susanne Bier's *Revenge* (2011).

Susanne Bier broke through in Denmark in 1999 with her dramatic comedy *Den eneste ene* (*The Only One*) with Sidse Babett Knudsen (later known for her role as the Danish Prime Minister in the TV show *Borgen*) in the lead role. The film was one of Denmark's biggest commercial successes at the box office (Schepelern) and depicts the complicated love life of two unfaithful married couples in Copenhagen faced with becoming first-time parents. The film marked a modern transition in Danish romantic comedies and received both the Robert and Bodil Awards as the best film of 1999. After the international success of Susanne Bier's *After the Wedding* (*Efter brylluppet*) in 2006, also with Mads Mikkelsen, which was nominated for Best Foreign Film but lost to Florian Henckel von Donnersmarck's *The Lives of Others* (2006), she also worked on the script for the Hollywood remake of her film directed by Bart Freundlich in 2019, making the women (played by Michelle Williams and Julianne Moore) the main protagonists. In the past few years, Bier has directed internationally acclaimed productions, including BBC's *The Night Manager* in 2016, Netflix's *Birdbox* with Sandra Bullock in 2018 and HBO Max' *The Undoing* with Nicole Kidman in 2020. Denmark has a long tradition of female filmmakers, including Alice O'Fredericks, Bodil Ipsen and Astrid Henning-Jensen as the veterans, followed by Helle Ryslinge, Jytte Rex, Linda Wendel, Lone Scherfig, Susanne Bier, Lotte Svendsen, Hella Joof, Annette K. Olesen, Charlotte Sieling, Pernille Fischer Christensen, Christina Rosendahl and May el-Toukhy, among others. Moreover, the Danish Film Institute continuously collaborates with the industry to "create greater diversity in Danish film" (Schepelern).

Copenhagen has been the location for many Danish and international film productions. According to IMDB, 1983 films, including short films, have been filmed there to date, but not all of them were set in the city. The city is featured most prominently in the titular *Copenhagen* (dir. Mark Raso, 2014), an independent US-Canadian drama-comedy about 28-year-old American William, who, while travelling in Europe with his best friend, meets a 14-year-old Danish girl, Effy, who works in a café and agrees to show him the city by bike, and over the course of a few days William also discovers his family's difficult past. This film is distinct from Danish films about Copenhagen as many foreign productions often perpetuate a tourist gaze on the city and its inhabitants. In terms of fashion, the casual look of jeans and t-shirts marks the daily attire of young people who need unpretentious, practical clothes to move around in the city, often on bike, because bicycle culture in old and new Copenhagen films is part of the inhabitants' identity. Most contemporary films set in Copenhagen confirm Marie Riegels Melchior's finding that "casual wear is [still] the norm" (Melchior 2010).

The urban crime films *Pusher* (1996), *Pusher II* (2004) and *Pusher III* (2005) were all directed by Nicolas Winding Refn, who was born in Copenhagen in 1970 and currently enjoys a successful Hollywood career. The trilogy explores the dark underground drug world of Copenhagen that was not visible to everyone. Refn, a film school dropout and the son of Danish film director and editor Anders Refn and cinematographer Vibeke Winding, wanted to break with the norms of filmmaking of the 1990s, hiring unknown actors, such as Mads Mikkelsen and Kim Bodnia, who also wanted change rather than fame (Kofod 2016), which ironically made them very famous in Denmark and beyond. The clothing styles of the main characters in the three films include track suits, leather jackets and gold chains, while animal prints are used to emphasize the raw attitude and carry strong working-class connotations. To achieve maximum authenticity, Refn and screenwriter Jens Dahl visited the Copenhagen underworld and talked to drug dealers and sex workers in Vesterbro, around Vesterbrogade and Istedgade, a neighbourhood next to the main train station that, before gentrification, used to have many strip clubs, porn shops and ethnic restaurants (Kofod 2016). The films achieved cult status, especially in Copenhagen, shining a light on its notorious nightlife and sparking a fascination with its underground counterculture.

Other films we found with connections to Copenhagen that we did not select as case studies include *Smilla's Sense of Snow* (dir. Bille August, 1997), which starts in Copenhagen and ends in Greenland. Howard Davies' television film *Copenhagen* (2002) is an adaptation of Michael Frayn's award-winning stage play about the meeting between the physicists Niels Bohr and Werner Heisenberg in 1941 in Copenhagen at which they discuss their research in nuclear energy, but the whole film takes place indoors. *Anja and Viktor* (dir. Charlotte Sachs Bostrup, 2001, 2003, 2008) is about two high school sweethearts who move to Copenhagen together to start their careers, and, in the later films, start a family together. The films also achieved cult status in Denmark, encouraging viewers to take stylistic inspiration from the films' 1990s fashion (Lindqvist 2019), especially the overload of pastel colours. The films' one-liners and quotes entered the daily vernacular of its viewers.

No history of Copenhagen film and fashion would be complete without mentioning the work of its most prolific and award-winning costume designer, Manon Rasmussen (born 1951 in Horsens), who has created costumes for 85 feature films (Danish and international), and has been nominated for 34 costume awards, winning 18 (including 15 Robert Awards) to date. She originally studied acting with the Solvognen theatre group and then began designing costumes in 1976 during her time at Københavns Tilskæreakademi (Copenhagen Tailoring Academy). In the late 1970s, she made and sold clothes through the collective shop Elverhøj. She started out as an assistant to costume designer Gitte Kolvig and in 1978 worked as a costume assistant on Anders Refn's historical film *The Family*, which launched her long career making costumes for film and television. She has worked closely with renowned Danish film directors, including Thomas

Vinterberg, Bille August, Susanne Bier and Lars von Trier. Her costume work on historical films and her close collaboration with actors have received particular recognition. "The clothing must support the psychological character of the protagonist, but at the same time it must be so discreet that it does not distract," she explained to the *Berlingske Tidende* newspaper in 2009 (quoted on the DFI website). Most of the films in our analysis feature her costumes, highlighting the close interconnections between the individual characters, their urban cultural settings and social class, and the role fashion plays in constructing personal and cultural development.

Historical films

Many historical films set in Copenhagen focus on important turning points in Danish history, usually involving social reforms, struggles for economic improvement, self-actualization or social mobility. Issues of class are at the forefront of these historical narratives, made visible through the protagonists' choice of clothing and their access (or lack thereof) to fashion and fashionable items. We focused our analysis on various cinematic examples in which class- and gender-coded clothing and fashion have been used as tools of transgression or social mobility. They provide a glimpse into the changing history of the city and its fashion. They address challenging social transformations and often focus on protagonists who stand out. In these films, clothing and fashion are often used as tools for marking inequalities and making differences visible. They present Copenhagen as progressive and open, despite its class restrictions, inequalities, lack of diversity and many other social problems. These films construct a cinematic portrait of Copenhagen as it evolved into a cosmopolitan, modernizing and gentrifying city. The films selected here are presented in chronological order of the historical period they portray. We also added contextual details from our research that help make broader thematic connections to the other chapters in this book.

En kongelig affære (*A Royal Affair*, 2012)

En kongelig affære, directed by Danish filmmaker and screen writer Nikolaj Arcel, takes place in the eighteenth century, when Denmark began implementing social reforms. The film is set mainly in Copenhagen at Christiansborg Castle (which burned down in 1794 – the current one, which today houses the Danish Parliament and was popularized by the TV show *Borgen*, was not completed until 1928). The film portrays a love triangle between King Christian VII (played by the Danish actor Mikkel Boe Følsgaard), his Queen Caroline Mathilde of England (played by the Swedish actor Alicia Vikander) and Christian's German doctor Johann Friedrich Struensee (played by Mads Mikkelsen), who becomes his advisor on matters of state. Struensee and Caroline Mathilde get involved romantically and set out to diminish the influence of the Danish aristocracy and launch social reforms by manipulating King Christian, who is mentally ill. However, the courtiers oppose these changes and regain power over the king and the country. The film gained wide international acclaim, including two Silver Bears at the Berlin International Film Festival, and was nominated for Best Foreign Language Film at the Academy Awards.

The clothing in the film highlights the aristocratic fashion of the eighteenth-century European royalty and courtiers' conspicuous consumption – a way of using fashion to symbolize status and wealth. Particularly the *robe à la Piémontaise* was popular among European aristocrats in the 1780s because of its elaborate use of expensive fabrics and because it showed off skin around the chest and neck. Originally popularized by aristocrats from the region of Piedmont, it was adopted as a fashion item by the French Queen Marie Antoinette, before spreading through the royal houses of Europe. Caroline Mathilde of England is thus positioned as a trendsetter when she arrives in Denmark for marriage. Her clothes distinguish her not only as European royalty but also as fashionable and progressive. Aristocratic women's clothing at this time was not meant to be practical, but on the contrary, it was designed to be decorative and designate women's status as displays of their family's wealth, leisure and access to the most fashionable styles and fabrics. The men in the film wear wigs, waistcoats, large lace cuffs and breeches with white stockings. Their clothes are also very ornate to show off their wealth and social status. The courtiers are visually distinctive in their use of jewellery, lace, decorative embellishments and upscale hairstyles. By comparison, Struensee dresses very humbly in brown and black suits, with no embellishments, which reflects his reformist mind-set and his push for social change. Despite Caroline Mathilde's involvement with Struensee and her support of welfare reforms, her royal elite wardrobe does not change throughout the film. She remains sartorially grounded in her position as Queen and trendsetter (Figures 6.2 and 6.3).

Another interesting finding was that copies of the original film costumes (designed by Manon Rasmussen) were displayed at the Koldinghus, a 750-year-old royal castle, originally founded by Christoffer I in 1268, and restored to function as a museum, during an exhibition entitled "Klæder skaber film" (Garments Create Films) that was on display from 21 October 2013 to 12 January 2014. The connection to Kolding Castle was interesting because Queen Caroline Mathilde stayed there for one night when she arrived in Denmark and King Christian also lived there for some time. The film costumes were again displayed outside the

FIGURE 6.2: Costume workshop at Koldinghus, 2020, photo by K. Sark.

FIGURE 6.3: Copies of the original costumes from *A Royal Affair* (2012) on display at Koldinghus, 2020, photo by K. Sark.

in-house costume workshop at the Koldinghus during Jim Lyngvild's exhibition of "Kongerækken" (the "Kings and Queens of Denmark"), and when the exhibition moved to Kronborg Castle north of Copenhagen in 2021, there was a special focus on Caroline Mathilde (Figure 6.4).

FIGURE 6.4: Koldinghus, 2019, photo by K. Sark.

Unge Andersen (Young Andersen, 2005)

Unge Andersen, directed by Rumle Hammerich, examines the teenage years of Hans Christian Andersen (HCA), who arrives in Copenhagen as a teenager to become a famous writer. The film opens with young HCA on his way to an upper-class party to show his new play to an influential patron. However, he is not welcomed into Copenhagen's high society, despite his friendship with a young woman who invites him. The rich men at the party call him a "country lad" and tell him to go back to work the "turnip fields" rather than write because he is rumoured to be "a failure as a singer, dancer, actor, and writer." HCA, the son of a poor shoemaker from Odense (Figure 6.5), stands out at the party because of his poor, shabby, dirty, old clothes – he clearly does not fit in among the well-dressed upper classes and cannot afford new clothes. However, the powerful State Councillor Collin offers to send young Andersen to the Slagelse Latin School, a boarding school run by the corrupt and abusive teacher, Meisling. There HCA encounters abuse and injustice but also discovers the gifts of friendship and the resilience of creativity against all odds. At the boarding school, Meisling asks the students in the geography class what the centre of the world is, implying magma, and HCA replies, Copenhagen because of its theatres, concerts and writers. Such remarks, along with his persistence in writing poetry, unleash the wrath and violence Meisling employs to quash his students' imaginations,

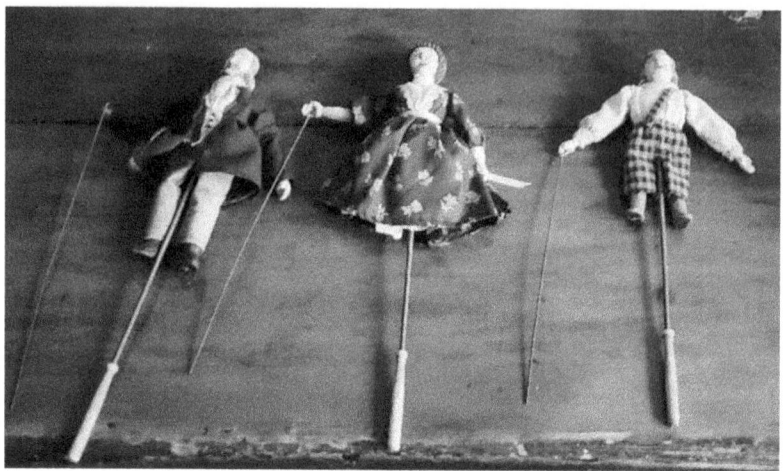

FIGURE 6.5: Dolls at HCA Childhood Home in Odense, 2021, photo by K. Sark.

which he equates with madness. But ultimately, through this formative and painful journey, HCA develops his poetic voice, confidence and talent as a storyteller.

Filmed in Gl. Færgestræde, an old street in the centre of Helsingør, north of Copenhagen, known as the location of Hamlet's Elsinore Castle, the old streets served as the historical backdrop for early nineteenth-century Copenhagen. The second boarding school to which Andersen and Meisling are transferred because of Andersen's letters of complaint is also in Helsingør (Figure 6.6), and we see Hamlet's castle just before HCA is about to jump into the sea in a desperate attempt to drown himself. Yet he emerges from the magical depth of the waters as a storyteller who can finally stand up to Meisling – his worst critic and tormentor – and thus liberate himself from his power through creativity.

The film won a Robert Award for best costumes (also designed by Manon Rasmussen) in 2006. The clothes in the film serve to clearly distinguish the upper and lower classes, which at that time also denoted the rural lifestyle of the poor and the urban life of the rich in Copenhagen. But the post-Napoleonic fashion of the 1820s – with cotton dresses, and cashmere shawls, and dropped waists and corsets instead of the girlish Empire waists, as well as the influence of the Industrial Revolution's mechanized cotton production in Europe – is apparent not only in the styles of the upper-class women's dresses but also in the ways fashion styles trickled down to the working classes. In the countryside, Meisling's wife wears white cotton dresses with low necklines, cone-shaped

FIGURE 6.6: Helsingør castle, north of Copenhagen, 2019, photo by K. Sark.

skirts, pinched sleeves and woolen shawls. Most men wore three-piece suits, ties, Garrick overcoats and Wellington high boots. It is the quality and vibrancy of the fabrics, attention to details and the use of accessories and jewellery that primarily distinguish the fashion of the upper classes and allow the wearer to be instantly decoded based on social class and position. When Andersen finally becomes famous through his fairy tales and plays at the end of the film, his clothes become more refined, better made and expensive. And so, clothing remained as the main marker of class and social position well into the twentieth century.

Lykke Per (*A Fortunate Man*, 2018)

Lykke Per is based on a turn-of-the-century, semi-autobiographical novel by the Danish Nobel-Prize winning author Henrik Pontoppidan (1857–1943), which was adapted by the Danish filmmaker Bille August. It takes place at the end of the nineteenth century and offers a glimpse into both the Danish countryside in Jutland and life in the capital city, as the protagonist is a 16-year-old teenager, who leaves his hometown, family and the expectations of becoming a local priest and moves to Copenhagen to study engineering instead. The film is set in the years 1898–1904, during Denmark's industrialization, when the distinctions between the living conditions in the countryside and in the city became even more apparent. It was a time of development and innovation resulting in shifts in social structures. Copenhagen is positioned as a more elitist part of

Denmark, but not unattainable if you work hard enough, as Per did. The film follows Per's social development, as he encounters women and men from different classes and becomes a gifted engineer, who wants to modernize Jutland and create economic growth with an energy project. Through his work, he meets the rich Jewish Solomon family, and their very independent daughter Jakobe. They finance his trip abroad to further develop his project, but the shadows from his past haunt and confuse him. The name *Lykke-Per* was given to him by his friend Fritjof Salomon, based on the folktale about a tender pig, who has been promised the princess and half the kingdom, but does not end up getting anything. Per cannot liberate himself from the religious shackles of his past and settle into the cosmopolitan and modern life he envisions for himself. The film ends with Per overlooking the ocean on the west coast of Jutland, on the opposite side of Denmark.

The film costumes (designed by Manon Rasmussen) highlight the class differences between the lower and upper classes but also the elements that both classes have in common due to the increasing mass production of clothing, such as men's shirts, vests and suits. It shows how the lower classes tried to imitate upper-class fashion, in the trickle-down effect of fashion. The fabrics worn by the lower classes are presented as worn-out from continuous use and have a brown colour palette for practical reasons, being less noticeable when stained or unwashed. The women in the lower classes have simpler clothing and more practical hairstyles while the upper-class women have more colourful clothes with ruffles, hats, gloves, jewellery, makeup and more elaborate hairstyles. The upper-class men have nicer suits with prints, accessories such as handkerchiefs, cufflinks, hats and golden buttons on their vests and gelled hairstyles. Through its costumes, the film sets up a clear dichotomy not only between the different urban classes but also between people from the countryside, who try to imitate the more refined styles from the city, signifying the ways in which class and prosperity have great significance for identities, behaviours, social interactions and careers. The clothing is used to indicate the parts of society Per moves through, and as he moves up, so does his clothing. In the beginning, he wears worn-out clothes in earth tones. Later in the film, he wears formal clothing with brighter colours and more refined fabrics, but the film ends with him clothed in darker clothes that resemble the practical clothing from the beginning, as he moves back to Jutland. As modernization and industrialization brought with it alienation from communities, religion and direct ties to the land that families had worked on for their daily food, textiles, furniture and other basic necessities for generations, the move away from commodifying Copenhagen also signifies a way of reconnecting with the traditions and practices that tend to go lost in rapid urbanization, industrialization and modernization.

The Danish Girl (2015)

Based on a true story, *The Danish Girl* is directed by British-Australian filmmaker Tom Hooper and takes place in Copenhagen in 1926. Partially filmed on location, we get a glimpse of the Royal Theatre, fish markets at Nyhavn, art galleries, department stores and other streets in the city centre. Based on a true story, it depicts the life of a transwoman, Lili Elbe, who became the first transgender person to undergo gender reassignment surgery in 1930 in Dresden. The film is inspired by the lives of the Danish painters Lili Elbe (played by Eddie Redmayne) and her wife Gerda Wegener (played by Alicia Vikander), after they met at the Royal Danish Academy of Fine Arts in Copenhagen and married in their early twenties. Gerda was an illustrator for books and fashion magazines, and in the film, we see her continuous support of Lili through her transition and until the end of Lili's life. Copenhagen is presented as an artistic city, with a vibrant creative class of artists, painters, performers and actors collaborating and supporting each other. In terms of social progress in gender equality, in 1929, Denmark adopted one of the first gender change laws in the world and de-criminalized same-sex sexual activity in 1933. Later, it became the first country in the world to grant legal recognition to same-sex partnerships in 1989. Discrimination on the grounds of sexual orientation was prohibited in 1996. Moreover, the scientific research on gender and sexuality conducted by the German physician and sexologist Magnus Hirschfeld in the 1920s at his *Institut für Sexualwissenschaft* in Berlin was ground-breaking but was destroyed in 1933 when the Nazis came to power, burned his books and forced him into exile in France, where he died in 1935. In the film, Copenhagen, Paris and Germany are presented as progressive and creative spaces on the cusp of the rise of fascism, where creative people could still self-actualize both through their work and their identities. After her transition in Germany, Lili, along with Gerda, returns to Copenhagen.

The film costumes, designed by the Spanish costume designer, Paco Delgado, who is known for his work with Pedro Almodóvar and on other Tom Hooper films, showcase both the everyday style and the more avant-garde fashion of the 1920s and were nominated for an Oscar. At the beginning of the film, Lili dresses in men's clothing in a blue, grey and black palette to show that she felt trapped in a male body. As the film progresses, Lili and Gerda move to Paris, where Lili begins to experience a new kind of freedom of expression, symbolized by more avant-garde and feminine fashion with flowing materials and warm colours. Although Copenhagen is presented as progressive, Paris is more cosmopolitan and provides more anonymity. Copenhagen is a relatively small metropolis with a small artistic circle where everyone knows each other. Paris symbolizes the modernity, diversity and creativity of the 1920s. The film's costumes take inspiration from Paul Poiret,

Lanvin and Coco Chanel with her more freeing and athletic fashion that defined Paris couture at that time. The scarf Lili wears is also a prop to hide her Adam's apple. Lili and Gerda often share scarves, which symbolizes their closeness. Both Lili and Gerda cut their hair short according to the latest flapper style, and their dresses change from having a turn-of-the-century, hour-glass shape to modern straight cuts with shorter skirts – they both actively follow the fashion trends and use them to express their femininity, modernity and individuality. They are also both artists who understand aesthetics and culture and use it to shape their work, art and fashionability. Lili and Gerda belong to the upper class, which allows them to follow the latest Parisian trends. During the Great Depression, when many people were losing jobs and currencies were losing value, the two protagonists had privileged access to couture, parties and art that was not accessible to most people. Both Copenhagen and Paris represent the cultural and aesthetic modernity of the roaring twenties and allow the protagonists to express their creativity through fashion.

Kispus (1956)

Directed by Erik Balling, one of the most prolific Danish post-war film and television directors, *Kispus* was the first Danish film made in colour. It depicts post-Second World War Copenhagen as a modern fashion city with a vibrant couture and ready-to-wear industry. The main protagonist is Eva Møller (played by Helle Virkner), a young working-class seamstress who works in a sewing studio in Christianshavn in Copenhagen's city centre. One day after work as she is walking home, she sees a couture gown in a store window at Gammel Strand, in the atelier of the fashion couturier Marcel (played by Angelo Bruun), based on the famous Copenhagen designer Holger Blom (1906–65). Eva enters the store and tries on the gown, which she cannot afford. Marcel (whose real name in the film is Marius) is gay and is positioned in the narrative as a fairy godmother with magical powers to transform through fashion. When he sees Eva in his gown, he feels inspired to start creating a new collection, and after a whole night's work gives her the gown as a present. In a Cinderella-esque fashion, the dress brings about change in Eva's life. She meets the good-looking Jakob (played by Henning Moritzen) but is scared that he will discover her real (class) identity and reject her because he drives a fancy car and appears to be wealthy. In reality, Jakob turns out to be a poor student who lives in Vesterbro, works as a chauffeur, and has to sell his books to take her out on a date at a fancy French restaurant. He is also scared that Eva will discover his humble social background, so they both continue pretending. The dress Eva received from Marcel was actually designed for an actress named Elisabeth, who lives in the rich neighbourhood of Strandvejen, and who exposes Eva out of spite. Meanwhile, Marcel invites Eva to participate in his new fashion show. After graduation, Jakob is determined to win Eva back. She runs into him at Nyhavn riding a cargo bicycle (a Copenhagen staple) and wearing a black-and-white graduation hat, a tradition that dates back to the 1850s in the Nordic countries (Figure 6.7).

In this comedy of errors and modern fairy tale, Copenhagen couture plays a transformative role as a symbol of the modern urban economy and social mobility. Copenhagen is positioned as a post-war cultural center, with luxuries like couture and French cuisine available to people with disposable incomes. Here, too, Paris lingers in the Danish imaginary as the production centre of luxury food, fashion, trends and cultural capital. The places where the protagonists live in Copenhagen designate their social position in society, but neither their work nor their clothes make it easy to discern their social backgrounds, class or career ambitions. They are members of the post-Second World War generation of baby boomers, for whom upward mobility was not only accessible through clothing but

FIGURE 6.7: Danish graduation hat, photo by Izabella Andersen.

also through the rapid modernization of Denmark. The gown that Marcel gives to Eva was inspired by Christian Dior's New Look, which became a sensation around the world in 1947 and defined the fashion silhouette of the 1950s. After years of fabric shortages, pragmatic masculine or unisex work wear, recycled or upcycled home-sewn clothes, and a general lack of luxury fashion items during the war years, the New Look came to symbolize post-war economic miracles in Europe and North America, a return to hyper-femininity in women's wear, and the return of disposable incomes and conspicuous consumption for the upper classes. The New Look was characterized by excessive fabric usage for full skirts, an emphasis on small waists, rounded soft shoulders and rounded hips – almost returning to the hourglass-shaped figure but with modern updates and shorter skirts. The couture gown that transforms Eva's life is a visible contrast to the dark uniform she wears at work in the sewing studio, indistinguishable from the other seamstresses, and to the blouse and skirt she wears at home. Colour is used to establish the sartorial contrast between Eva's two identities as a working-class seamstress and her new identity as a model in Marcel's colourful gowns. Modelling Marcel's couture designs is presented as her path to social mobility, despite the fact that she does not find a rich husband in Jacob. The use of colour in the film is another nod to post-war modernity: it is not a coincidence that the first Danish film made in colour is about the fashion industry, symbolizing the post-war modernization of its manufacturing sector. Most of the men in the film wear white shirts and ties, grey trousers and suits or tuxedos, while the women are dressed in different day or evening dresses. Fashion as a transformative commodity reorganized post-Second World War society, as the Danish textile and ready-to-wear manufacturing industry was being established in Herning in Jutland, while Copenhagen was becoming the capital of fashion salons, trade shows and couturiers.

The film is an homage to the Copenhagen fashion milieu of the 1950s. Eva's ex-fiancé works at a clothing and lingerie store, where she catches him kissing another woman. Eva works as a seamstress in the city centre, where she and many other women sit behind sewing machines all day. Marcel is presented as the Copenhagen couturier of the post-war era. Eva's sister-in-law Joan has a sewing machine at home (Figure 6.8) and dreams of making a fancy gown for herself – the omni-presence of the making, selling and buying of clothing, fashion and couture are presented as part of the everyday life, economy and culture in Copenhagen at this time, positioning the city as a fashion centre. The upper-class ladies invited to Marcel's salon fashion shows wear big fur coats, sip sherry, smoke cigarettes and eat pastries, as Marcel shows his new gowns on live models. Marcel's queerness is downplayed by his professional attire of grey suits, white shirts and black ties. With the exception of his silk scarfs, his queer identity remains under wraps. Instead, he pours his creativity into colourful gowns for his female clients. Marcel's final fashion show takes place

FIGURE 6.8: Old sewing machine, Tidens Samling Museum, Odense, 2020, photo by K. Sark.

at the fancy French restaurant where Eva's brother works as a waiter, and where Jacob took Eva on their first date. Eva models Marcel's new collection, including a wedding gown for the finale. When Jacob arrives to win her over, he tells the waiter who informs him there are no more tables available at the restaurant during the fashion show: "Je suis Christian Dior!" In the last scene of the film, Jacob takes Eva on his cargo bike to his tiny attic apartment, riding along the Hans Christian Andersen Boulevard in the centre of Copenhagen (Figure 6.9). In his apartment, they begin to kiss and undress on his couch, and it is implied that they live happily ever after. The film is quite progressive for its time and a testament to the city's fashion culture.

FIGURE 6.9: HCA Boulevard, Copenhagen, 2010, photo by K. Sark.

Olsen Banden (The Olsen Gang, 1968–98)

Olsen Banden, also created by Erik Balling, is a collection of fourteen "folk comedy" films that depict the working classes of Copenhagen in the late 1960s, 1970s and 1980s before the city was gentrified. It centres on a criminal gang comprised of Egon, Benny and Kjeld, whose criminal pursuit of wealth, prosperity and social mobility is always brought to an end. Egon Olsen sees himself as a criminal mastermind, developing new criminal plans each time he gets arrested and spends time in prison. Each film starts with Egon's prison release, followed by making new plans in the living room of Kjeld and Yvonne's dilapidated home in the rundown Valby neighbourhood on the outskirts of Copenhagen. Egon's friends faithfully follow his plans and never give up hope of becoming millionaires, no matter how many times things go wrong. Interestingly, the main antagonists are not the police but other criminals, who usually manage to outwit the gang, leaving them with nothing, and so each film starts with a new criminal adventure in pursuit of wealth. We also meet the police detective Mortensen, who provides slapstick comic relief in the early films and usually gets Egon back into prison. In the first film, from 1968, Mortensen investigates a sex shop that sells pornographic materials. Pornography was legalized in 1969 in Denmark, just a year after the first film came out. Several of the early films play with a new genre that emerged after the decriminalization of pornography, *Sengekantsfilm* (bedside films), with suggestive sexuality represented by provocatively clad women but never addressed explicitly. Kjeld is a family man with a wife and a son, whom he often brings along on his capers because he and Yvonne share parental duties. His wife Yvonne has expensive tastes and habits, such as buying a fridge and a television set on credit in the first film, that fuel their desire to become rich. She is often sceptical of their plans and is usually the first to get angry when everything falls apart. Some of the luxury items that Yvonne and the gang aspire to include trips to Mallorca, a white mink coat for Yvonne, a new convertible for Benny and a model train set for Kjeld. But they rarely retain any of their stolen riches, as they are outsmarted by other criminals, who are presented as more sophisticated and in luxurious surroundings, such as a modern hotel suite at the Sheraton-Copenhagen, outfitted in Danish designer furniture and lamps (perhaps a nod to Arne Jacobsen's total design of the Royal Copenhagen Hotel). The films depict the post-Second World War struggle for upward mobility from the comedic and ironizing perspective of small criminals who never make it big (Lindberg 2018).

In the early films of the late 1960s, Copenhagen still looks very grey, shabby and not yet refurbished. Many of the buildings, especially in the industrial harbour, are dilapidated ruins, while others, like the Copenhagen Airport, are modern and new. The early films also show many sex shops, half-naked women and nude magazines and posters, which became less frequent in the later films to suit younger audiences. By the mid 1970s, the streets of Copenhagen begin to look more cosmopolitan and stylish, with women in colourful mini dresses on bicycles and on the sidewalks. The third film from 1971, entitled *The Olsen Gang in Jutland*, presents the humorous contrast between city dwellers and people from Jutland's west coast. The film's irony is communicated through its choice of clothing, as the Copenhageners wear the smartest clothes they can get, while the simply clad country folk are in fact the sneaky ones with all the money and trick them in the end. It is also hard to forget Yvonne's iconic response when the Olsen gang suggest that she joins them on the trip to Jutland, and she asks, "go abroad!?" This reveals the show's (and Copenhageners') attitudes towards the rest of Denmark. By 1977, Yvonne becomes a feminist and makes Kjeld do all the housework, while she is getting her drivers' licence. The 1979 film features an automated Lego vehicle and a robot as a prop in a break-in – an effective advertisement for the Danish toy brand. In the same episode, the gang plans to steal shares Magasin du Nord (Figure 6.10), Copenhagen's oldest department store in Kongens Nytorv (since 1879). Before they can even begin with their plans, Yvonne instantly begins planning to get new furniture and new clothes from Magasin – her ambitions and spending habits are always one step ahead of what the gang can actually accomplish.

By the 1980s, Copenhagen was visibly transformed into a cosmopolitan center for culture, commerce and fashion trends. The city was urbanized with international hotel chains such as Scandinavian Air Lines (SAS) and graffiti that reads "Travolta kids." While Yvonne and Egon pretend to be chamber maids in the new SAS Hotel Scandinavia, Egon cross-dresses as a woman. The last film, made in 1998, shows how the three friends have been separated for many years, have grown considerably older, but meet by chance and plan one last coup together. Difficulties arose as Poul Bundgaard, the actor portraying Kjeld, died during the filming. The producers had to think creatively, choosing to finish the film anyway, with Tommy Kenter made up to resemble Kjeld in some of the scenes as a stand-in (DR).

The costumes of the main characters are the most iconic part of the films, as the three main protagonists are presented as archetypes rather than a reflection of fashionable practices. They always wear the same outfits for comedic effect. As stereotypes, aspects of their dress draw on the conventions of Danish folk comedies from the 1920s and 1930s. Egon Olsen is relatively short compared to Benny and Kjeld and can be recognized by his pinstriped, brown suit, yellow shirt, flowery tie, bowler hat and the cigar in his mouth. Benny is the tall, thin one

FIGURE 6.10: Magasin du Nord in Copenhagen, 2010, photo by K. Sark.

with a very characteristic giggle. He wears a chequered brown blazer, a red turtleneck (and later a pink shirt with a yellow tie), brown pants, a threadbare hat and most importantly bright yellow socks and brown leather shoes. He represents the clown of the group. Kjeld is overweight and wears glasses, a brown velvet jacket over a white (later light blue) shirt with a bow tie, grey trousers, a grey cap and white shoes, and he usually carries a brown leather bag containing the tools for their break-ins. Yvonne follows the latest fashion trends and wears colourful minidresses, large clip-on earrings, geometric Vidal Sassoon-inspired coiffed hairstyles and oversized hats. Her most iconic outfit is a hot pink dress with a giant matching pink hat, decorated with white daisies. She is often dressed in bright pink, salad green, crisp yellow and orange, colours typical for the 1970s. The police detective Mortensen wears large, thick-rimmed glasses, a checkered brown suit with capri pants and dark long socks, leather shoes, a white shirt with cuff links and a striped tie. The characters' clothes reflect their aspirations to rise above their class. Ironically, their fashion-forward outfits, which represented stylish, avant-garde fashion in the late 1960s and 1970s, became caricature-esque over the course of the show, as the characters' clothing froze in time, while their urban and social milieu evolved. Their clothes became a trope for the protagonists' never-ending comedic attempts and aspirations to become millionaires and live a life of leisure, but when they briefly get their hands on a briefcase full of money and manage to escape to a villa with a pool in Spain, they soon get bored and want to go home and get a job, and then lose the money. Thus, their unchanging clothes can be interpreted as the visual representation of their continuous, and often parodic and absurd aspirations to become millionaires, that never succeed.

Lille Spejl (*Mirror Mirror*, 1978)

Lille Spejl (literally, *Little Mirror*), directed by the Danish filmmaker Edward Fleming, was the first Danish film with an openly gay main protagonist. Set in the Copenhagen queer and working-class community of the late 1970s, the film portrays a gay factory worker, Bent (played by Frits Helmuth), who has a complicated relationship with his mother Gloria Gibson (played by the famous Bodil Kjer), a failed cabaret dancer who has always wanted a daughter. Bent lives in a small apartment in a rundown, working-class neighbourhood in Copenhagen, in a building managed by his gay friend Sandra (Preben Kaas), who creates a supportive community for diverse characters. Gurli (Margrethe Koytu), a sex worker, lives upstairs and other neighbours are gays and drag queens. The characters often meet for tea and dinners in Sandra's large apartment. In Denmark, the 1970s witnessed an opening of cultural mores, which is reflected in the film's celebration of diversity, making this one of the pioneering films in queer film history. When Bent's mother becomes terminally ill, he has to take care of her. During one of his visits, she reminisces about the past while putting makeup on both herself and Bent, and, with the help of a red wig, she makes herself look like her younger self, as she appears on the poster next to her bed. Her small attic apartment is decorated with theatre props, red velvet curtains, a throne armchair and a giant bed. Bent begins to renovate his tiny apartment to resemble his mother's, including a giant bed that take up most of the space.

The film depicts Bent's struggles as a caregiver living without money and unsuccessfully exploring the gay dating scene of the late 1970s. Much of the action takes place at a local queer bar, where the occupants of the house come to party and pick up potential partners; as well as at the corner store and the neighbourhood pub, where Bent's friends work. Bent openly flirts with all men, including the university student Conny, who moves into a spare room in Sandra's large apartment and who is more interested in Gurli, as well as with the local grocer Tom, which does not go over well with Tom's pregnant wife Else. Dating life for both the queer characters and for Gurli is not always presented as safe and is at times marked by violence, while Copenhagen queer life and culture is portrayed as rather eccentric. The film culminates with the protagonists going to a drag ball with cabaret and drag performances on stage. Bent's drag is an homage to his mother Gloria, using the same makeup and red wig she used to wear as a cabaret dancer and wearing a lavender gown he repurposed from a vintage dress from the neighbourhood antique shop.

The 1970s in fashion were marked by ready-to-wear fashion sold in boutiques, mod street styles and the beginnings of rebellious counterculture styles, which eventually culminated in punk aesthetics. The film costumes were designed by Keld Rex Holm and Ulla-Britt Söderlund. Brown, beige, orange and yellow colours of the 1970s characterize the style of the film. Whether in the street scenes, in the hospital or at the corner store, the men wear shirts, trousers and wool blazers with either brown or chequered patterns. The women wear flowery dresses. But at the queer bar and at the drag ball they, dress up in elaborate pastel-coloured gowns, large fur coats, wigs and costume jewellery. The theatricality of their drag costumes pays homage to Hollywood celebrities such as Marilyn Monroe and Bob Fosse's *Cabaret* (1972). The drag ball is a free, inclusive and vibrant space to dress up and celebrate diversity. Their drag costumes signal aspirational wealth by trying to make cheap clothes look expensive. As Bent says about his mother's possessions to an antique dealer who tells him that none of them are real or worth anything: "well, for her it was real [...] and that's what matters." Thus, the performative and aspirational role of fashion outweighs its practical or social restrictions and becomes a tool of authentic self-expression and desire, rather than a traditional marker of class or gender. In the final dramatic scene, after the drunken party night following the drag ball and another failed attempt to find a meaningful connection with a date, Bent is shamed for his appearance and lifestyle choices by his friend Tom and walks to his mother's apartment only to see her old furniture being thrown onto a truck to be discarded. Bent gets up onto the truck and sits on her throne armchair and is driven through the streets of Copenhagen imagining himself dressed as a queen and waving to the neighbourhood inhabitants and friends. Thus, the transformative power of drag here has a similar effect as couture did in *Kispus*, allowing the characters to dream themselves out of their social and emotional circumstances. In 1984, the BENT Award was inaugurated by MIX Copenhagen (Bentprisen website), named after the main protagonist and awarded to films and TV series for authentic portrayals of gay, bisexual and transgender people.

Contemporary films

Since the early 2000s, Copenhagen went through extensive gentrification, barely escaping bankruptcy of the 1980s and 1990s, and transforming into one of Europe's most innovative design hubs, architectural and culinary attractions, and a city that focuses on innovation. In contrast to the films presented in the historical section, contemporary Danish films set in Copenhagen reverse the traditional codes of trickle-down styles and break down the boundaries between street style and couture, casual and formal wear, as well as who has access to what type of fashion. In fact, the way clothing and fashion are used in *The Model* (2016), *In the Blood* (2016), *Darkland* (2017) and *Druk* (2020) reveals that contemporary life in present-day Copenhagen is not easy to decode through sartorial codes of conspicuous consumption and that members of different classes can mix their wardrobes with a postmodern pastiche of cheap and expensive, elegant and careless, practical and impractical, luxury and fast fashion, without revealing too much about their social background or identities. The lifestyle of young people in the capital is not as romanticized as it was in Erik Balling's romantic comedies of the 1950s and 1960s or in Susanne Bier's relationship dramas of the 1990s. Recent films also show what we describe as the dark side of hygge culture, based on exclusion due to either social or ethnic backgrounds or various types of addiction. A focus on young people struggling with their identities, relationships, belonging and their place in the contemporary city and economy is particularly strong. The Nordic Noir crime genre also touches on the dark side of urban life in Copenhagen, exposing the social and economic problems of class and race, and the dark side of social marginalization, criminality and addiction in the land of hygge. The films selected for analysis are presented in the chronological order of their release and provide a glimpse into gentrified Copenhagen through its fashion.

The Model (2016)

The Model, directed by Mads Matthiesen, is about 16-year-old Emma from Copenhagen, who moves to Paris for modelling work, where she is immediately confronted with the harsh, exploitative reality of the contemporary fashion world. Her efforts to connect emotionally with a photographer fail and force her onto a destructive path of lies, sex and drugs to maintain a hold on her career and personal life. Again, Paris in the Danish imaginary is a stand-in for glamour, fashion, luxury, opportunity and a more *laissez-faire* lifestyle; but unlike its trendsetting modernity in the 1920s and the 1950s, contemporary Paris is presented as a treacherous, exploitative and unromantic place, far from Danish hygge, coziness and comforts. The juxtaposition between Paris as the capitalist metropolis that exploits and traumatizes its creative-class workers and Copenhagen as the comfortable and more balanced home is also reflected in the clothes that Emma wears in the two cities: the hyper-sexualized outfits in Paris make her look older than she is, while the casual jeans and t-shirts she wears at home in Copenhagen remind us that she is just a teenager.

The film costumes were designed by the award-winning costume designer Stine Thaning. The fashion in the film is presented as formal at the high fashion events in Paris, with tuxedos and dresses; while the domestic scenes when Emma is at home with her family or boyfriend are marked by relaxed clothing – a classic everyday look in many contemporary Copenhagen films. In Paris, we see Emma at photoshoots in stylized high fashion and couture and at parties wearing a little black dress, which attracts the attention of influential men in the industry. Her time in Paris progressively worsens, her efforts to connect with people repeatedly fail, she is objectified and sexually abused by the men in the fashion industry, her mental health begins to deteriorate and she begins to do drugs and take sexual risks. She becomes obsessed with a top photographer, dependent on him both for an emotional connection and her professional success as a model. But the film suggests that both romantic encounters and modelling careers are disposable and unsustainable in the world of the global fashion business. This is a very different take on a modelling career as a glamorous passage to upward mobility, as depicted in *Kispus*. This minimalist style also constructs her as an empty canvas, the way models tend to be seen by the modelling industry. Their bodies serve as tools to be styled, photographed, branded and eventually replaced by the next it-girl. Emma does not have any agency in her style, or in her life, and is continuously used by others for projections of desires, objectification and commodification. At the end of the film, she returns to her parents' home and her childhood bedroom in Copenhagen, traumatized by her experiences in Paris and in need of real emotional connection, healing and hygge. She slowly begins to regain her sense of self and live out her life as a teenage girl.

I Blodet (*In the Blood*, 2016)

I Blodet, directed by Rasmus Heisterberg, is a film that follows four students who share an apartment in the Nørrebro neighbourhood in Copenhagen, one of the city's most culturally diverse areas and increasingly trendy, gentrified and a popular living area for students. The multiculturality communicates a dynamic atmosphere and a sense of urban coolness. The film focuses primarily on Simon's struggles to remain young and carefree, which backfire when all his friends embark on adult lives with increasing responsibilities. Simon rebels against becoming an adult by getting wilder and taking things to extremes, which increasingly isolates him from his friends. In his attempt to remain a part of the party culture Copenhagen provides, Simon ends up losing everything in the end, including friendships, love and his internship.

Summer in Copenhagen shows the city at its best, with green parks full of young people having picnics and drinks, enjoying the vibrant nightlife, strolling through the streets, riding bikes across the Queen Louise Bridge at sunrise, drinking in bars, clubs and at music festivals and having sex. But there is also a tinge of melancholy, loneliness and a darker side to the self-destructive drinking and partying culture, as a carefree existence turns into carelessness and betrayal. Alcohol and drug addiction and the consequent toll on mental health and relationships is a common theme in many contemporary Danish films. Simon's apartment has an Absinth poster and a fully stocked bar. Simon is studying medicine, doing an internship at a hospital, and attends lectures at the university. In his free time, he meets up with friends for drinks and hangs out with his friend and roommate Knud. They go to bars, sneak into an outdoor music festival, go swimming at Amager Beach, go to dinner parties with wine and cigarettes, and backyard garden parties with baby announcements, as some of his friends are starting families. Simon gets drunk and sleeps with Knud's girlfriend Mia. As the summer winds down, he has a hard time confronting the reality of his studies, his failed relationships and friendships and cannot let go of the summer intoxication. The social isolation Simon begins to experience is in direct contrast with the hygge culture of Copenhagen summer lifestyles.

The clothes in the film follow the casual jeans and t-shirt style of young Copenhageners, combined with jackets with rolled-up sleeves and sneakers. Their multifunctionality is used in constructing the young protagonists as Copenhageners, without any visible difference in the clothing the characters wear in their everyday life, at home, or at parties. The women also wear simple t-shirts, jeans and sneakers, but sometimes they mix it up with loose summer dresses, still worn with sneakers – a "boho" comfort look. Even when the young women dress up for parties, it is still casual and relaxed, toned down with sneakers and loose hairstyles. This relatively casual, minimalist and functional fashion is emblematic of the young urban Copenhagen style that persists to this day.

Underverden (Darkland, 2017)

Underverden (literally, *Underworld*), directed by Iraqi-Danish filmmaker Fenar Ahmad, presents Copenhagen's multiethnic underground world, in which the life of a successful brain surgeon Zaid is suddenly uprooted when his little brother Yasin is killed by the gangsters to whom he owed money. Zaid becomes obsessed with getting revenge because he refused to bail out Yasin when he asked for help. Zaid oscillates between his daily life as a surgeon, husband and father-to-be, who lives in a gentrified part of Copenhagen in an expensive and stylish apartment, and the violent reality of his brother's underground world of crime, drugs, violence and murder. Zaid's education and career gave him access to privilege, whereas Yasin got mixed up with the criminal world, which provides a glimpse into the different experiences of immigrant lives in Copenhagen. Zaid is the only person of colour in his social circle. His pregnant Danish wife organizes dinner parties for their friends. They go to gallery openings and expensive restaurants. He wears button-up shirts and dark trousers, and black or beige raincoats, representing a polished and styled look of an upper-class Copenhagener. His style is very proper and allows him to fit into the minimalist aesthetic of contemporary Copenhagen fashion. By contrast, the young gang members wear expensive tracksuits, belt bags, duvet jackets, vests, designer sneakers and sunglasses to show off their branded urban street style.

The film gives us a glimpse into an underground subculture with its own fashion codes. The juxtaposition of classes is now blurred by the expensive brands the gang members wear as a way to signify power, conspicuous consumption and disposable income, which was not accessible to them growing up. The Nordic Noir genre (often applied to many Danish TV shows, discussed in the next chapter) usually presents a dark, grey, cold and violent environment that is in direct opposition to the hygge culture. It exposes a very different view of Copenhagen, often portraying a melancholy and dark mood, influenced by the mental heaviness and darkness of the long winter months in the North, with only limited hours of daylight. The sartorial style in these films can be characterized by a simple, minimalist and often cold or dark colour spectrum in blue, black and brown colours. These films usually include very practical indoor and outdoor clothes that are not meant to make a statement or stand out. Zaid's understated minimalist style in his regular life contrasts both with his black combat attire when he enters the crime world and with the eccentric urban street style of the gangsters he pursues. The dark side of hygge based on social, economic and political exclusion is communicated through fashion.

Druk (Another Round, 2020)

Druk (literally *Drinking*), directed by Thomas Vinterberg, is about four high school teachers in Copenhagen having a mid-life crisis. Their lives, work and relationships are stagnating, and they decide to consume alcohol daily to see how it may affect their social and professional lives. At first, all four members of the group find both their work and private lives more enjoyable, but soon, as with all addictions, things begin to go wrong on all fronts, and end in the tragic death of one of the teachers. In the final scene of the film, after the funeral of their friend, they join a group of high school graduates who are binge-drinking and celebrating in the city centre by the water, all wearing the iconic Danish graduation hats (Figure 6.7) that date back to the mid nineteenth century. Martin (played by Mads Mikkelsen) dances frenetically in a cathartic attempt to let go of life's heavy burdens and finally jumps into the habour water, as many Copenhageners do on hot summer days. The dangers of addiction and especially alcoholism have been a major theme in Danish cinema since at least the 1950s with Bodil Ipsen's *Café Paradis* (1950). Vinterberg provides a social commentary on Danish cultural taboos and hypocrisies, especially the alcohol-binging culture that starts as early as high school and is often linked to mental health problems and high suicide rates. Nominated for Best Foreign Film (which it won) and Best Director at the 2021 Academy Awards, four awards at the 74th British Academy Film Awards (BAFTAs), including Best Non-English-Language Film and Best Actor in a Leading Role for Mads Mikkelsen, the film is based on a play Vinterberg wrote while working at the Burgtheater in Vienna. The film was also inspired by Vinterberg's daughter, Ida, who wanted to tell a story about the Danish binge-drinking culture among young people and was planning to play the main protagonist's daughter but was tragically killed in a car accident four days into filming. Following the tragedy, the script was reworked to become more life affirming. The film is dedicated to Ida and was partially filmed in her classroom with her classmates (Jones 2021).

The costumes were designed by Ellen Lens and Manon Rasmussen. The male characters in the film switch between functional, understated casual clothing – checkered shirts, grey t-shirts and jeans, which they wear at school and at home – and formal attire – suits and button-up shirts when they go out to restaurants together, and dark suits with black shirts and ties at the funeral at the end. The film opens and closes with images of high school graduates partying and drinking excessively, which is socially justified by the ritualistic passage to maturity and symbolized by their pristine graduation hats that over the course of several weeks of partying become increasingly damaged. In 1903, when the modern high school system was introduced, the colour schemes for the graduation hats began to vary, depending on the specializations of the high schools. Today, the unwritten rule is to wear the hat until all the student parties are over, which usually lasts for a couple of weeks and thus leaves the hats with traces of deliberate wear and tear. In the old days, the caps also signified belonging to various fraternities and clubs, so many people would wear them for many years after graduation (West Madsen 2016) (Figures 6.11 and 6.12).

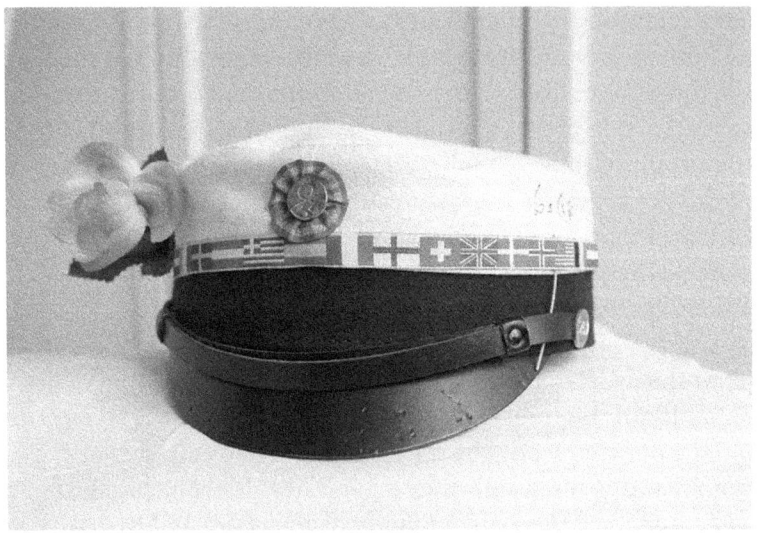

FIGURE 6.11: Danish graduation hat, photo by Mia Petersen, with permission.

FIGURE 6.12: Danish graduation hat, photo by Mia Petersen, with permission.

Despite the COVID lockdowns that interrupted the film's release, it was very successful with audiences in and beyond Denmark. Writing for *Time Magazine*, Stephanie Zacharek pointed out that beyond celebrating male friendship, the film presents a "mild tragedy of middle-aged invisibility," which women often experience with age, but we rarely see portrayals of men struggling with it (Zacharek 2021). The culture critics of the *Slate* magazine, Stephen Metcalf and Dana Stevens, noted that the film presents the dilemma of middle-age existence for privileged white men in a "Kierkegaardian contemplation of life and death, at a time when their privileges are gradually being decentered," as their "self-mythologizing especially around alcohol and sex is out the window," and "the epic of self pity that white men have been writing for millennia now is over, [and] no one wants to hear it" (*Slate Culture Gabfest* podcast 2021). Dana Stevens, the *Slate* film critic, pointed out that this film attempts a "Dogme type of experiment to make a movie about main characters conducting an experiment" (with alcohol). She also noted that the film "won an Oscar in a year when other nominated films dealt with black history and human rights in response to the Black Lives Matter events, and other large social and political issues were at the center of most nominated films", and thus "the Danish win seemed very 'low stakes' for the North American audiences" (Stevens 2021: n.pag.). The dark side of hygge is explored here through various negotiations and commentary on addiction, mental health struggles and suicide, which in Denmark are particularly high, despite its international reputation for being one of the "happiest" countries. In line with the disruptive Dogme aesthetics and approach, Vinterberg holds up a mirror to the problematic undercurrents in Danish society. It is not without a hint of irony that around the same time Mads Mikkelsen was featured in Carlsberg beer commercials, promoting and endorsing one of the giants of the Danish domestic and export industry.

Conclusion

From the films selected here, we can see how clothing is a way to express (sometimes conflicting) multiple identities. Fashion has always reflected social, economic, cultural and political change, and perhaps the current disavowal of class, culture and gender markers in clothing, especially in young and urban fashion styles, and the gravitation towards simplicity and minimalism in clothes has to do with our changing relationships to our environments and urban spaces.

In many ways, Copenhagen films are not particularly experimental in terms of playing with fashion, but they do reflect social and economic changes, often reinforcing or even exaggerating stereotypes, with or without self-irony or humour. The characters are usually very expressive, but their clothing is plain and simple, perhaps not to take away the focus from the social issues at hand. Danish and Copenhagen films are critical of their society and culture – they present social and political critique that fashion discourses, especially fashion journalism, shy away from. This is also evident in many Danish television shows (discussed in the next chapter). Yet, Danish cinema and films are still not very diverse, with only a few actors of colour cast as main protagonists. Clothing in Copenhagen films still functions as representation of class, social power and status – for street gangs and leisure classes – and is still used to represent social stereotypes and tropes, which have traditionally been exaggerated with extra irony or dark and hyperbolic humour. Unlike *Kispus* and other iconic classics, contemporary Copenhagen films do not engage with fashion directly – that is mostly done on social media and on the streets. Rather, the focus in most contemporary films is on social issues, relationships, character struggles and personal growth, and thus the influence of the Dogme 95 aesthetic minimalism persists and the reluctance to distract audiences from the messages in films.

REFERENCES

Aarhus University History. "A Little about the History of the Danish Student Hat." www.auhist.au.dk/showroom/praesentationer/lidtomstudenterhuen/. Accessed 20 Oct. 2022.

Bentprisen. Om Bentprisen, www.bentprisen.dk/om-bentprisen/. Accessed 20 Oct. 2022.

Bodilprisen, www.bodilprisen.dk. Accessed 20 Oct. 2022.

Cinema of Denmark. *Wikipedia*, www.en.wikipedia.org/wiki/Cinema_of_Denmark. Accessed 20 Oct. 2022.

Copenhagen Fashion Film Festival, www.copenhagenfashionfilm.dk/. Accessed 20 Oct. 2022.

Copenhagen Film Festival, www.annualcphfest.com/. Accessed 20 Oct. 2022.

CPH DOX – Documentary Film Festival, www.en.cphdox.dk/. Accessed 20 Oct. 2022.

Copenhagen Short Film Festival, www.filmfreeway.com/CopenhagenShortFilmFestival. Accessed 20 Oct. 2022.

Det Danske Filminstitut (DFI). "Manon Rasmussen." www.dfi.dk/viden-om-film/filmdatabasen/person/manon-rasmussen. Accessed 20 Oct. 2022.

Filming Location – Copenhagen, Denmark. IMDB, www.imdb.com/search/title/?locations=Copenhagen,%20Denmark&ref_=adv_prv. Accessed 20 Oct. 2022.

Ganeva, Mila. *Women in Weimar Fashion: Discourses and Displays in German Culture, 1918–1933*. Rochester: Camden House, 2008, www.cambridge.org/core/books/women-in-weimar-fashion/weimar-film-as-fashion-show/14B74A2B107E5EDBFACEA3226E0973CC. Accessed 20 Oct. 2022.

Hartvigson, Niels Henrik. "Det homoseksuelle København: Fra Bundfald og Kispus til i dag." *Kosmorama*, vol. 55, no. 244, 2009, pp. 56–71, www.kosmorama.org/kosmorama/arkiv/244/det-homoseksuelle-kobenhavn. Accessed 20 Oct. 2022.

Jones, Emma. "Another Round: How a Film about a Drinking Experiment Became a Celebration of Life." *BBC News*, 7 Apr. 2021, www.bbc.com/news/entertainment-arts-56647795. Accessed 20 Oct. 2022.

Kofod, Mikkel. "'Pusher' 20 År: Da Dansk Film Blev Fucket – Fortalt Af Nicolas Winding Refn, Mads Mikkelsen, Zlatko Burci M. Fl." *Soundvenue*, 16 Nov. 2016, www.soundvenue.com/film/2016/11/pusher-20-aar-da-dansk-film-blev-fucket-fortalt-af-refn-mads-mikkelsen-zlatko-buric-med-flere-228420. Accessed 20 Oct. 2022.

Kosin, Julie. "Paco Delgado on Dressing *The Danish Girl*: 'We Were All Contained by the Bravery of Lili.'" 25 Dec. 2015, www.harpersbazaar.com/culture/film-tv/a13461/paco-delgado-interview-the-danish-girl-costumes/. Accessed 20 Oct. 2022.

Lindqvist, Sofie. "That's Why You Should Dress like Anja and Viktor." *Costume*, 2019, www.costume.dk/mode/tendens/derfor-skal-du-klaede-dig-som-anja-og-viktor. Accessed 20 Oct. 2022.

Lyngvild, Jim. "I Actually Do Not Care Much about Queen Margrethe." *Berlingske*, 6 Nov. 2021, www.berlingske.dk/aok/jim-lyngvild-jeg-er-faktisk-temmelig-ligeglad-med-dronning-margrethe. Accessed 20 Oct. 2022.

Melchior, Marie Riegels. "Denmark." *Berg Encyclopedia of World Dress and Fashion*. Vol. 8 – Western Europe, edited by Lise Skov. New York: Bloomsbury Fashion Central, 2010, pp. 330–335.

Nickel, Christiane. "Episode 3, Weimar Fashion: Made in Germany." *German Fashion History* podcast, Anchor 2021, www.anchor.fm/gfhp/episodes/Weimar-Fashion-Made-in-Germany-Ep-3-ese03r. Accessed 20 Oct. 2022.

Schepelern, Peter. "Dansk Filmhistorie 1896–2019." Det Danske Filminstitut, www.dfi.dk/viden-om-film/filmhistorie/dansk-filmhistorie-2000-2009. Accessed 20 Oct. 2022.

Slate Culture Gabfest Podcast. *Slate*, 24 Mar. 2021, www.slate.com/podcasts/culture-gabfest/2021/03/why-spaghetti-is-the-worst. Accessed 20 Oct. 2022.

Visit Kolding website. "Kongerækken med Jim Lyngvild." www.visitkolding.dk/kolding/planlaeg-din-tur/kongeraekken-med-jim-lyngvild-gdk1118491. Accessed 20 Oct. 2022.

West Madsen, Fie. "Har du også undret dig? Derfor er studenterhuen og hueregler blevet en tradition." *Berlingske*, 24 Jun. 2016, www.berlingske.dk/samfund/har-du-ogsaa-undret-dig-derfor-er-studenterhuen-og-hueregler-blevet-en-tradition. Accessed 20 Oct. 2022.

Wille, Jakob Ion. "Understanding Fashion Film, Form and Genre." *Kosmorama*, 29 Jan. 2019, www.kosmorama.org/kosmorama/artikler/understanding-fashion-film-form-and-genre. Accessed 20 Oct. 2022.

Wilson, Elizabeth. *Adorned in Dreams: Fashion and Modernity*. London: I.B. Tauris, 2013 (1985).

Zacharek, Stephanie. "Mads Mikkelsen Can Do Anything. But He's Stuck in the Boring Oscar-Nominated *Another Round*." *Time Magazine*, 19 Mar. 2021, www.time.com/5947965/another-round-review/. Accessed 20 Oct. 2022.

FILMOGRAPHY

After the Wedding. Directed by Bart Freundlich, Produced by Joel B. Michaels, Julianne Moore, Ingenious Media, 2019.

Anja & Viktor. Directed by Charlotte Sachs Bostrup. Produced by Regner Grasten Film. Performed by Charlotte Sachs Bostrup, 1999.

Babettes gæstebud [*Babette's Feast*]. Directed by Gabriel Axel. Produced by Just Betzer, Bo Christensen, 1988.
Ballade på Christianshavn [*Our Home is Our Castle*]. Directed by Erik Balling, Henning Bahs, Copenhagen, 1971.
Birdbox. Directed by Susanne Bier, Produced by Clayton Townsend, Chris Morgan, Netflix, 2018.
Café Paradis. Directed by Bodil Ipsen, Produced by Lau Lauritzen, Jens Dahl, Nicolas Winding Refn.Jr. ASA Film, 1950.
Casino Royale. Directed by Martin Campbell, Produced by Barbara Broccoli, Michael G. Wilson, 2006.
Coco Chanel & Igor Stravinsky. Directed by Jan Kounen, Produced by Chris Greenhalgh, Eurowide Film Production, Wild Buch, 2009.
Copenhagen. Directed by Mark Raso, Produced by Mauro Mueller, Mette Thygesen, Fidelio Films, Scorched Films, 2014.
Das Leben der Anderen [*The Lives of Others*]. Directed by Florian Henckel von Donnersmarck, Produced by Max Wiedermann, Quirin Berg, Wiedemann & Berg, 2006.
Den eneste ene [*The One and Only*]. Directed by Susanne Bier, Manuscript by Kim Fupz Aakeson, Metronome Productions, 1999.
Druk [*Another Round*]. Directed by Thomas Vinterberg, Tobias Lindholm, Directed by Kasper Dissing, Sisse Graum Jørgensen, Zentropa, 2020.
Efter brylluppet [*After the Wedding*]. Directed by Susanne Bier, Manuscript by Anders Thomas Jensen, Produced by Sisse Graum Jørgensen, Zentropia, 2006.
En kongelig affære [*A Royal Affair*]. Directed by Nikolaj Arcel, Manuscript by Rasmus Heisterberg, Nikolaj Arcel, Zentropia, 2012.
Festen [*The Celebration*]. Directed by Thomas Vinterberg, Produced by Nimbus Film, 1998.
Frøken Smillas fornemmelse for sne [*Smilla's Sense of Snow*]. Directed by Bille August, Manuscript by Ann Biderman, Constatin Film, 1997.
Hævnen [*In a Better World*]. Directed by Susanne Bier, Produced by Sisse Graum Jørgensen, Manuscript by Anders Thomas Jensen, Zentropia, 2010.
I Blodet [*In the Blood*]. Directed by Rasmus Heisterberg, Produced by Caroline Schlüter Bingestam, Scanbox Entertainment, 2016.
Kispus. Directed by Erik Balling, Nordisk Film A/S, 1956.
Lille Spejl [*Mirror, Mirror*]. Directed by Edward Fleming, Produced by Nina Crone Edward Fleming Produktion, Crone Film, 1978.
Lykke Per [*A Fortunate Man*]. Directed by Bille August, Produced by Anders Frithiof August, Nordisk Film Distribution, 2018.
Olsen Banden. Henning Bahs Erik Balling. Directed by Erik Balling, Produced by Nordisk Films Kompagni, 1968–1998.
Pelle erobreren [*Pelle the Conqueror*]. Directed by Billie August, Manuscript by Bille August, Per Olov Enquist, Bjarne Reuter, Per Holst Filmproduktion, Svensk Filmindustri, 1989.

Pusher. Directed by Nicolas Winding Refn, Manuscript by Nicolas Winding Refn, Jens Dahl, Produced by Balboa Entertainment, 1996.

Pusher II, Directed by Nicolas Winding Refn, Manuscript by Nicolas Winding Refn, Jens Dahl, Produced by Balboa Entertainment, 2004.

Pusher III. Directed by Nicolas Winding Refn, Manuscript by Nicolas Winding Refn, Jens Dahl, Produced by Balboa Entertainment, 2005.

Roswolsky's Mistress. Directed by Felix Basch, Written by Henrik Galeen, Hans Janowitz, Messter Film GmbH, 1921.

The Danish Girl. Directed by Tom Hooper, Produced by Tim Bevan, Eric Fellner, Anne Harrison, United International Pictures, 2015.

The Model. Directed by Mads Matthiesen, Produced by Jonas Bagger, Nordisk Film Distribution, 2016.

The Night Manager. Directed by Susanne Bier, Written by David Farr, The Ink Factory BBC, 2016.

The Undoing. Directed by Susanne Bier, Written by David E. Kelley. HBO, 2020.

Underverden [Darkland]. Directed by Fenar Ahmad, Produced by Jacob Jarek, Scanbox Entertainment, 2017.

Unge Andersen [Young Andersen]. Directed by Rumle Hammerich, Produced by Tina Dalhoff, Nordisk Film, 2005.

7

Fashion in TV Shows

Katrina Sark and Izabella Andersen

Danish TV shows have gained popularity in the global television and streaming industry and enjoyed widespread acclaim from international critics and audiences largely because of their innovative plots, strong female characters and the suspenseful plots of the Nordic Noir crime genre (Jacobsen 2017: 326). Particularly the strong female leads demonstrate how women work in fields traditionally dominated by men, while often wearing what has been traditionally considered "masculine attire," such as suits, jeans and other practical clothes. Many of the popular series' action takes place in and around Copenhagen and often uses the characters' clothes as a distinct signifier and representation of class, career and position in society. The representation of fashion in Copenhagen TV shows has changed noticeably over time. There is still a focus on class but also a perceptible difference in lifestyle and political attitudes, as well as how people relate to other classes in their everyday lives.

In this chapter, we examine several TV shows from various genres, including historical and social dramas, Nordic Noir crime series, political dramas, as well as situational comedies about contemporary life in and around Copenhagen, with a particular focus on the role and meaning of clothing and fashion. The fashion in these TV shows reveals that Copenhagen inhabitants are very conscious of their traditions, history and position in Danish society. However, the developments in society and in fashion demonstrate that the fashion system has not only become much more complex but also less hierarchical, especially in the shows that depict Danish society before 1970 with a clear sartorial and visual representation and division of social classes. In contrast, the newer Nordic Noir and contemporary lifestyle shows represent social classes less distinctly, but the social stratification is still there, as in most societies. Many of these shows can be seen as time capsules for the period in which they were produced and the social contexts they reflect, allowing us a glimpse into the everyday representations of clothing and fashion in Copenhagen over several decades.

We have divided the chapter into three sections, starting with historical costume dramas, where the focus is very much on class divisions and aspirations for post-war prosperity often represented through clothing choices. The second section focuses on the representations of strong female characters often dressed in masculine attire in contemporary Nordic Noir shows and political dramas. The last section examines various representations of contemporary life and lifestyles in situational comedies, in which the main protagonists are usually dressed in functional casual wear that allows them versatility in their daily lives and professions and often blurs the lines between social classes. All in all, we found that the representations of Danish protagonists on TV reflect the same sartorial trends and habits observed in the previous chapters, with a strong focus on functionality, pragmatism and the understated or minimalist aesthetic of the so-called "Scandi" of Copenhagen chic.

Representations of Danish history, class and society

Historical TV shows have enjoyed great popularity with Danish viewers over the years, including popular shows such as *Huset på Christianshavn* (*House at Christianshavn*, 1970–77), *Matador* (*Monopoly*, 1978–82) and *Krøniken* (*The Chronicle*, 2004–07). Most historical costume dramas are produced for the domestic market and are rarely translated into English. *Matador* is perhaps the best-known Danish costume drama. It takes place around the Second World War, and it is central to the plot of the show that it does not take place in Copenhagen, but rather in a small town nearby, a stand-in for Danish society of that time. Several characters serve as direct links to the capital city and its fashion world, especially the character of young Daniel Skjern, who wants to be a fashion designer and gets an apprenticeship with Hr. Jørn (a designer based on Holger Blom). In contrast, *Krøniken* and *Huset på Christianshavn* show the post-Second World War period, which was marked by economic development and modernization, and clothing often serves as a representation of class and social stereotypes. These shows often focus on working-class families and communities, their everyday struggles and aspirations, and the post-war generation's rebuilding of Danish society into a prosperous and progressive welfare state society, which, as these shows reveal, was not always easy and took many years of hard work and determination. We examine several key themes and scenes, and how they relate to the fashion of the times portrayed and the culture that produced it. The TV shows we chose to analyze here reveal the struggles of everyday people, often with a great deal of humour and self-irony and a persistent determination to rise above one's rank in society and create a better future for the next generations. All three shows discussed below reveal the social, economic and sartorial transformation that Denmark and Copenhagen experienced after the Second World War.

Huset på Christianshavn (House at Christianshavn, 1970–77)

Created by the prolific Erik Balling (director of *Kispus* and the *Olsen Banden* films), *Huset på Christianshavn* was an 84-part show about the tenants of a small, old apartment building in Christianshavn, an area of small islands between the islands of Zealand and Amager, separated from the rest of the city centre by the Inner Harbour. Today the area is known for its cafes and canals lined with colourful houseboats and the neighbouring Freetown Christiania, an alternative community of squatters who have been living there since the 1970s, but at the time the show was filmed, it was primarily a working-class neighbourhood. The show features most of the same actors as in *Olsen Banden*. The first episode opens with a young couple with a baby moving into an attic apartment, and as they are carrying their trunk up the stairs, they meet most of their new neighbours. Gradually we get to know all the families and protagonists, their daily struggles and the building gossip.

The clothes the main characters wear reflect the simple, everyday clothes of working-class Copenhageners of the 1970s. Both men's and women's clothes are practical, functional and comfortable without any extravagance. Even though the show focuses on character development and relationships rather than on fashion trends, it is still an indicative time capsule for 1970s everyday casual wear. Although there is nothing extravagant about the style of clothing in the show, as it is relatively typical of the working classes of the time, there is still a focus on important changes in, for example, gender roles. Many of the women in the series were housewives, but at some point, Ellen Olsen (played by Helle Virkner, the protagonist of *Kispus*) gets a job as a bus driver (DR). The series also depicts how Danes suddenly started going on charter holidays, commenting on the growing success of the post-Second World War welfare state economy and the growing middle classes.

Matador (Monopoly, 1978–82)

Matador is a television series created by Erik Balling and Lise Nørgaard about social mobility, spanning the years 1929 until 1947, as the upper classes become less equipped to adapt to modernization and the working classes create new businesses. The first episode of *Matador* opens in 1929 in a fabric store in the fictional Danish town of Korsbæk (a compound of Korsør and Holbæk), where upper-class ladies buy fabrics to have their clothes custom-made. Filmed on location around Sjælland in the towns of Gedser, Hillerød, Holte and Køge, it follows the lives of several characters from across the social spectrum, focusing on the rivalry between the families of two businessmen: the banker Hans Christian Varnæs and the self-made entrepreneur Mads (Andersen-)Skjern, who builds a ready-to-wear fashion business. Here, we see the juxtaposition of old and new money, the Conservative Party and the Venstre (Left), Jutland and Sjælland, as well as insiders and outsiders. The name *Matador* was taken from a local edition of the Monopoly board game and is often used to describe a business tycoon.

Class distinctions are made particularly apparent in the episodes set during the interwar years, as the high-society families spend their leisure time at dinner parties, dressed in tuxedos and evening gowns, talking about gossip from Copenhagen, while the working-class folk meet in the local family-run pub after a work's day to talk about local events. The pub's proximity to the train station is central to understanding this type of provincial town – *Stationsdanmark* – and thus the relationship of these suburban communities to Copenhagen. Clothes for upper-class women are a status symbol: there is a clear distinction between those who wear fur coats and wool ones. Cotton fabrics are used for working-class women's wear, while silk, crepe de Chine and other expensive fabrics are used for upper-class women's clothes. The women who entered the labour market stopped wearing corsets. The high-society ladies wear mink and fox fur wraps, muffs, feathers, pearls, broaches, gloves and lace collars. Their decorative looks represent their husband's wealth as conspicuous consumption. The husbands wear three-piece suits, uniforms or tuxedos, silk and wool scarfs and woollen coats. They represent the leisure classes with disposable income. Working-class women wear very functional and practical clothes, while most working-class men have work uniforms. The contrast between the older and younger generations also becomes apparent: older women wear wide-shaded hats with embellishments and even some turn-of-the-century pieces of clothing, while the young women wear bell-shaped hats, flapper dresses and short haircuts. Upper-class fashion is embodied by the character of Maude Varnæs, who has her dresses tailored in Copenhagen by the designer Hr. Jørn, a stand-in for Copenhagen couturier Holger Blom.

The series begins with the arrival of the travelling textile salesman Mads Skjern and his little son from a small town in Jutland. Immediately rejected by the fabric store owners and the local banker, he opens his own ready-to-wear clothing store right across from the fabric store, which causes a minor uproar. Over time, the clothing store becomes more and more successful, while the fabric store loses customers, becoming increasingly outdated. After the war, when Mads' son Daniel is grown up, he gives up his education in trades to become a fashion designer. Mads travels to the United States to learn about the modernization of retail (as many Danish textile entrepreneurs did in the post-Second World War years). Daniel turns down an offer to run Mads' textile business and moves to Paris, and then comes home with a male "friend." Having no apparent heir to his business, Mads visits one of his former employees, Agnes Jensen, at her sewing studio to offer her the job he had intended for Daniel. Agnes is apprehensive about having to give up her own business, but Mads offers to buy it so that her seamstresses can continue their work. Agnes accepts Mads' offer, but with the condition that she will get a share of the family business, to which Mads agrees. Thus, we get a glimpse into post-war Danish society, the small business owners' lives and work, contradictions between pre-war and post-war values, the stratification of society, changing gender roles, especially for working-class women, the consumption practices of the new middle classes, and the rapidity of social changes after the Second World War, through the perspective of 1970s filmmakers and costume designers.

Krøniken (The Chronicle, 2004–07)

Krøniken, created by Stig Thorsboe and Hanna Lundblad, reflects the development of the Danish post-war society starting in 1949 and spanning 25 years, by following the lives of four protagonists, who are the grown children of a generation that does not care much for social change and had to endure the wartime rationing and the occupation (DR). The series was inspired by *Matador*, which was often referenced in the marketing of *Krøniken*. The generational conflicts become apparent in the careers, life choices and the new post-war social challenges of mass unemployment and housing shortages. The show chronicles the story of television coming into Danish households and is centred around the *Radiofabrikken* Bella in Copenhagen, which manufactures new media devices known as televisions and grows from just 50 employees in 1949 to 500 employees in 1965 when most households have a television (Figure 7.1). By the 1960s, Denmark began to experience economic prosperity, thanks in part to the expansion and modernization of manufacturing. But then the oil crisis caused a sudden downturn in the early 1970s. The post-war creation of the Danish welfare state also plays a key role, and politically the show spans important international milestones for Denmark, when it joined NATO in 1949 and the European Community in 1972, becoming a more European and globally connected country by the end of the show (Bollerup 2003).

The four young lead roles are played by Anders W. Bertelsen (Palle), Anne Louise Hassing (Ida), Maibritt Saerens (Søs) and Ken Vedsegaard (Erik). The show revolves around the main characters' lives and confrontations with their social heritage. Palle grew up in a working-class family. Palle is often dressed in a white shirt, brown blazers, hat and generally formal business attire, which is reflected in his daily life as an economics student and his political activity as a Social Democrat. Like Palle, Ida grew up in a family with a working father and

FIGURE 7.1: Old television sets, on display at the Horsens Industry Museum, 2020, photo by K. Sark.

a homemaking mother, which was typical of the time. Her parents expect her to start vocational training, but she soon drops out to get a job as an office worker. Ida is often neatly dressed in brown shirts, knee-length skirts and small hats. In other contexts, such as leisure and parties, she wears bright pastel colours, especially blue, and dresses with discreet floral patterns. Søs and Erik are siblings from an upper-class family. Søs is the younger of the two, has dark hair, often wears very characteristic red lipstick and does not hold back from wearing embroidered and patterned dresses or clothing in warm green and pink tones. She also wears beige blazers and suits. Desiring to become an actress, she is more experimental with her style and appearance than her older brother Erik, who is more traditional and stays true to his social heritage by imitating his father's classic suits, ties or bowties, and a pair of large, distinctive black glasses. His hair is carefully styled with hair wax, and his general look communicates his sense of propriety and his ambition to maintain his status in society. The colour palette of the show remains within a brown and beige universe, with small breaks of pastel green, blue and pink. However, the clothing also reflects the various breaks from traditional roles, as the young people have other aspirations than their parents. They want to get away and start their education, and the women especially do not want to be homebound. The four young characters' clothes reveal the generational shifts among the various social classes and communicate the attempts of the younger generation to break away from their heritage and social expectations.

Strong female characters in masculine attire

In our analysis of Copenhagen shows, we also found a particular focus on strong female characters and how they use clothing in their work and everyday life. In *Matador*, for example, we see how things go downhill for most of the male characters, while the women get increasingly stronger as they go through divorces, start their businesses and become financially independent. We also see the contrast between working-class women, who dress in very functional and practical clothes and climb the ranks by creating successful businesses. Functional clothing also plays a significant role in more recent Danish television, especially in the internationally renowned Nordic Noir shows like *The Killing* (*Forbrydelsen* 2007–12) and *The Bridge* (Broen 2011–18), as well as the political drama *Borgen* (*The Castle* 2010–13 and 2022), all of which feature strong women as the main protagonist: Sarah Lund in *The Killing*, Birgitte Nyborg in *Borgen*, and the Swede Saga Norén in *The Bridge*. All three protagonists break the unwritten cultural rules in their fields of work and become role models for young women identifying with them.

The Killing (*Forbrydelsen*, 2007–12) and *The Bridge* (*Broen*, 2011–18)

A defining element of the Nordic Noir genre is that the action takes place in dark environments, which most Nordic countries experience in the fall and winter months, and which can often be a cause of depression and anxiety. The genre mobilizes this sense of gloom by focusing on crime-solving narratives with a mystery at its core that needs to be brought to light and is not always visible to the average inhabitant of the welfare state society. The suspense of crime-solving work builds until it releases a cathartic sense that order is restored again. Traditionally reserved for male protagonists, this crime and detective genre has been re-imagined with strong women in the lead roles, who not only know how to help themselves but also rescue and assist others. They are the empowered daughters of strong post-war mothers, who were hard-working, outspoken and helped build the contemporary welfare state society that the new generations benefit from.

The Killing, created by Søren Sveistrup, Torleif Hoppe, Per Daumiller and Michael W. Horsten, features several Copenhagen locations, including a police headquarters, which fans of the show can visit (it is the Police Museum), and the building where the main protagonist, Sarah Lund, lives in Østerbro on the corner of Middelfartgade and Vardegade. Sarah Lund mainly wears an Icelandic sweater and blue jeans and does not go to great lengths to think about her appearance, apart from the fact that everything must be practical so that there is nothing in the way when she solves crimes. An unintended consequence of her wardrobe choice was the immense popularity of her sweater. The knitting patterns for it sold out, and its designers Guðrun & Guðrun even had to sue another knitting company for copying, producing and selling it. It may not be coincidental that Sarah Lund wears her iconic sweater in just about every episode – it is a deliberate choice as the sweater is gender-neutral and neither a tight suit nor part of an ornate and feminine wardrobe. Popularized by Nordic fishermen, it highlights her casual style and her attempt to sneak away not only from the stereotypical attire expected of women in her job but also from the Nordic Noir crime genre convention of professional women in suits.

The Bridge, created by Hans Rosenfeldt and Camilla Ahlgren, refers to the Øresund tunnel-bridge that connects Denmark and Sweden, just outside Copenhagen and Malmö (Figure 7.2), which in the first episode becomes a crime scene, bringing together two police investigators, the Danish Martin Rohde (Kim Bodnia) and the Swedish Saga Norén (Sofia Helin). Filmed on location in both Denmark and Sweden, the show is a co-production that became very popular first in the United Kingdom, and then worldwide. The female protagonist Saga Norén acts very rationally and does not show emotions. She wears dark, practical, yet professional clothes and has the same type of jacket as her male counterparts. Indeed, her sartorial style is almost identical to her male co-star. Saga is just one of the examples of female leads in the Nordic Noir genre, in which the female protagonist typically lives alone, immerses herself in her work and appears emotionally cold. Another element that has contributed to the show's success is the often humorous

FIGURE 7.2: Øresund tunnel-bridge that connects Denmark and Sweden, 2019, photo by K. Sark.

contrast between the emotionally cold Saga, who generally does not know how to interact with others, and her Danish male counterpart, Martin, who is a family man and diligently tries to create a connection with Saga as they need to be able to work well together. This gender inversion complements both their characters as they grow and become a competent team. The show also reveals the criminal underworld and the violent environment that is in direct opposition to the celebrated hygge culture associated with Nordic countries. It exposed a very different view of Copenhagen, often portraying a melancholy and dark mood, influenced by the mental heaviness and darkness of the long winter months, with only limited hours of daylight. The sartorial style reflects this mood and can be characterized by a simple, minimalist and often cold or dark colour spectrum in blue, black and brown colours and functional attire.

Borgen (The Castle, 2010–13) and *Borgen: Riget, magten og æren (Borgen: Power and Glory*, 2022)

Borgen, created by Adam Price, mainly takes place at the Christiansborg Palace (nicknamed the Castle) in Copenhagen, which houses the Danish Legislature, the Supreme Court and the Prime Minister's Office (Figure 7.3). In the show, Birgitte Nyborg (played by Sidse Babett Knudsen) is the first female Prime Minister of Denmark (a few years before Helle Thorning Schmidt was elected in real life). She wears business suits that are similar to those of many Danish and European Union female politicians, but she also includes her own colourful and feminine touch with tight skirts, tights and blazers in red, purple and green. Denmark's first female Prime Minister, Helle Thorning Schmidt, was nicknamed "Gucci-Helle" and "Brothel Nut" (Bakalus) because of the challenge she posed to the gender equality debate with her feminine appearance and because she was the first in that position, but she nonetheless paved the way for Mette Frederiksen (Denmark's current and second female Prime Minister). Thorning Schmidt was criticized for dressing in a too feminine manner and having her hair loose, instead of living up to the idea of a female politician in a business suit with her hair up. Yet, she proved that a woman can easily dress nicely and nonetheless be professional. Today, she still actively participates in the gender equality debate and has starred in a rap video and dyed her hair pink. This was the start of an ongoing debate about how dress reflects the competencies and qualifications of female politicians, which is founded on the sexist preconception that "male" attire is the "norm" in professional contexts.

The reboot of *Borgen – Power & Glory* (*Borgen: Riget, magten og æren* [literally, Kingdom, Power, and Glory] also created by Adam Price in collaboration with DR and Netflix, released in the spring of 2022) picks up ten years later and brings back Birgitte Nyborg as the newly appointed Foreign

FIGURE 7.3: Christiansborg Palace, Danish Parliament, 2010, photo by K. Sark.

Minister under a female Prime Minister Signe Kragh (played by Johanne Louise Schmidt). When a Canadian drilling company discovers oil in Greenland, a former Danish colony, an international power struggle breaks out in the Arctic. The show examines power and its pressure on personal and professional lives in a time of political turmoil in Europe and has heightened significance in light of Europe's reliance on Russian oil and gas, not to mention the global climate crisis. Brigitte Nyborg's and Signe Kragh's power suits and blouses, as well as their pulled-back hairstyles, are inspired by current Danish Prime Minister Mette Frederiksen's professional attire and appearance. They are in their prime years: Nyborg is 53, while Kragh is 41 when the new season opens. In addition to being highly professional and competent, Nyborg is presented as very international – bilingual in Danish and English, and also fluent in French and German. Nyborg is positioned as more progressive on the environment than Kragh, but the geopolitical pressure of Russia, China and the United States pressuring Denmark over the oil in Greenland quickly makes Nyborg change her official position on climate and unleashes other turmoil in her work and private life. The climate debate is further complicated through the character of Birgitte's 21-year-old son

Magnus (Lucas Lynggard Tønnesen), who joins a political climate movement. Their public and private disagreements reflect the current generational gap in climate politics.

In a parallel narrative, Katrine Fønsmark (played by Birgitte Hjort Sørensen) takes over the leadership of the news department at a local television network, starting out with the ambition to hold Danish politicians accountable to democratic values but very quickly crumbling under pressure from all sides of the media business. In the end, both Birgitte Nyborg and Katrine Fønsmark voluntarily resign from their high-ranking positions and both struggle with the perception of failure. The show touches on the intersections of the climate crisis, oil, environmental degradation, colonialism and energy politics, and presents these issues from the political and journalistic perspectives of female leadership. The colonial undertones grow more and more apparent during the negotiations between Danish politicians and diplomats with Greenlandic leadership that pushes for independence, which is continually denied through threats of no longer providing security against China, Russia and the US, and shaming Greenlanders for high addiction and suicide rates and for not having a creative class of intellectuals, political and entrepreneurial leaders. The show holds up a very critical mirror to Danish society and politicians, with the implication that Denmark may not be as progressive as it can and should be.

Comprised of dark suits and silk blouses, Birgitte Nyborg's clothes present a more severe, powerful and tough version of her, as she struggles to hide the vulnerability she feels with the onset of pre-menopause, her lack of personal and romantic life after her divorce, and her general loneliness after her children have moved out. She puts on a tough front, tries to appear youthful and claims to enjoy the freedom and energy she can put into her work, but that backfires when her work becomes unsustainable, burns her out and alienates her from her family and allies. The strong women in the show reveal what it takes to constantly have to balance between power and vulnerability and success and failure in both the private and public spheres. Their clothes serve as professional armour. Not meant to reveal their humanity and vulnerability, it allows them to maintain a level of professionalism and constructed imperviousness. In several scenes, Nyborg's assistant has a change of clothes ready for her when she is experiencing hot flashes or needs to change into a pantsuit because she suddenly gets her period again. In these instances, clothes express more than the protagonists are willing to admit even to themselves. They become a vehicle to navigate between the personal and professional worlds and struggles, and they visualize the psychological toll of high-pressure jobs under constant public scrutiny. In this season, the black power suits of Copenhagen's power elite mask old colonial-capitalist undercurrents that are holding on to power at all costs, and stepping away from power is constructed as essential for well-being and survival to avoid personal, ethical and environmental extinction.

Comedic representations of contemporary lifestyles

Other interesting examples of the use of practical, functional clothing, as well as women's ownership of typically "male attire," can be found in many Danish sitcoms, including *Rita* (2012–17), created by Lars Kaalund and Jannik Johansen, about a schoolteacher, who is a divorced mother of three and does not follow the rules in either her job or her personal life in the suburbs of Copenhagen. Her daily attire combines masculine and feminine aesthetics with tight jeans, plaid shirts over a grey cotton tank top, a leather jacket and yellow high-heel sandals. She positions herself as a minimalist punk rebel, in contrast to everyone else in the show, who is represented through pastels and primary colours. In the opening shot of the first episode, we are introduced to Rita smoking in the school bathroom, and what we see first is her yellow high heels. Rita makes her own rules about her life, her appearance and her sexuality. Her relationship with the men in her life is very pragmatic (she frequently has sex with her colleague Rasmus in his office), and she takes articles of men's clothing and makes them her own (Kruse 2012). Another teacher, Hjørdis, wears colourful, floral patterns and loose-fitting clothes, while the school principal Helle wears a "Scandi chic" wardrobe of grey, geometric, minimalist sweaters and dresses. While Rita's clothing communicates strength and rebellion but also a kind of unapproachability, Hjørdis' "boho-chic" look makes her the show's comic relief. It also contrasts with Rita's confidence in her own body. Helle's style is the most sophisticated and chic of the three female protagonists; she represents leadership and power, but unlike the usual political, authoritative power of Nordic Noir women, her grey palette and minimalist geometric cuts show her attention to Scandinavian fashion trends in an understated but very confident and empowered manner.

In 2015, four episodes of a spin-off show at the same suburban school were released under the title *Hjørdis* (2015), created by Christan Torpe, in which the title character puts on a variety show for the school's two-week-long anti-bullying campaign by mobilizing and inspiring the school's more socially awkward kids, who are considered outsiders by the other kids. When the Crown Princess of Denmark promises to make an appearance, the variety show takes on greater importance for the school. Unlike Rita, who is no longer part of this series, Hjørdis has a much softer feminine look and prefers to wear loose floral and potato-sack dresses and leggings, flowy blouses and embroidered vests. Her clothes signify not only her kind positivity and approachability but also practicality and functionality with a bit more colour to reflect her quiet but vibrant personality. Both shows portray suburban Copenhagen and its welfare-state-funded school system as idyllic, focusing more on the comedic aspects of a situational workplace comedy than the serious social or racial issues of a globalizing society.

Klovn (*Clown* 2005–18), created by Casper Christensen and Frank Hvam and directed by Mikkel Nørgaard, is a sitcom set in Copenhagen about two friends, Casper Christensen and Frank Hvam (their real names), who play a version of themselves, giving us insight into their embarrassing everyday lives. Inspired by the US sitcom *Curb Your Enthusiasm* by Larry David, the main plotline focuses on a semi-retired comedian encountering humorous and embarrassing situations, along with his wife, friends and celebrity acquaintances. Playing with the concepts of reality, realness and authenticity, the two protagonists navigate many awkward or embarrassing situations, and each time try to push the boundaries of audience expectations. The show presents contemporary men from Copenhagen who find themselves in today's crisis of masculinity: often wealthy (or at least they would like to appear so) in white shirts, vests and ties, representing the "creative classes" populating contemporary Copenhagen. Their clothes signal that they can afford to be in the "right circles" and eat at popular restaurants. They exude a certain kind of snobbery about clothing, as they aspire to a higher status, while things tend to go comedically wrong and develop into extremely embarrassing situations. Frank Hvam often appears in awkwardly fitting underwear, including a white tank top and white boxer shorts that are too big for him. The protagonists' awkward relationship with their clothes and lack of elegance is used to amplify the humour. Their self-ironizing self-presentation as "clowns" or anti-heroes is made more complex by their infidelity, drinking, smoking and partying in Copenhagen, which is juxtaposed with their more polished suburban lives.

Both *Rita* and *Klovn* focus on the imperfect lives of their multi-layered protagonists, revealing that everyday life in Copenhagen is far from idyllic. The humour in these shows allows them to focus on the fun elements in the problems their characters encounter and make fun of in their everyday lives. By allowing the audiences to identify with the complex character flaws of their anti-heroes, the shows establish a cathartic escape for the audience, and fashion assists in building that identification, humanizing the protagonists in very nuanced and subtle ways, even when they behave in morally dubious ways.

Conclusion

Many TV shows have helped to construct a visual and sartorial image of Copenhagen, and because of their international popularity, they set a tone for what

Copenhagen fashion means not only to the rest of the country but globally. There are several contemporary productions that directly or indirectly address diversity of Danish and Copenhagen society, for example *Taxa* (DR), *Om Natten Lyver Jeg Aldrig* (DR), *Når Støvet Har Lagt Sig* (DR), and some shows do represent "immigrant" or Muslim experiences, but overall, there is still a noticeable lack of racial diversity in Copenhagen shows. Nonetheless, these shows can provide glimpses into urban street styles and professional attire across the social and economic spectrum; they can reveal the underlying gender and class tensions, and they can also set aspirational goals for future generations. Copenhagen has positioned itself at the forefront of cultural representation, constructing narratives, characters and fashion that are simultaneously not only relaxed and daring but also non-traditional for stereotypical gender perceptions. The shows we examined here confirm that as Copenhagen's cultural influence grows, it approaches fashion in a more practical sense (Dam 2017). More than half of the city's inhabitants ride a bike, so practical clothing is often in focus (Dam 2017). As represented in these TV shows, Copenhagen fashion blurs gender binaries and makes clothing choices more playful and also more functional.

It is evident from these shows that women have adopted and perfected practical fashion, and that many female characters use their clothing to challenge traditional perceptions of gender and sexuality and play with gender boundaries. By wearing what is traditionally considered "men's" clothes, these women navigate their roles as strong women in their jobs, relationships, families and sexual encounters. This is a very different representation of women than in historical shows, where upper-class women dress decoratively to represent their husband's wealth and disposable incomes, while working-class women dress more practically. In contemporary shows, the wardrobes of the female protagonists do not detract from their functionality – for them, it is their character traits that determine the way they stand out, rather than what they wear. Furthermore, the presence of strong female characters is linked to positive export patterns while series with low production values and simple narrative structures are less successful (Jacobsen 2017: 328). Perhaps the strong female leads in Danish television, and their more practical approach to fashion, contribute to the international success of these television representations of Copenhagen and its fashion.

REFERENCES

Bollerup Jacobsen, Birgitte. "KRØNIKEN – ny dramaserie af Stig Thorsboe." *DR Press*, 26 Nov. 2003, www.dr.dk/presse/kroeniken-ny-dramaserie-af-stig-thorsboe. Accessed 20 Oct. 2022.

Dam, Rikke Agnete. "Derfor elsker hele verden dansk mode." *Costume*, 24 Dec. 2017, www.costume.dk/mode/tendens/derfor-elsker-hele-verden-dansk-mode. Accessed 13 Mar. 2023.

Jacobsen, Pia Majbritt Jensen, and Ushma Chauhan. "Danish TV Drama: Behind the Unexpected Popularity." *Critical Studies in Television, The International Journal of Television Studies*, vol. 14, no. 4, 2017, pp. 325–330.

Kruse, Marie Wiuff. "Kvinderne scorer på skovmandsskjorten." *Børsen*, 27 Nov. 2012, www.borsen.dk/nyheder/pleasure/kvinderne-scorer-paa-skovmandsskjorten-6afro. Accessed 13 Mar. 2023.

Lindberg, Kristian. "50 år med Olsen-banden: Olsen-banden er alle danske mænd – og Yvonne alle danske kvinder." *Berlingske*, 10 Oct. 2018, www.berlingske.dk/kultur/50-aar-med-olsen-banden-olsen-banden-er-alle-danske-maend-og-yvonne-alle. Accessed 13 Mar. 2023.

TV SHOWS

Borgen: Riget, magten og aeren. Tobias Lindholm, Adam Price Jeppe Gjervig Gram. Perf. Adam Price. *DR*, 2010–13.

Borgen. Tobias Lindholm, Adam Price Jeppe Gjervig Gram. Perf. Adam Price. *DR & Netflix*, 2022.

Broen Camilla Ahlgren, Nikolaj Scherfig, Björn Stein, Astrid Øye, Måns Mårlind, Erik Arhnbom, Marie Louise Käehne, Morten Dragsted Hans Rosenfeldt. *Filmlance, Nimbus Film, SVT, DR, ZDF*, 2011–18.

Forbrydelsen. Torleif Hoppe, Michael W. Horsten, Per Daumiller Søren Sveistrup, *DR*, 2007.

Hjørdis. Christian Torpe. *TV2, Netflix*, 2015.

Huset på Christianshavn. Ebbe Langberg, Erik Balling, Tom Hedegaard. Nordisk Film, *DR*, 1970–77.

Klovn. Frank Hvam Casper Christensen. Perf. Frank Hvam Casper Christensen, *TV2*, 2005–18.

Krøniken. Hanna Lundblad Stig Thorsboe. *DR* (TV-Drama), 2003–06.

Matador. Erik Balling, Paul Hammerich, Jens Louis Petersen, Karen Smith Lise Nørgaard. Directed by Lise Nørgaard, Produced by Nordisk Film, 1978–81.

Rita. Christian Torpe. Perf. Marie Østerbye Christian Torpe, *TV2*, 2012–20.

8

Innovation and Technology

Katrina Sark, Bjørn Utoft Sørensen and Emilie Thomsen

The seed of all innovation is creativity, and Denmark is known for the creative talent nurtured by its many design schools and universities. Despite the historical and regional divide between Denmark's two fashion industries in Copenhagen and Jutland, Copenhagen regularly showcases Denmark's innovations at international events and trade shows. There are several innovative fashion companies based in Copenhagen; for example, the team behind the Copenhagen-based brand OUR SHIFT (comprised of creative director and designer Milan Florián Flíček, a graduate of the Royal Academy and CEO Barbora Surá, a graduate of Copenhagen Business School), whose fully upcycled collection, "Make less, thanks!" is the answer to many of the current challenges fashion faces in an age of a global climate crisis. But their clever and provocative catchphrase is only the beginning of their brand and fashion culture. They put conscious and deliberate actions into their fashion activism and creativity by repurposing upcycled fabrics come from the tents left by the visitors of the annual Roskilde music festival that would normally end up in landfills or burned as waste, including the tent zippers and windows, washed and repurposed materials, reused and tailored into raincoats, jackets, pants, suits and dresses, and playfully and masterfully enhanced with deadstock fabrics mindfully sourced and creatively reimagined as functional, innovative and stylish.

Son of a Tailor shirts are made to order online to eliminate waste and overproduction. Their approach allows customers to choose sizes, materials and colours. They do not keep a stock of any of their clothing and are working on reducing their waste (Lynglund 2018). Using a laser cutter to cut out the patterns for the shirts, they introduced a zero-waste pullover via three-dimensional (3D) printing and launched a Kickstarter campaign for a 3D knitting machine, which eliminates overproduction and textile waste, reaching their target goal in only 39 minutes (Staley 2019).

Another Copenhagen-based brand, KERNE.MILK, was founded in 2019 by Marie Mark, focusing on high-quality garments that last longer through upcycling and repurposing of quality materials (KERNE.MILK website). They have a minimal waste policy and have a line of one-of-a-kind scrap styles made of their leftover materials, which are combined in new ways and sewn together by hand in their studio in Nørrebro (KERNE.MILK website) (Figure 8.1). They also work together with Huset Venture, a social non-profit enterprise that seeks to create jobs for people with reduced working abilities.

While there are many other examples of innovative brands that use technology to further the circularity of fashion and textiles, in this chapter, we focus on Kvadrat/Really, a frontrunner when it comes to innovative textile technology. We also examine the work of MANND, a creative virtual reality studio that aims to challenge the use and understanding of extended reality (XR), or real-and-virtual combined environments, to "create the next era of branded content, communication and entertainment" (MANND website). Among their many projects is a virtual reality (VR) film, *X-Ray Fashion: Seeing through a Toxic Industry* (dir. Francesco Carrozzini, 2018), which focuses on the working conditions in the global fashion industry. They worked

FIGURE 8.1: Kerne Milk storefront in Nørrebro, Copenhagen, 2022, photo by K. Sark.

with the VIA University College to create an immersive augmented reality (AR) fashion catwalk experience and also together produced a VR and AR fashion project called *ERA360* in January 2020. They have collaborated with a British production company, MAD Productions, to sell AR fashion experiences.

Finally, we analyze the exhibition "Fashion Tech & Fashion's Sustainable Growth Layer" organized by the Lifestyle & Design Cluster, a Danish organization whose mandate is to promote Danish fashion and furniture design, help Danish brands transition towards circularity and support the future generation of creative talent emerging from the Danish design schools. They provide an important link between graduates and local businesses and try to bridge gaps between industry and researchers. Their mandate is to promote new thinking and alternative solutions for the fashion industry. They organize exhibitions, trade shows, workshops, showcasing events and annual career fairs, bringing together students from all the Danish design schools and universities to allow them to network and talk to representatives from Danish fashion, textile and design companies. This exchange facilitates mentorships, internships and future employment for the new generations of design professionals, as they begin to transition from schools to workplaces. Our research and analysis in this chapter are based on articles, online information and interviews conducted with two business developers: Wickie Meier Engström, a director and partner from Really, and Signe Ungermand, co-founder of MANND, as well as team leaders Christian Chapelle, Heidi Svane Pedersen, Johanne Stenstrup and Lone Haumann from the Lifestyle & Design Cluster. Our goal is to examine the important innovative work being done in the Danish fashion sector.

It should be noted that we specifically refrain from labelling these innovative brands as "sustainable" because Danish law, as well as other international marketing laws, prohibits specific materials and products from being promoted as "sustainable" as it is nearly impossible to document these claims, especially given that documentation for such general terms must consider the entire lifecycle of a garment, in both social and environmental terms (Danish Consumer Ombudsperson 2014). Fashion has problems with documentation, traceability and transparency, as well as a continued lack of various lifecycle data beyond the point of purchase, and hence, promoting some materials as more sustainable than others in general terms proves to be problematic. In guidelines from 2014, the Danish Consumer Ombudsperson (*Forbrugerombudsmanden*) points to the difficulty of documenting sustainability and advises against marketing in such terms, while in 2021, the Consumer Ombudsperson went as far as to openly state that it would be ill-advised for businesses to market products as "sustainable." Currently, fashion brands are not accountable for, for example, extended producer responsibility, such as having a recycling system built into their business model, and most do not take sufficient responsibility for products after purchase, which perpetuates planned obsolescence and overproduction. Furthermore, data on the use phase, which is integral to fashion's lifecycle, remains under-researched. But we do want to acknowledge the creative and innovative work that continues to push for new possibilities in fashion cultures.

Kvadrat/Really

Kvadrat is a textile company located in the Nordhavn area in Copenhagen, an up-and-coming waterfront design hub. It has collaborated with Stan Smith and Adidas, among others, as well as with the Danish slow fashion brand Artikel København, which produces fashion pieces on a made-to-order basis (Figures 8.2–8.4). Artikel uses Kvadrat's furniture fabric leftovers, which have a high Martindale (the unit used to measure the abrasion resistance of textiles), making their designs durable (Mchangame & Larsen 2021). Kvadrat's factories are located in Denmark, and their upcycled materials do not involve any dyeing, water or hazardous chemicals, and only produce recyclable waste (Figures 8.5 and 8.6).

Kvadrat merged with Really, which develops recyclable textiles that are designed for circularity and aimed at the high-end industry for furniture, design, textiles and architecture. Their first product was a series of benches designed by Max Lamb. Launched in 2017 at the Milano Design Week (Ministry of the Environment and Food 2019), it used Really's Solid Textile Board, which consisted of discarded textiles from the fashion industry. Really does not produce any new materials; they only upcycle end-of-life textiles from the fashion industry. The material they create is made for circulation, which means an extension of the materials' life (Brunner-group website), further noting that "we need resources to remain in the use loop for as long as possible and to replace new (virgin) materials" (Meier Engström 2020). She noted that Really identifies as a Danish, a Scandinavian and a Copenhagen brand. She believes that Copenhagen is a key location in relation to its international network and customers because of its ease of access. They have already collaborated with other Danish brands, such as Maria Black, Organic Cotton, Montana, &Tradition, Norm Arkiteter and Mads Nørgaard. In the future, they would like to be a central part of the fashion industry's circular ambitions by supplying materials to the fashion industry based on the waste from the industry (Meier Engström 2020). Their circularity-based approach to textile upcycling is currently at the forefront of innovation-driven change.

FIGURE 8.2: Artikel København store in Copenhagen, 2021, photo by K. Sark.

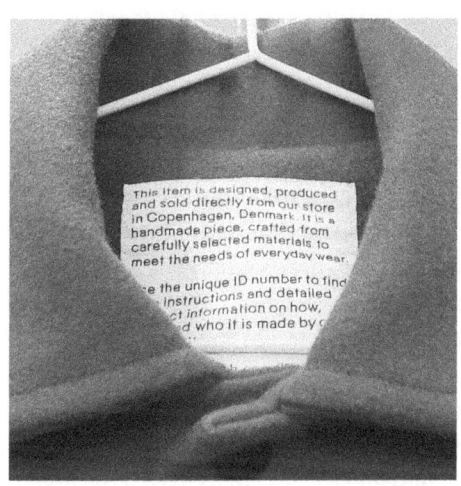

FIGURE 8.3: Artikel København, 2021, photo by K. Sark.

FIGURE 8.4: Artikel København, 2021, photo by K. Sark.

 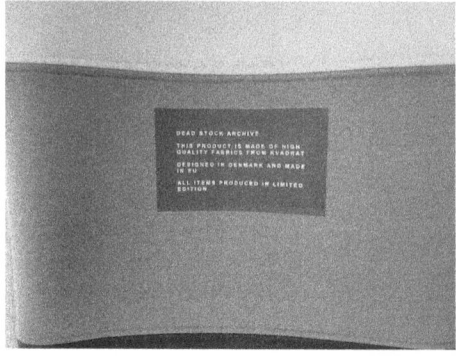

FIGURE 8.5: Kvadrat fabrics at Illum Bollinghus in Copenhagen, 2022, photo by K. Sark.

FIGURE 8.6: Kvadrat logo on a bag at Res Res conscious fashion store in Copenhagen, 2022, photo K. Sark.

MANND – X-Ray Fashion

MANND is the XR production studio that in collaboration with Connect4Climate, a global climate organization, made *X-Ray Fashion: Seeing through a Toxic Industry* (dir. Francesco Carrozzini, 2018), a documentary VR film experience about the dark side of fast fashion and garment production. MANND currently has offices in Aarhus and Copenhagen, having joined the new Lifestyle Lab collaborative workspace, after presenting their VR documentary at the "Fashion Tech & Fashion's Sustainable Growth Layer" exhibition at the Geological Museum during Copenhagen Fashion Week in August 2019, and then at many other festivals and exhibitions around the world.

X-Ray Fashion was part of the official selection at the Venice Biennale Film Festival in the VR competition in 2018. It was nominated for two VR Webby Awards, and for the London VR Award for Best VR Social Impact Award (film by Arhus 2019). *X-Ray Fashion* shed light on the problems associated with the production of textiles and fashion and demonstrated how contemporary technology can reveal and confront aspects of the fashion industry that are normally hidden from consumers. The experience was provided by a physical installation that used a VR headset and combined interactive computer-generated imagery environments and live-action 360 scenes. Visitors to the installation could feel different physical effects related to the various stages of fast fashion production, including changing terrain, wind, heat and water (MANND website). The virtual experience drew attention to physical sensations, such as water running through your toes when you see a stream near a factory, or the heat, smell and air when you look at a factory with hundreds of seamstresses, all to make consumers realize the realities of the garment industry and its effects on people and the environment, especially in the Global South (Teatret Svalegangen 2020) (Figures 8.7–8.9).

FIGURE 8.7: *X-Ray Fashion* installation, 2018, photo by MANND, with permission.

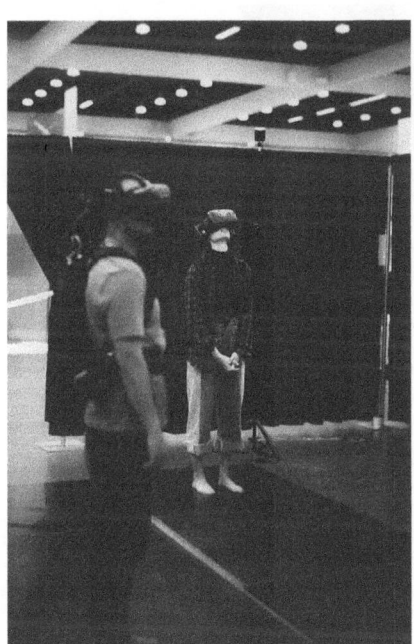

FIGURE 8.8: *X-Ray Fashion* installation, 2018, photo by MANND, with permission.

FIGURE 8.9: *X-Ray Fashion* installation, 2018, photo by MANND, with permission.

One of the founders of MANND, Signe Ungermand, pointed out that

> we think that we as consumers have a huge responsibility. We became accustomed to a sweater costing only 50 DKK (about 7 Euros). Are we even ready to pay 500 DKK (about 70 Euros) for something that does not harm the environment or people? We hope a film like *X-RAY Fashion* can open people's minds up to that.
>
> (Teatret Svalegangen 2020)

The documentary puts the viewer in the shoes of supply-chain workers "to make them experience a deep state of presence and take the message to heart" (MANND website). It places viewers eye-to-eye with the workers who make their clothes, aiming to be an "eye-opener, a conversation-starter, and hopefully the beginning of a changed mindset" (MANND website). In 2017, when they made the film, they believed that people did not talk enough about the problems of clothing production. The film's VR sensory elements were meant to provide more transparency about consumption as an emotional journey, which stays with the body for a long time, according to Ungermand (Figures 8.10–8.12).

FIGURE 8.10: *X-Ray Fashion* poster, photo by MANND, with permission.

INNOVATION AND TECHNOLOGY

FIGURE 8.11: *X-Ray Fashion*, photo by MANND, with permission.

FIGURE 8.12: The making of *X-Ray Fashion*, photo by MANND, with permission.

Lifestyle & Design Cluster

According to Heidi Svane Pedersen, director of the Lifestyle Lab and lead of the technology team at the Lifestyle & Design Cluster, an organization funded by the Danish government to promote the Danish fashion and design industries, "there is a new generation of fashion companies in Denmark that understand that online representation is key," and that their main competencies are no longer just design- or collection-centred but also include diversity, circularity, tech-minded competencies, digital (3D) design, textile innovations and blockchain technology for greater transparency (Pedersen 2021). In 2021, Pedersen and her team opened an incubation lab in Copenhagen to facilitate more collaborative activities and events between the tech industry and fashion and design. The Lifestyle Lab includes a showroom for exhibition and displays of innovative designs, workspaces for innovative start-ups and meeting rooms. Their goal is to connect technology with circularity practices across the industries. Their proximity to the Danish Design Museum also allows them to collaboratively foster a stronger connection between Danish design history and current innovation in design and fashion.

Furthermore, the Lifestyle & Design Cluster collaborates with all Danish fashion design schools and universities on an annual Career Day, where they invite Danish fashion companies with openings for internships or apprenticeships and students from across Denmark to network together. The event usually features a keynote speaker or a discussion panel from the industry to help students professionalize and have a smoother transition into the Danish job market (Figure 8.13).

FIGURE 8.13: Career Day at the Aarhus City Hall (designed by Arne Jacobsen) organized by the Lifestyle & Design Cluster in collaboration with Danish design schools and universities, 2019, photo by K. Sark.

In August 2019, the Lifestyle & Design Cluster organized an exhibition of innovative fashion collections in Copenhagen entitled "Fashion Tech & Fashion's Sustainable Growth Layer," in collaboration with the Royal Danish Academy of Fine Arts, School of Design, VIA University College, KEA School of Design and Technology and Design School Kolding. For this exhibition, three talents from each fashion design program were selected to work specifically on innovative fashion, using smart textiles, tech design and new production methods (Lifestyle & Design Cluster 2019). Christian Chapelle, Head of Fashion at the Lifestyle & Design Cluster, explained that the exhibition allowed them to "pinpoint the newest trends" and facilitate innovation through the collaboration between students and the industry (Chapelle 2021). The collaborative designs were on display during Copenhagen Fashion Week, and the showcase was open to the public. According to Chapelle, "technology is shaping the future of fashion especially within e-commerce, but also in regard to artificial intelligence, data analytics, personalization, and so on" (Chapelle 2021). For this project, Danish fashion companies including Guðrun & Guðrun, Coze Aarhus, Gabba, Blanche and Tobias Birk Nielsen were matched with the students participating in the talent programme, and together they produced collections that were then exhibited at the Geological Museum (part of the Natural History Museum of Denmark) in Copenhagen (Bergquist 2019). The collaboration created opportunities for contemplation and reflection, experimentation and the creation of physical prototypes (Dansk Mode & Textil 2019) (Figure 8.14).

Precisely these types of collaborations are important in terms of making the fashion industry more innovative. They provide opportunities to share knowledge, expertise, research and experience. Many companies do not have research and development departments that can work in an experimental and exploratory format, so it is important for organizations like the Lifestyle & Design Cluster to bridge innovation and circularity, bringing together new talent and established brands, as well as education and the future of the industry. Some examples at this collaborative exhibition included textiles that changed colour when exposed to heat and fibre made from old milk (Lifestyle & Design Cluster 2020). Milk fibres were spun from a residual product to produce a soft yarn that has been used in collaboration with Guðrun & Guðrun (Dansk Mode & Textil 2019).

In 2021, the collaborative activities and projects of the Lifestyle & Design Cluster and the Danish fashion design schools were reorganized around the lifestyle industry. The focus areas were divided into circular economy, digitization and new technologies, and design and entrepreneurship. Within these areas, the teams looked at new materials, furniture and interior design, and clothing and fashion. One of the projects was called "Green Circular Transformation," which

FIGURE 8.14: "Fashion Tech & Fashion's Sustainable Growth Layer" exhibition in Copenhagen, August 2019, photo by K. Sark.

helped companies to get started on a green transition free of charge. This mix of education, consulting and business promotion, which brands get for free from the Danish government to help them transition to circular business models, was started after the COVID-19 lockdowns and the letter that the brands wrote to the Danish government asking for bailouts (quoted in Chapter 3). In essence, the government responded by paying for their transition to circular business practices.

In another project, they brought together 25 local textile companies and Herning Municipality to develop a strategy for textile waste. The idea was to create new circular business models and value chains through collaborations between entrepreneurs and students in the textile and fashion industry. Chapelle pointed out that the fashion and design students are "very innovative, so the established brands can learn from the students. On the other hand, the brands are commercial and know all about procedures, production, and sales, so the students can of course learn a lot from them" (Chapelle 2021). Again, it is in the collaborative nature of these projects that innovation and creativity meet.

Other collaborative projects focused more in-depth on materials. Collaborations with the Design School Kolding and VIA University College examined how to create less toxic colour and dye methods, technologies and processes, while a collaboration with VIA University College, the Royal Academy and KEA Copenhagen Business Academy developed a project for testing recycling technologies. The collected knowledge and research were used to make concrete recommendations to the fashion industry about material and design choices.

The Lifestyle & Design Cluster has organized and developed many other important projects, including the "Circular Fashion Days" exhibitions at the Copenhagen International Fashion Fair (CIFF) during Copenhagen Fashion Week in 2021 and 2022, where they showcased 26 Danish brands that have incorporated circularity into their production practices. Even more Danish brands are expected to join the initiative and exhibit at upcoming CIFF presentations. In addition, Johanne Stenstrup of the circularity team at the Lifestyle & Design Cluster organized a series of panel discussions during CIFF to educate and inspire international buyers and other brands to work more circularly and regeneratively (Sark 2021). All these examples show how important it is to have bridging organizations like the Lifestyle & Design Cluster to connect businesses, students and researchers to generate innovative solutions (Figures 8.15 and 8.16).

FIGURE 8.15: "Circular Fashion Days" exhibition and panel discussion on regenerative practices organized by Johanne Stenstrup at CIFF during Copenhagen Fashion Week in August 2021, photo by K. Sark.

FIGURE 8.16: "Circular Fashion Days" exhibition and panel discussion on regenerative practices organized by Johanne Stenstrup at CIFF during Copenhagen Fashion Week in August 2021, photo by K. Sark.

Conclusion

Innovation, creativity and technology matter now more than ever, and it is clear from our research that the most innovative results come from interdisciplinary, multimedia and multigenerational collaborations, and strategic partnerships across industries. Denmark is in the very privileged position of being able to produce exceptionally talented students of design and fashion through its many state-funded design schools and universities. Organizations such as the Lifestyle & Design Cluster facilitate important collaborations not only across the generational divide but also across industries, including an emphasis on technology, innovation and circularity. Their work is essential in facilitating progress in the fashion industry, which is in urgent need of reforming. Their own decentralized operational structure, with offices in Herning, Aarhus and Copenhagen and strategic teams covering the areas of technology, circularity, research and development, contribute greatly to their effectiveness. Our research also revealed that while Copenhagen's role in advancing innovation across domains is important, it is not exclusive, as not all of the innovative fashion tech companies in Denmark are based there, in part because of the high cost of real estate and labour, in part because of a lack of financial support and incentives for innovative start-ups to move there, and in part because of the historical fragmentation and decentralization of Denmark's fashion and textile industries. It also shows that innovation in fashion and technology happens not only in Copenhagen but across all of Denmark. The examples we examined here represent only a small glimpse into what can be done locally in terms of innovation and technology. Denmark ranks high among global innovation countries and can be a leader in mobilizing knowledge, research and development skills towards a stronger knowledge-based economy, and Copenhagen is well positioned to expand its fashion culture through creativity and innovation.

REFERENCES

Bergquist, Karin. Magasinet 360, www.magasinet360.dk/magasiner/2019-4/slow-fashion. Accessed 13 Mar. 2023.

Brunner-group. kvadrat really, www.brunner-group.com/en-DE/products/materials-and-fabrics/material-kvadrat-really/. Accessed 20 Oct. 2022.

Challenges.dk, 2019, www.challenges.dk/da/ide/x-ray-fashion-vr. Accessed 13 Mar. 2023.

Chapelle, Christian. Lifestyle & Design Cluster. Email interview, 7 Apr. 2021.

Connect4Climate, www.connect4climate.org/video/x-ray-fashion-virtual-reality-installation-francesco-carrozzini. Accessed 13 Mar. 2023.

CSR. Ny klimavenlig teknologi på vej til modeindustrien, www.csr.dk/ny-klimavenlig-teknologi-på-vej-til-modeindustrien. Accessed 13 Mar. 2023.

Danish Consumer Ombudsperson. Environmental and Ethical Statements, 2014, www.forbrugerombudsmanden.dk/media/46475/2016-miljmssige-og-etiskeudsagn.pdf. Accessed 13 Mar. 2023.

Danish Consumer Ombudsperson. Quick Guide on Environmental Marketing, 2021, www.forbrugerombudsmanden.dk/media/56731/kvikguide-om-miljoemarkedsfoering.pdf. Accessed 13 Mar. 2023.

Dansk Mode & Textil, www.dmogt.dk/branchenyt/oplev-fashion-tech-og-fremtidens-baeredygtige-mode. Accessed 13 Mar. 2023.

Film by Aarhus, www.filmbyaarhus.dk/x-ray-fashion-premieres-in-aarhus-at-this-2019/. Accessed 13 Mar. 2023.

Haa, Emma Ahlgreen. Århusianske Pond i nyt samarbejde med Bestseller-ejer: Skal udvikle miljø venligt tøj, www.stiften.dk/artikel/århusianske-pond-i-nyt-samarbejde-med-bestseller-ejer-skal-udvikle-miljøvenligt-tøj. Accessed 13 Mar. 2023.

Jørgensen, Christian Bjerggaard. Pond: Vi skal samarbejde med naturen i stedet for at modarbejde den, 18 Jul. 2017, www.incuba.dk/hvad-sker-der/nyheder/pond-samarbejder-med-naturen-i-stedet-for-at-modarbejde-den/. Accessed 13 Mar. 2023.

Kerne.Milk. *Kernemilk*, n.d., www.bit.ly/3xIOAEK. Accessed 13 Mar. 2023.

Kerne.Milk. *Kernemilk*, n.d., www.bit.ly/3CMlatd. Accessed 13 Mar. 2023.

Kvadrat. REALLY, www.kvadrat.dk/en/REALLY. Accessed 13 Mar. 2023.

Lifestyle & Design Cluster. Fashion Tech & Modens Bæredygtige Vækstlag, www.ldcluster.com/wp-content/up-loads/sites/4/2019/11/Case-Fashion-tech.pdf. Accessed 13 Mar. 2023.

Lifestyle & Design Cluster. Fashion Tech & Modens Bæredygtige Vækstlag, www.ldcluster.com/en/portfolio-item/fashion-tech-2/. Accessed 13 Mar. 2023.

Lynglund, Olivia. *DM&T*, 2018, www.bit.ly/2VRXa6F. Accessed 13 Mar. 2023.

MANND, www.mannd.dk/projects/xray-fashion. Accessed 13 Mar. 2023.

MANND, www.mannd.dk/press. Accessed 13 Mar. 2023.

Meier Engström, Wickie. Really representative. Email interview, 23 Nov. 2020.

Mchangama, Moussa, and Frederik Larsen. "Sustainable Fashion in Action." *In futurum*, 2021.

Miljø- og Fødevareminsteriet. Formstøbning med upcycled tekstilaffald fra Really. 2019.

Pedersen, Heidi Svane. Lifestyle & Design Cluster. Phone interview, 13 Apr. 2021.

Sark, Katrina. "Lifestyle & Design Cluster – Innovation and Technology." *Chic Podcast*, episode 27, 8 Sept. 2021, www.anchor.fm/chic-podcast/episodes/Episode-27--Lifestyle--Design-Cluster--Innovation-and-Technology-e172i82. Accessed 13 Mar. 2023.

Sark, Katrina. "Circular Fashion Days at Copenhagen Fashion Week." *Chic Podcast*, episode 26, 31 Aug. 2021, www.anchor.fm/chic-podcast/episodes/Episode-26--Circular-Fashion-Days-at-Copenhagen-Fashion-Week-e16nq7o. Accessed 13 Mar. 2023.

Selchau Majlund, Mathias. Pond Textile, Email interview, 24 Nov. 2020.

Staley, Ruby. *fashionjournal*, 2019, www.bit.ly/3yICCw4. Accessed 13 Mar. 2023.

Teatret Svalegangen, www.svalegangen.dk/events/gaesteforestillinger/2020-2021/x-ray-fashion/. Accessed 13 Mar. 2023.

Ungermann, Signe. MANND co-founder. Interview, 23 Nov. 2020.

Conclusion

Katrina Sark

If we apply Hans Christian Andersen's metaphor of the naked emperor to the current global fashion industry in the global climate crisis, then many political leaders remain naked in their lack of information, action, legislation, and inability to identify and rely on the right advisers; the courtiers who want to maintain their positions of power and privilege continue to perpetuate greenwashing, unethical behaviour and colonial exploitation, while citizens and activists continue to draw attention to the fact that the climate emergency remains unresolved and the emperor is – still – naked. The power of this fairy tale persists because of its critique of power manipulation, which is as old as human nature.

Andersen's childhood spent in poverty, his feelings of being an outsider during his school years, and his difficult climb to social recognition informed his creativity and the observational skills that facilitated this weaving of social, political, economic and cultural critique into children's fairy tales. Moreover, his love for Copenhagen and its culture fueled his perseverance and resilience through all the setbacks, ridicule, hostility and violence he experienced on his path to fame. By the time Copenhagen accepted him as one of its own, he was no longer a young teenager with an overactive, creative imagination, but the mark he made on the city and its culture was lasting (Figure C.1).

The persistent strength of his cautionary tale reminds us to re-examine our relationship to power, people and the planet. As our industries have become unsustainable and require de-growth to avert environmental degradation and ecological and climate catastrophes, we all need to learn how to stop pretending and how to re-focus our knowledge and creativity towards non-exploitative practices. As the young Gen Z activists have taught us, continuing business as usual in a climate emergency is no longer ethical or sane – even if, for now, it remains profitable.

Copenhagen fashion culture has a long and vibrant history. The main takeaway for the readers of this book is that without fully understanding how fashion cultures of cities are formed, how they develop and how they need to be preserved, no amount of concentrated effort invested in the fashion economy will make it economically, socially or ethically sustainable. We hope that this book can assist with that understanding and make Copenhagen's fashion culture more transparent, creative and just. We hope that this book can inspire future generations of fashion and design creatives to make their businesses more ethical by reconceptualizing how we understand fashion and culture. Finally, we also hope that this book inspires readers to see fashion and culture in new ways and to expand the limits of creativity and sustainability in their own work.

FIGURE C.1: HCA statue with kids, Copenhagen, 2010, photo by K. Sark.

Contributors

IZABELLA ANDERSEN has a degree in design culture and economics from the University of Southern Denmark (SDU) in Kolding, with a specialization in design and fashion. Her BA thesis focused on fashion and identity, concentrating on socially constructed cultural norms in relation to gender. In 2020, she was a member of the editorial team and contributing writer at *The Critical Pulse* magazine. In addition to her research interests in fashion, gender and drag queens, she works with sustainability, communication, PR management, branding and marketing.

* * * * *

TRINE BRUN PETERSEN is the head of research at The Royal Danish Collection. Her current research project focuses on the material culture of childhood with a particular interest in children's clothing as a commercial and cultural phenomenon. She has published articles on children's fashion and dress in international journals and edited the *Green Design Culture* anthology with Rosita Satell and Tau Ulv Lenskjold.

* * * * *

ANDERS LARSEN holds an MA in history from the University of Copenhagen. He has published on the history of gay men in Denmark and drag culture. He currently teaches at DIS in Copenhagen, where he focuses on visual and fashion studies, as well as queer history with a strong focus on Copenhagen. Anders is also an award-winning drag performer as Chantal al Arab, who is frequently featured on Danish TV and radio.

* * * * *

FREDERIK LARSEN is an independent researcher with a Ph.D. from the Copenhagen Business School and the co-founder of the consultancy In futurum. Frederik has conducted research on the fashion industry, sustainable business practices and second-hand markets. As a consultant, Frederik advises companies, organizations and public institutions on sustainability and social justice.

* * * * *

MARIA MACKINNEY-VALENTIN is an associate professor at the Royal Danish Academy. She holds an MA in English Literature from the University of Copenhagen and a Ph.D. from the Royal Danish Academy of Fine Arts, School of Design. Her main research interests include identity construction and issues of gender, status, power and trend mechanisms. She has published widely on fashion and identity, including the monograph *Fashioning Identity: Status Ambivalence in Contemporary Fashion* (Bloomsbury 2017).

* * * * *

MARIE RIEGELS MELCHIOR is an associate professor in European ethnology at the University of Copenhagen. Her research interests concern mainly fashion and design culture, cultural history from the nineteenth century onwards, heritage and museum studies. She has written extensively on Danish fashion and design history in the twentieth and twenty-first centuries as well as on museological issues when fashion enters museums. She is on the editorial board of *Ethnologia Scandinavica, Journal of Scandinavian Ethnology* and *Critical Studies of Fashion & Beauty* (Intellect).

* * * * *

KATRINA SARK is an associate professor in the Department of Media, Design Learning, and Cognition at the University of Southern Denmark (SDU). She specializes in cultural analysis, cultural history, media, gender studies, sustainability and decoloniality. She is the founder of the Canadian Fashion Scholars Network, the co-founder of the Urban Chic book series and the co-author of *Berliner Chic: A Locational History of Berlin Fashion* (2011), and *Montréal Chic: A Locational History of Montreal Fashion* (2016). Her other publications include *Branding Berlin* (2023), an edited volume on *Social Justice Pedagogies* (2023) and a special issue on *Ethical Fashion and Empowerment in Clothing Cultures* (2021). She also hosts the *Chic Podcast*, dedicated to fashion, design, culture, sustainability, media and technology.

* * * * *

ELSE SKJOLD is an associate professor in design and sustainability at the Royal Danish Academy, and Head of the MA programme *New Landscapes for Change: Fashion, Clothing & Textiles*, which was launched in September 2020. She has been part of developing the wardrobe method and typically combines this with a design entrepreneurial approach in her action-based research on green transition in fashion and textile companies.

* * * * *

EMILIE THOMSEN has a BA in design culture and economics with a specialization in fashion, and graduated with distinction. She is completing her MA in web communication at the University of Southern Denmark (SDU). Her interests include sustainability and fashion, and she is a co-founder and member of the editorial team of *The Critical Pulse* magazine, where she designs the layout, maintains the website and contributes articles and artwork. She also teaches graphic design workshops at SDU.

* * * * *

BJØRN UTOFT SØRENSEN has a BA in design culture and economics with a specialization in fashion, where he graduated with distinction, and is currently completing his MA in web communication at the University of Southern Denmark (SDU). Since 2020, he has been a co-founder and part of the editorial team of *The Critical Pulse* magazine, where he does the layout and writes articles about sustainability in the fashion industry.

www.ingramcontent.com/pod-product-compliance
Ingram Content Group UK Ltd.
Pitfield, Milton Keynes, MK11 3LW, UK
UKHW031432200225
455368UK00026B/451